THE BOOK OF THE CHURCH.

THE

Book of the Church.

BY

ROBERT SOUTHEY, Esq. LL.D.

POET LAUREATE,

HONORARY MEMBER OF THE ROYAL SPANISH ACADEMY, OF THE ROYAL SPANISH ACADEMY OF HISTORY, OF THE ROYAL INSTITUTE OF THE NETHERLANDS, OF THE CYMMRODORION, OF THE MASSACHUSETTS HISTORICAL SOCIETY, OF THE AMERICAN ANTIQUARIAN SOCIETY, OF THE ROYAL IRISH ACADEMY, OF THE BRISTOL PHILOSOPHICAL AND LITERARY SOCIETY, &c.

IN TWO VOLUMES.

VOL. I.

LONDON:

JOHN MURRAY, ALBEMARLE-STREET.

MDCCCXXIV.

LONDON:
PRINTED BY WILLIAM CLOWES,
Northumberland-Court.

TO THE

REVEREND PETER ELMSLEY, D.D.

PRINCIPAL OF ST. ALBAN'S HALL,

CAMDEN PROFESSOR OF ANCIENT HISTORY, &c. &c.

THESE VOLUMES ARE INSCRIBED, AS A MEMORIAL

OF RESPECT AND FRIENDSHIP.

A shorter work than the present was designed by the Author when he commenced his task; but in his progress he found facts too important to be omitted, and details which could not be abridged without injury to the general purport and effect. References have not been given, because the scale is not one which would require or justify a display of research. He believes, however, that there is not a single statement in these Volumes which his collections would not enable him readily to authenticate.

Crediton, Jan. 10, 1824.

CONTENTS.

FIRST VOLUME.

CHAPTER III.

CHAPTER IV.

CHAPTER V.

CHAPTER VI.

CHAPTER VII.

CHAPTER VIII.

CHAPTER IX.

CHAPTER XI.

SECOND VOLUME.

CHAPTER XII.

CHAPTER XIII.

CHAPTER XIV.

CHAPTER XV.

CHAPTER XVI.

CHAPTER XVII.

CHAPTER XVIII.

THE BOOK OF THE CHURCH.

THE BOOK OF THE CHURCH.

THE

BOOK OF THE CHURCH.

MANIFOLD as are the blessings for which Englishmen are beholden to the institutions of their country, there is no part of those institutions from which they derive more important advantages than from its Church Establishment, none by which the temporal condition of all ranks has been so materially improved. So many of our countrymen would not be ungrateful for these benefits, if they knew how numerous and how great they are, how dearly they were prized by our forefathers, and at how dear a price they were purchased for our inheritance; by what religious exertions, what heroic devotion, what precious lives, consumed in pious labours, wasted away in dungeons, or offered up amid the flames. This is a knowledge which, if early inculcated, might arm the young heart against the pestilent errors of these distempered times. I offer, therefore, to those who regard with love and reverence the religion which they have received from their fathers, a brief but comprehensive record, diligently, faithfully, and conscientiously composed, which they may put into the hands of their children. Herein it will be seen from what heathenish delusions and inhuman rites the inhabitants of this island have been delivered by the Christian faith; in what manner the best interests of the country were advanced by the clergy even during the darkest ages of papal domination; the errors and crimes of the Romish Church, and how when its corruptions were at the worst, the day-break of the Reformation appeared among us: the progress of that Reformation through evil and through good; the establishment of a Church pure in its doctrines, irreproachable in its order, beautiful in its forms; and the conduct of that Church proved both in adverse and in prosperous times, alike faithful to its principles when it adhered to the monarchy during a successful rebellion, and when it opposed the monarch who would have brought back the Romish superstition, and together with the religion, would have overthrown the liberties, of England.

CHAPTER I.

RELIGION OF THE ANCIENT BRITONS.

THE light of God, which at the creation was imparted to man, hath never been extinguished. From the patriarchs it descended to the prophets, and from the prophets to the apostles ; but there were many who wandered and lost the light, and their offspring became inheritors of darkness. Thus it fared with our fore-fathers. We know not when, or from whence, they reached the British Islands ; Scripture hath not recorded it, and it was in times beyond the reach of other history. There is reason to believe that they brought with them some glimmerings of patriarchal faith, and some traditional knowledge of patriarchal history. Other tribes followed at various times and from various places, some from the Baltic and from Germany, some from the opposite coasts of Belgium and Gaul, others from Spain; the Phenicians also traded here; and our fathers being ignorant, and far removed from those among whom the truth was preserved, received the fables and superstitions of the new comers, and blended them with their own, till they fell at length into the abominations of idolatry.

Their priests, the Druids, are said to have retained the belief of one supreme God, all-wise, all-mighty, and all-merciful, from whom all things which have life proceed. They held also, the immortality of the soul: whatever else they taught was deceit or vanity. Thus, it is said, they believed that the soul began to exist in the meanest insect, and proceeded through all the lower orders of existence, ascending at each new birth, to a higher form, till it arrived at its human stage; this, according to their philosophy, being necessary, that it might collect, during its progress, the properties and powers of animal life. This lower state was a state of evil; but there could be no sin there because there could be no choice, and therefore death was always the passage to a higher step of being. But when the soul had reached its human form, it then possessed the knowledge of good and evil, for man is born to make his choice between them; he is born also to experience change and suffering, these being the conditions of humanity. The soul, thus elevated, became responsible, and if it had chosen evil instead of good, returned after death to the state of evil, and was condemned to an inferior grade of animal life, low in proportion to the debasement whereto it had reduced itself. But they who had chosen the better part, which it is free for all to choose, passed into a state from whence it was not possible to fall; for when death had delivered them from the body, evil had power over them no longer, because they had experienced it, and knew that it was evil: and they were no longer subject to suffering, neither to change; but continuing the same in goodness and in heavenly affections, they increased in knowledge, and thereby in happiness through all eternity. They believed also that the beatified soul retained the love of its country and its kind; and that the spirits of the good sometimes returned to earth, and became prophets among mankind, that they might assist their brethren, and by teaching them heavenly things, oppose the power of Cythraul, or the Evil One.

These were but the conceits of imagination; and they who impose upon the people their own imaginations, however innocent, prepare the way for the devices of deceit and wickedness. Good men may have mingled these fancies with the truth; bad ones feigned that there were other gods beside Him in whom we live and move and have our being; Teutates, whom they called the father, and Taranis the thunderer, and Hesus the god of battles, and Andraste the goddess of victory: Hu the mighty, by whom it is believed that Noah the second parent of the human race, was intended; Ceridwen, a goddess in whose rites the preservation of mankind in the ark was figured; and Beal or Belinus,...for the Phenicians had introduced the worship of their Baal. By favour of these false gods, the Druids pretended to foretell future events, and as their servants and favourites they demanded gifts and offerings from the deluded multitude. The better to secure this revenue, they made the people, at the beginning of winter, extinguish all their fires on one day, and kindle them again from the sacred fire of the Druids, which would make the house fortunate for the ensuing year: and if any man came who had not paid his yearly dues, they refused to give him a spark, neither durst any of his neighbours relieve him; nor might he himself procure fire by any other means, so that he and his family were deprived of it till he had discharged the uttermost of his debt. They erected also great stones so cunningly fitted one upon another, that if the upper one were touched in a certain place, though only with a finger, it would rock; whereas no strength of man might avail to move it if applied to any other part: hither they led those who were accused of any crime, and, under pretence that the gods would, by this form of trial, manifest the guilt or innocence of the party, directed him where to touch and make the proof: and thus at their discretion they either absolved the accused, or made them appear guilty.

The mistletoe, the seed whereof is eaten and voided by the birds, and thus conveyed from one tree to another, they affected to hold in veneration. When it was discovered growing upon an oak, upon which tree it is rarely to be found, the Druids went thither with great solemnity, and all things were made ready for sacrifice and for feasting. Two white bulls were fastened by their horns to the tree; the officiating priest ascended, and cut the mistletoe with a golden knife; others stood below to receive it in a white woollen cloth, and it was carefully preserved, that water wherein it had been steeped, might be administered to men, as an antidote against poison, and to cattle for the sake of making them fruitful. The sacrifice was then performed. The best and most beautiful of the flocks and herds were selected for this purpose. The victim was divided into three parts: one was consumed as a burnt offering; he who made the offering feasted upon another, with his friends; and the third was the portion of the Druids. In this wise did they delude the people. But they had worse rites than these, and were guilty of greater abominations. They were notorious, above the priests of every other idolatry, for the practice of pretended magic. They made the people pass through fire in honour of Beal; and they offered up the life of man in sacrifice, saying that when the victim was smitten with a sword, they could discover events which were to come by the manner in which he fell, and the flowing of his blood, and the quivering of his body in the act of death. When a chief was afflicted with sickness, they sacrificed a human victim, because they said the continuance of his life might be purchased if another life were offered up as its price; and in like manner, men were offered up when any calamity befel the people, and when they were about to engage in war. Naked women, stained with the dark blue dye of woad, assisted at these bloody rites. On greater occasions, a huge figure in the rude likeness of man, was made of wicker-work, and filled with men: as many as were condemned to death for their offences were put into it; but if these did not suffice to fill the image, the innocent were thrust in, and they surrounded it with straw and wood, and set fire to it, and consumed it, with all whom it contained.

Their domestic institutions were not less pernicious than their idolatry. A wife was common to all the kinsmen of her husband, a custom which prevented all connubial love, and destroyed the natural affection between child and father; for every man had as many wives as he had kinsmen, and no man knew his child, nor did any child know its father. These were the abominations of our British fathers after the light of the Patriarchs was lost among them, and before they received the light of the gospel.

CHAPTER II.

RELIGION AND PHILOSOPHY OF THE ROMANS.—FIRST INTRODUCTION OF CHRISTIANITY.—PERSECUTION.—FIRST ESTABLISHMENT OF CHRISTIANITY.—RELIGION OF THE ANGLO-SAXONS.

When the Romans established themselves as conquerors in Britain, the authority of the Druids was destroyed, and one system of idolatry was exchanged for another as far as Roman civilization extended. The heathenism, which was thus introduced, contained fewer remains of patriarchal truths than that which it displaced: it was less bloody, because, during the progress of knowledge and refinement, the more inhuman of its rites had fallen into disuse; and it was not so fraudulent, because for the same reason it had in great measure ceased to obtain belief, or to command respect; but inasmuch as it had any influence over the conduct of the people, its effect was worse, because the fables which were related of its false Deities, gave a sanction to immoralities of every kind, even the foulest and most abominable crimes. So gross indeed was this iniquitous mythology, that none except the most ignorant of the multitude gave ear to it: the priests who performed the service of the temple laughed in secret at the rites which they practised and the fictions upon which their ceremonies were founded, and the educated ranks looked upon the credulity of the vulgar with scorn. Religion had no connexion with* morality among the Greek and Roman heathens, and this was one main cause of their degeneracy and corruption. Religion consisted with them merely in the observance of certain rites, and the performance of sacrifices; and men were left to the schools of philosophy, there to choose their system of morals, and learn a rule of life. And in those schools the blind led the blind. Some of the bedarkened teachers affirmed that there were no Gods; others, that if there were any, they took no thought for this world, neither regarded the affairs of men. By some, the highest happiness was placed in sensual gratification; by others, in the practice of a cold stern virtue, of which pride was the principle, and selfishness the root. A miserable condition of society, in which the evil-disposed had nothing to restrain them but the fear of human laws; and the good, nothing to console them under the keenest sorrows which man

* I owe this remark to STILLINGFLEET, by whom it is coupled with this weighty caution, "Let us have a care of as dangerous a separation between faith and works."

is born to; no hope beyond this transitory and uncertain life; nothing to disarm death of its sting; nothing to assure them of victory over the grave. Yet the Romans became fiercely intolerant in support of a mythology wherein they had no belief: they admitted other idolatries, and even erected altars to the Gods of the Britons: but when the tidings of salvation were proclaimed, they were kindled with rage, and persecuted the Christians to death.

It cannot now be ascertained by whom the glad tidings of the gospel were first brought into Britain. The most probable tradition says that it was Bran, the father of Caractacus, who, having been led into captivity with his son, and hearing the word at Rome, received it, and became on his return the means of delivering his countrymen from a worse bondage. There is also some reason to believe that Claudia, who is spoken of together with Pudens, by the Apostle Paul, was a British lady of this illustrious household: because a British woman of that name is known to have been the wife of Pudens at that time. Legends, which rest upon less credible grounds, pretend that a British king called Lucius, who was tributary to the Romans, was baptized with many of his subjects. These things are doubtful: "the light of the word shone here," says Fuller, the church historian, "but we know not who kindled it." It is said that the first church was erected at Glastonbury; and this tradition may seem to deserve credit, because it was not contradicted in those ages when other churches would have found it profitable to advance a similar pretension. The building is described as a rude structure of wicker work, like the dwellings of the people in those days, and differing from them only in its dimensions, which were threescore feet in length, and twenty-six in breadth. An abbey was afterwards erected there, one of the finest of those edifices, and one of the most remarkable for the many interesting circumstances connected with it. The destruction of this beautiful and venerable fabric is one of the crimes by which our Reformation was sullied.

The first man who laid down his life in Britain for the Christian faith, was Saint Alban; Saint he has been called for that reason, and the title may be continued to him in mark of honour and respect, now that it has ceased to carry with it a superstitious meaning to our ears. During the tenth, and most rigorous of the persecutions, which was the only one that extended to this island, a Christian priest flying from his persecutors, came to the city of Verulamium, and took shelter in Alban's house; he, not being of the faith himself, concealed him for pure compassion; but when he observed the devotion of his guest, how fervent it was, and how firm, and the consolation and the joy which he appeared to find in prayer, his heart was touched; and he listened to his teaching, and became a believer. Meantime the persecutors traced the object of their pursuit to this city, and discovered his retreat. But when they came to search the house, Alban, putting on the hair-cassock of his teacher, delivered himself into their hands as if he had been the fugitive, and was carried before the heathen governor; while the man whom they sought had leisure and opportunity to provide for his escape. Because he refused either to betray his guest, or offer sacrifices to the Roman gods, he was scourged, and then led to execution upon the spot where the abbey now stands, which, in after-times, was erected to his memory, and still bears his name. That spot was then a beautiful meadow on a little rising ground, "seeming," says the venerable Bede, "a fit theatre for the martyr's triumph." There he was beheaded, and a soldier also at the same time; who, it is said, was so affected by the resignation and magnanimity of this virtuous sufferer, that he chose to suffer with him, rather than incur the guilt of being his executioner. Monkish writers have disfigured the story with many fictions in their wonted manner, but there is no reason to question that the main facts are historical truths. Others of our countrymen, some few whose names alone are preserved, and more of whom all memory has perished, laid down their lives under the same persecution. Concerning them, the worthy Fuller has beautifully said, " it was superstition in the Athenians to build an altar to the unknown God, but it would be piety in us here to erect a monument in memorial of these unknown martyrs, whose names are lost. The best is, God's kalendar is more complete than man's best martyrologies; and their names are written in the book of life, who, on earth, are wholly forgotten."

This was the last persecution under the heathen emperors: shortly afterwards Christianity became the religion of the Roman empire, in an evil age, when corruptions of every kind, both in religious and in secular affairs, were making a rapid and destructive progress; and when the Christian world was disturbed with acrimonious disputes concerning high mysteries, and abstruse points, which the limited intellect of man cannot comprehend, which have been left indefinite by the revealed word of God, and which for us to attempt to define is equally presumptuous and vain. No records of the British church during that age are extant; for the existing legends of the British and Irish saints, who are placed in those times, are as little connected with historical truth, as the stories of the Round Table, the romances of Amadis and his descendents, or the ideal state of pastoral Arcadia, as imagined by the poets. Thus much, however, is known, that these islands did not escape the contagious errors which were then prevailing. Monachism, in its first stage, when it had nothing useful or ornamental to compensate for its preposterous austerities, was introduced here; and pilgrims went from hence, not only to visit Jerusalem, whither a pardonable, if not a meritorious, feeling of devotion might lead them,...but to behold and reverence, like a living idol, a maniac in Syria, who, under that burning climate, passed his life upon the top of a lofty column, and vied with the yoguees of India in the folly and perseverance with which he inflicted voluntary tortures upon himself. This too is known, that the ancient British heathenism was zealously preserved and progagated by the Bards, and by the remains of the Druids; of whom some taught it in its original state, and others mingled with it some things which they borrowed from Christianity. And it may be presumed that the heathenism of the Romans also still lingered here, though it was not cherished with the same zeal, being unconnected with old remembrances and national feeling, and having never made its way into the northern, nor perhaps into the mountainous, parts of the island. This certainly was losing ground; and the old national heathenism was probably gaining it, in proportion as the Roman power declined, and the Caledonian tribes extended their invasion southward; when to repel these invaders the Saxons were invited, and settling in the land as conquerors, introduced with them another system of heathen idolatry.

The Saxons, Angles, and other kindred tribes, to whom we are indebted for the basis and the character of our fine language, and of our invaluable civil institutions, were at the time of their establishment here a ferocious people, but not without noble qualities, apt for instruction, and willing to be instructed. The heathenism which they introduced bears no affinity either to that of the Britons, or of the Romans. It is less known than either, because while it subsisted as a living form of belief, the few writers who arose in those illiterate ages were incurious concerning such things: but it has left familiar traces in our daily speech, and in many of those popular customs which in various parts of the country still partially maintain their ground. They had idols wrought in wood, stone, and metals of different kinds, even in gold:...this fact implies considerable proficiency in art, beyond that to which the ancient Britons had attained. One of these idols was designed as standing upon a fish, others as having many heads; a gross but intelligible mode of representing to the senses of a rude people that the Gods whom they worshipped beheld the actions which were done on all sides. The latter images may be thought to imply by their fashion a Tartaric origin; the former may not improbably be referred through the same channel to India, and perhaps to the corrupted tradition of the Deluge, which seems to have been preserved wherever ancient traditions are found. They had temples, a ritual worship, and a regular priesthood. The rites were bloody. The Saxons on the continent are known to have decimated their prisoners for sacrifice. But there is some reason to infer, that the priests, when they accompanied the conquerors hither, had attained to that stage of intellectual advancement, wherein it became their wish so to direct their influence as to mitigate, rather than increase, the evils to which their fellow-creatures were liable in an age of violence and incessant war. From the Saxons it is that we derive the holy name of God; its literal meaning was the Good; and we must acknowledge the propriety of that reverential feeling which induced them thus to express goodness and divinity by the same word. The enclosures of their temples were held to be profaned if a lance were thrown into them: and the priests were not permitted to bear arms; nor to ride like warriors on horseback, ...only upon mares. When the image of their goddess Hertha, or Mother Earth, was borne abroad in a covered carriage, so long as it continued without the consecrated precincts, all hostilities were suspended, and nothing was thought of but festivity and joy. At the expiration of this festival, which otherwise might seem to have been instituted in favour of humanity, the vehicle, the garment which covered it, and the idol itself, were washed by slaves in a lake which none but the servants of the Goddess were allowed to approach, and after this ceremony, the slaves were sacrificed by drowning. They worshipped the Sun and Moon, the Thunderer, and Odin, the favourite God of those who settled in this island, because he was a deified warrior, from whom the kings of the different kingdoms of the Heptarchy traced their descent. Of the other objects of their mistaken worship little more than a few names can now be ascertained. That of the goddess Eostre, or Eastre, which may probably be traced to the Astarte of the Phenicians, is retained among us in the word Easter, her annual festival having been superseded by that sacred day.

The change produced in Britain by the Saxon conquest was greater than that which took place in any other part of the Western Empire, when it was broken up, and divided among the Gothic conquerors. Every where else they soon conformed to the religion, and intermingled with the inhabitants, of the conquered provinces, so that a mixed speech presently grew up, retaining more traces of its Roman than of its Barbaric origin. But the Roman tongue, and the Roman religions, the unfashionable and unpatronised rites of its perishing Paganism, as well as the flourishing forms of its corrupted Christianity, were at once swept away from that largest and finest portion of Britain in which the conquerors fixed themselves; and the Saxons established their heathen superstition and their language, without any compromise or commixture. Some mixture of races there must have been, but it was too partial to produce any perceptible effect. This remarkable and singular fact is to be explained by the condition in which they found the island. During the decline of the Roman empire, then in the last stage of its decay, the Britons had shaken off an authority, which, easy and greatly beneficial as it had proved upon the whole, was insufferable to their national feeling,...a stubborn and haughty feeling, but of a noble kind. They succeeded to their own undoing. A deplorable state of anarchy and intestine war ensued, during which the greater part of those persons who considered the Latin as their mother tongue,...in other words, the cultivated part of the population,...either fled the country, or were cut off. The Britons themselves were divided into an unknown number of petty kingdoms, and their princes were animated with as much hostility against each other as against the invaders. But they were too high-minded to brook that forced and ignominious incorporation to which the Gauls, and Spaniards, and Italians, had submitted; and gradually retiring to the western peninsula, to the land of Lakes, and to the Highlands of Scotland, their language ceased to be spoken in that great division of the island which now obtained the name of England from its Anglian conquerors. The priests and monks withdrew with them, as well as the less placable votaries of the old Druidical faith; and Christianity, as a public establishment, disappeared from the kingdoms of the Heptarchy for about an hundred and fifty years.

CHAPTER III.

CONVERSION OF THE ANGLO SAXONS.

That Gregory, who was afterwards raised to the Popedom, and is distinguished from succeeding Popes of the same name (one alone excepted), by the rank of Saint, and from him by the appellation of the Great, was one day led into the market-place at Rome, with a great concourse of persons, to look at a large importation of foreign merchandise, which had just arrived. Among other articles, there were some boys exposed for sale like cattle. There was nothing remarkable in this, for it was the custom everywhere in that age, and had been so from time immemorial: but he was struck by the appearance of the boys, their fine clear skins, the beauty of their flaxen or golden hair, and their ingenuous countenances; so that he asked from what country they came; and when he was told from the island of Britain, where the inhabitants in general were of that complexion and comeliness, he inquired if the people were Christians, and sighed for compassion at hearing that they were in a state of Pagan darkness. Upon asking further, to what particular nation they belonged, of the many among whom that island was divided, and being told that they were Angles, he played upon the word with a compassionate and pious feeling, and said, "Well may they be so called, for they are like Angels, and ought to be made co-heritors with the Angels in heaven." Then demanding from what province they were brought, the answer was, "From Deira;" and in the same humour he observed, that rightly might this also be said, for *de Dei irâ*, from the wrath of God they were to be delivered. And when he was told that their king was named Ælla, he replied, that Hallelujah ought to be sung in his dominions. This trifling sprung from serious thought, and ended in serious endeavours. From that day the conversion of the Anglo-Saxons became a favourite object with Gregory. He set out from Rome with the intention of going among them as a missionary himself; but the people, by whom he was greatly admired, rose almost in insurrection because of his departure, and by their outcries compelled the Pope to send after him, and recall him*; and when, upon the death of

* There is an anecdote relating to this recall, which is worthy of notice, as confirming Gregory's character for a punster, and thereby authenticating that string of puns

Pelagius, he was elected to the papacy, he took the first opportunity of beginning the good work on which he was intent. Accordingly he despatched thither forty missionaries from a monastery which he had founded at Rome. When they had proceeded as far as the city of Aix in Provence, the reports which they heard concerning the barbarous kingdoms of the Heptarchy, intimidated them so much, that they halted, and deputed Augustine, who was their chief, to return to the Pope, and represent to him the danger of the

which must always be remembered in the Ecclesiastical History of England. I give it in the words of his anonymous but contemporary biographer. *Sed antequam missi eum adissent, trium dierum jam confecto itinere, dum idem vir Domini B. Gregorius, ut iter agentibus moris est, circa sextam horam in prato quodam sociis quibusdam quiescentibus, aliis autem illi assistentibus vel necessariis rebus occupatis, sederat et legerat; venit ad eum locusta, et dans saltum, paginæ quam percurrebat insedit; cernensque cam beatus vir Domini Gregorius tam mansuetè loco quo assederat, permanere, cœpit, collætans sodalibus, ipsius nomen reciprocans quasi interpretari;* Locusta, *inquam, hæc dici potest, quasi* loco sta. *et subjungens, sciatis, inquit, non progressius nos iter cœptum licere protendere: verumtamen surgite, et jumenta sternite, ut quantum licuerit, quò tendimus properemus. Cum autem hinc mutuò confabularentur, et secum quærerent; pervenerunt missi apostolici equis sudantibus; statimque illi cum magnâ celeritate epistolam, quam detulerant, porrexerunt; quâ perlectâ, Ita est, inquit, socii, ut prædixeram: Romam celerius remeabimus.*—Acta Sanctorum. Mart. T. ii., 133, 134.

attempt and the little probability of succeeding among a ferocious people whose language they did not understand. But Gregory, in reply, enjoined them to proceed: forasmuch, he said, as it is better not to begin a good work, than to withdraw from it. He recommended them also to the French bishops, and to the protection of Theodorick and Theodebert, who were then reigning in France; and he sent an agent into that country to redeem Anglo-Saxon youths from slavery, and place them in monasteries, where they might be carefully educated, and thereby trained to assist in the conversion of their countrymen.

The attempt, which had been represented as so formidable to the missionaries, was in reality free from danger, and political circumstances prepared the way for its success. In the dismembered parts of the great Roman empire, the northern conquerors were no sooner settled in possession of their dominions, than they adopted the religion of the inhabitants, as they did the other customs which were preferable to their own. This change had taken place in France: at that time there was no rivalry or hostility of feeling between France and Britain; each had war enough at home to employ all its restless and turbulent strength; and neighbourhood, therefore, had led to an amicable intercourse, useful to both countries, but most so to Britain, which had preserved less from the wreck of its Roman civilization. Ethelbert, king of Kent, or Oiscinga, as the kings of that province were called, from Oisc, the son of Hengist, whom they regarded as the founder of their dynasty, had married Bertha (otherwise named Aldeberga), daughter of Charibert, king of Paris. Her father is reproached for voluptuousness: if that reproach be deserved, which there seems reason to doubt, even his vices would in such an age be favourable to the milder habits of life; but it is certain that he was of a gentle and generous nature, the liberal patron of arts and literature, and distinguished for his proficiency in Latin. Queen Bertha, therefore, when removed to Kent, might sigh for the refinements of her father's court, and wish that they could be introduced at her husband's. The clergy were in that age the only persons by whom improvements could be brought about; the churches and monasteries were the schools of the ornamental arts, as well as of all the learning that existed; and if the Queen had had no other desire than that of refining the manners of her husband, and softening the barbarity of his subjects, that alone would have induced her joyfully to welcome the missionaries on their arrival, and give them all the encouragement and assistance which it was in her power to bestow. But there was also the sense of duty to influence her. It had been stipulated upon her marriage, that she should be allowed the free and public exercise of her religion. She had brought over with her from France a household establishment of clerks, with a prelate, by name Liudhard, at their head; and a church without the walls of Canterbury, built in the time of the Romans, dedicated to a certain St. Martin, and since the Saxon conquest fallen to decay, had been repaired and fitted up for her use.

When, therefore, Augustine and his companions landed in the Isle of Thanet, they were sure of the Queen's favour: they came also not as obscure men, unprotected and unaccredited; but with recommendations from the Kings of France, and as messengers from a potentate, whose spiritual authority was acknowledged and obeyed throughout that part of the world, to which the northern nations were accustomed to look as the seat of empire and superior civilization. They made their arrival known to Ethelbert, and requested an audience. The King of Kent, though not altogether ignorant of the nature of his Queen's religion, nor unfavourably disposed towards it, was yet afraid of that miraculous power which the Romish clergy were then believed to possess, and which they were not backward at claiming for themselves. For this reason, he would not receive them within the walls of his royal city Canterbury, nor under a roof; but went into the island with his nobles, and took his seat to await them in the open air: imagining that thus he should be secure from the influence of their spells or incantations. They approached in procession, bearing a silver crucifix, and a portrait of our Saviour upon a banner, adorned with gold, and chanting the litany. The King welcomed them courteously, and ordered them to be seated: after which, Augustine stood up, and, through an interpreter, whom he had brought from France, delivered the purport of his mission, in a brief, but well-ordered, and impressive discourse. He was come to the King, and to that kingdom, he said, for their eternal good, a messenger of good tidings; offering to their acceptance perpetual happiness, here and hereafter, if they would accept his words. The Creator and Redeemer had opened the kingdom of heaven to the human race: for God so loved the world that he had sent into it his only Son, as that Son himself testified, to become a man among the children of men, and suffer death upon the cross, in atonement for their sins. That incarnate divinity had been made manifest by innumerable miracles. Christ had stilled the winds and waves, and walked upon the waters: he had healed diseases, and restored the dead to life: finally, he had risen from the dead himself, that we might rise again through him, and had ascended into heaven, that he might receive us there in his glory; and he would come again to judge both the quick and the dead. "Think not," he proceeded, "O most excellent King, that we are superstitious, because we have come from Rome into thy dominions, for the sake of the salvation of thee and of thy people; we have done this, being constrained by great love: for that which we desire, above all the pomps and delights of this world, is to have our fellow-creatures partakers with ourselves in the kingdom of heaven, and to prevent those from perishing who are capable of being advanced to the fellowship of the Angels. The grace of Christ, and of his Spirit, hath infused this charitable desire into all his ministers; so that, regardless of their own concerns, they should burn for the salvation of all nations, and, regarding them as children and brethren, labour to lead them into the ways of eternal peace. This they have done through fire and sword, and every kind of torments and of death; till, through their victorious endeavours, Rome and Greece, the Kings and Princes of the Earth, and the Islands, have rejoiced to acknowledge and worship the Lord God, who is the King of kings. And, at this day, no fear of difficulties, or pain, or death, would deter Gregory, who is now the Father of all Christendom, from coming himself to you, so greatly doth he thirst for your salvation, if it were lawful for him (which it is not) to forsake the care of so many souls committed to his charge. Therefore, he hath deputed us in his stead, that we may shew you the way of light, and open to you the gate of heaven; wherein, if ye do not refuse to renounce your idols and to enter through Christ, ye shall most assuredly live and reign for ever."

The king replied prudently and not unfavourably. Their words and promises, he said, were fair; but what they proposed, was new and doubtful, and therefore he could not assent to it, and forsake the belief in which all the English nations had for so long a time lived. Nevertheless, because they had come from such a distant country, for the sake of communicating to him what they thought true and excellent, he would not interfere with their purpose; on the contrary, he would receive them hospitably, and provide for their support.

Augustine and his companions were accordingly entertained in Canterbury, at the king's expense. They officiated in the church which had been repaired for queen Bertha's use; and it was not long before Ethelbert himself became their convert. After such an example, their success was as rapid as they could desire; for though Ethelbert declared that he would not compel any person to renounce his idols, and profess the new religion, having learnt from his teachers that the service of Christ must be voluntary, he gave notice, that the converts might expect his favour, as persons who had made themselves co-heritors with him of the kingdom of heaven.

Fortunately for the progress of Christianity, Ethelbert held at this time that pre-eminence over the other kings of the Heptarchy, which carried with it the title of Brætwalda: his authority was acknowledged as far north as the Humber. This gave him a wider influence than any of the kings of Kent possessed after him; and, under his protection, the missionaries extended their endeavours into the neighbouring kingdoms. Sebert, his nephew, who reigned in Essex, was the second royal convert. London was the capital of his petty state, and soon after the conversion of its king, Ethelbert (who had previously founded a monastery at Canterbury) built a church there, in honour of the great apostle of the Gentiles, upon a rising ground, where, under the Romans, a temple of Diana had stood; and where successive edifices, each surpassing the former in extent and splendour, have retained the name of St. Paul's from that time to this. Redwald, the Uffinga of East-Anglia (as the kings of that province were called from Redwald's grandfather Uffa), was the third king who professed the new religion. He became a convert when on a visit at the Brætwalda's court; but he was unable to introduce Christianity into his own kingdom on his return, because his wife, and the principal chiefs, adhered obstinately to their old idolatry; compromising, therefore, and perhaps hesitating between the two modes of belief, he set up an altar to Christ in a heathen temple, and mingled christian prayers with sacrifices to the Anglian idols. For this he has been severely censured; but if the concession proved that his knowledge was imperfect, and his faith weak, it prepared an easy way for the general reception of Christianity, when an attempt to have forced it upon the country might have ended in his expulsion from the throne. It was now brought face to face with the idolatry of the Heathens: and the people, seeing it admitted to equal credit, were induced to inquire, and to compare, and choose between them. This was a slow, but necessary, consequence: one which led to more immediate good incidentally resulted. Edwin, the rightful king of Deira, having been expelled in childhood from his kingdom, by Ethelfrith of Bernicia, was then a fugitive at Redwald's court. Ethelfrith, who had made greater conquests from the Britons than any other of the Anglo-Saxon conquerors, and was confident in his power, and elated with success, required Redwald to deliver up the exile, tempting him by three repeated embassies with large offers of silver and gold, and threatening war and destruction if he refused or demurred. The same infirmity of character which had made the Uffinga prevaricate in his religion, now nearly prompted him to the commission of an atrocious crime: moved not by avarice, but by fear, he promised either to put his guest to death, or to expel him. This resolution was taken at nightfall, and immediately communicated to Edwin by a faithful friend, who went to his chamber, called him out of doors, exhorted him to fly, and offered to guide him to a place of safety.

But Edwin would not again encounter the perpetual danger and anxiety of a wandering life. To fly, he said, would be a breach of confidence on his part; he had trusted to the Uffinga Redwald, who, as yet, had offered him no wrong; and if he were to be delivered up, better that it should be by the Uffinga himself than by an ignoble hand. And, indeed, whither could he betake himself, after having, for so many years, in vain sought an asylum through all the provinces of Britain? Resolving therefore to abide his fate, whatever it might be, he sate down mournfully upon a stone before the palace, when a venerable person, in a strange habit, is said to have accosted him, and inquired wherefore he was sitting there, and keeping watch at an hour when all other persons were asleep? Edwin, somewhat angrily, replied, that it could be no concern of his whether he chose to pass the night within doors or without. But the stranger made answer, that he knew the cause, and bade him be of good cheer, for Redwald certainly would not betray him; he assured him further, that he should regain his father's throne, and acquire greater power than any of the Anglo-Saxon Princes had possessed before him; and he asked of him, in requital for these happy fore-tidings, that when they should be fulfilled he would listen to instructions which would then be offered him, and which would lead him into the way of eternal life. This Edwin readily promised; with that the stranger laid his hand upon the head of the royal exile, saying, when this sign shall be repeated, remember what has passed between us now, and perform the word which you have given. And then, according to Bede, he disappeared. By Catholic writers this is represented as a miraculous appearance; others suppose it to have been a dream; a more possible solution is, that the person in whom Edwin afterwards recognised the gesture and garb of the apparition, may actually have been in Redwald's court, though unknown to him, and that it was a real interview. This might be admitted without difficulty, if it were not that in books which abound with gross and palpable fables, whatever appears fabulous is, with too much appearance of probability, accounted so; and thus the writers who in one age impose upon the credulous multitude, provoke, in another, too indiscriminate an incredulity.

Redwald's nature was weak, but not evil; and on this occasion he was saved from guilt and infamy by the brave counsel of his wife. Animated by her he bade defiance to Ethelfrith, marched against him before the Northumbrian had collected the whole of his advancing army, gave him battle on the banks of the river Idel in Nottinghamshire, and defeated and slew him, though with the loss of his own son, Regner, in the battle. Edwin bore a conspicuous part in the victory; it gave him the united kingdoms of Deira and Bernicia, and it placed Redwald in the rank of Brætwalda, which after his death was assumed by Edwin. It led also to more lasting consequences. Edwin sought in marriage Edilburga, or Tata (as she was also called), a princess of Kent, daughter to Ethelbert, and sister to Eadbald, who had succeeded him. The new Oiscinga had cast off Christianity, because he was impatient of its restraints, and had chosen, together with the kingdom, to take unto himself the wife whom his father Ethelbert had wedded after Queen Bertha's death. The three sons of Sebert, his cousins, who had jointly inherited the kingdom of the East Saxons, encouraged by his example, expelled Mellitus, the Bishop of London, because he would not admit them to the communion, while they refused to be baptized; and they restored the old idolatry in their dominions. Mellitus, therefore, and his companion Justus, repaired to Canterbury, to consult with Laurentius, the successor of Augustine, what might best be done. In their despair of effecting any good while circumstances were so unpropitious, they are said to have resolved upon abandoning the island, and Mellitus and Justus, in pursuance of this resolution, sailed for France. Laurentius gave out it was his intention to follow them on the morrow, and he ordered his bed to be laid that night in the church of St. Peter and

St. Paul. In the morning he went into the presence of Eadbald, and instead of taking leave on his departure, as was expected, threw off his habit, and exposed to the astonished King his back and shoulders bloody, and waled with stripes. Being asked who had dared maltreat him in that manner, he made answer, that the Apostle Peter had appeared to him during the night, and punished him thus severely for his purpose of abandoning the flock which had been committed to his charge. It is added, that Eadbald was struck with horror and compunction at what he saw and heard; and in consequence of the effect thus produced upon his mind, he put away his father's widow, received baptism, and prohibited the old Saxon worship, ... which had been tolerated during Ethelbert's reign, but which, by Eadbald's authority in his own dominions, and his influence over the adjoining kingdom, was from that time for ever abolished in Kent and Essex. This story must be either miracle, or fraud, or fable. Many such there are in the history of the Anglo-Saxon, as of every Romish church; and it must be remembered, that when such stories are mere fables, they have for the most part been feigned with the intent of serving the interests of the Romish church, and promulgated, not as fiction, but as falsehood, with a fraudulent mind. The legend which is here related, is probably a wonder of the second class. The clergy of that age thought it allowable to practise upon the ignorance and credulity of a barbarous people, if by such means they might forward the work of their conversion, or induce them, when converted, to lead a more religious life. They may have believed themselves to be acting like parents, who deceive children for their good, when it would be in vain to reason with them. Whether they thought thus or not, it is certain that thus they acted; and it is not less certain, that a system which admitted of pious fraud opened a way for the most impious abuses.

Whether Eadbald was, in this instance, the dupe of Laurentius; or whether, being tired of his step-mother, and perhaps ashamed of his actions, yet more ashamed of exposing himself to the imputation of fickleness and infirmity of purpose, he had concerted with the prelate a scene which might account for, and justify, his sudden change of conduct; from that time he became a zealous supporter of the new religion: and when Edwin solicited his sister Edilburga in marriage, objected to giving her to a heathen. A stipulation, however, was made, as in the case of Queen Bertha, that she should be allowed the free exercise of Christianity for herself and her household; and Edwin declared that he would not hesitate to embrace that faith himself, if, upon due examination, it should be found holier, and worthier of the Deity, than the service of those gods whom he had hitherto worshipped after the manner of his fathers. When, therefore, the chosen Queen departed for the court of her intended husband, Paulinus, one of the last missionaries whom Gregory had sent to assist Augustine, was raised to the episcopal office on this important occasion, that he might accompany her, in the hope of becoming the Apostle of the Northumbrians. Gregory had selected fit men for the service to which they were appointed. Paulinus, instead of urging the King upon the subject of his meditated change, by which he might have offended and indisposed him, left it to time and opportunity, and the silent operations of his own active and meditative mind; and made it his chief business to preserve Edilburga and her attendants from becoming indifferent to their religion in a land of Heathens. He had thus obtained a character for prudence, as well as for talent; when an attempt to assassinate the King was made by an emissary of Cwichelm, King of Wessex, and Edwin was saved from certain death by the fidelity of one of his Thanes, Lilla by name, who, throwing himself between his royal master and the murderer, received the poisoned short sword in his own body. That same night, Edilburga was delivered of a daughter: Edwin returned thanks to his gods * for her favourable delivery. Paulinus was present, and ventured to tell the King, that it was not to those idols, but to the God of the Christians, and his prayers, that he was beholden for this propitious event. The skilful missionary had chosen his time well, while the impression of his providential preservation was fresh, and when the King's heart was softened by the birth of his child. Yielding to these feelings, and to the mother's wishes, he permitted Paulinus to baptize the infant, and twelve of the royal household. The child was named Eanfleda; (among the Anglo-Saxons, the fashion never obtained of introducing scriptural or religious names:) she was the first who received baptism in the kingdom of Northumbria. The King promised also for himself, that if the same God to whom he gave this pledge of his intentions, would preserve

* Cressy says, that he intended to sacrifice the child to these idols. I know not on what authority he states it, for, contrary to his usual practice, he has given no reference here. But it is not mentioned by Bede, and is so inconsistent with Edwin's character, and with the conditions of his marriage, that it may safely be rejected as fabulous.

him, and favour him with victory in the war which he was about to make on Cwichelm, in vengeance for the late murderous attempt, he also would be baptized.

The expedition was successful, and his vengeance was complete: all who were concerned in the intended assassination, were either slain in battle, or delivered into his hands for punishment. From that day, Edwin never offered sacrifice to his idols, but he hesitated concerning the new faith; his mind was perplexed and troubled; he was a man of strong understanding, in middle age, when the intellectual faculties are mature, and least liable to be led astray; he conversed often with Paulinus, and with the most intelligent persons of his court, upon the truth of Christianity; and often retired to meditate upon the awful subject in solitude. At this time, there came letters and presents for him and the Queen, from Pope Boniface, whom Paulinus had made acquainted with the state of his mind. The Pope said to him, that although the wonders of Divine Power could never be adequately explained by the words of man, being incomprehensible by human wisdom, it had pleased God, in his mercy, to infuse into mankind a saving knowledge of himself; and, through the influence of that redeeming mercy, the Father, the Son, and the

Holy Spirit, were now worshipped as One Trinity, from the rising of the sun to the going down thereof, all powers and empires being subject to that Holy Name. He held out to him the example of Eadbald, with whom he was allied by marriage; spake of his Queen as one who, by baptism, had been born again, and thereby made heiress to a glorious immortality; and in the earnestness of paternal love, admonished him to cast away his idols, and, rejecting their vain worship, and the superstition and deceits of their augurs, to believe in the Father who created, the Son who had redeemed, and the Spirit who would enlighten him. The gods which he had hitherto served, had neither sense nor power of motion; they were mere images, made by man, and it behoved him to demolish and destroy them. But he possessed a living spirit; and the Pope invited him to the knowledge of that God who had created him, had breathed into him an immortal soul with the breath of life; and had sent his Son to redeem him from the effects of original sin, and from the powers of evil, and to reward him with everlasting happiness. In his letter to the Queen, the Holy Father expressed his regret that her husband, who was a part of herself, should still remain in the darkness of Heathenism; and he exhorted her to pray earnestly, and persevere in praying, that they might be joined together in faith as in marriage, that so their union might continue after this perishable life. The presents for the King, consisted of a *camisia*, or under garment, with an ornament of gold, and a certain vesture, called *læna anciriana;* those for the Queen were a silver mirror, and an ivory comb, inlaid with gold.

One day, when Edwin had retired alone, as was his manner, to brood over the momentous question which these letters had pressed upon his immediate attention, Paulinus entered the room, and laying his hand upon the King's head, asked him if he remembered that token? Startled at the appeal, as if a spirit was before him, the King fell at his feet. "Behold," said Paulinus, raising him up, "thou hast, through God's favour, escaped from the enemies of whom thou wert in fear! Behold, through God's favour, thou hast recovered thy kingdom, and obtained the pre-eminence which was promised thee! Remember now thine own promise, and observe it: that He who hath elevated thee to this temporal kingdom, may deliver thee also from eternal misery, and take thee to live and reign with himself eternally in heaven!" Edwin, overcome as if by miracle, hesitated no longer. He called his chiefs to council, that, if they could be persuaded to think and believe as he did, they might be baptized at the same time: and when they were assembled, he required them each to deliver his opinion concerning the new religion which was preached among them, and the propriety of receiving it.

Coifi, the Chief Priest of Northumbria, was the first who spake: "As for what the religion is, which is now propounded to us," he said, "O King, see thou to it! For my part, I will assert what I certainly know, that that which we have hitherto held, is good for nothing. For, among all thy people, there is no one who has given himself more diligently to the worship of our gods than I; and yet many have received greater benefits, and obtained higher dignities, and prospered better in whatever they undertook. But if these gods had possessed any power, they would rather have assisted me, who have endeavoured so carefully to serve them. If, therefore, after due examination, you have perceived that these new things, of which we are told, are better and more efficacious, let us, without delay, hasten to adopt them."

Another speaker delivered an opinion, more creditable to his disposition and understanding than that which had been given by the Chief Priest: "O King, the present life of man, when considered in relation to that which is to come, may be likened to a sparrow flying through the hall, wherein you and your chiefs and servants are seated at supper, in winter time: the hearth blazing in the centre, and the viands smoaking, while without is the storm and rain or snow; the bird flies through, entering at one door, and passing out at the other; he feels not the weather during the little minute that he is within; but after that minute, he returns again to winter, as from winter he came, and is seen no more. Such is the life of man; and of what follows it, or of what has preceded it, we are altogether ignorant. Wherefore, if this new doctrine should bring any thing more certain, it well deserves to be followed." The rest of the assembly signified their assent to the change; and it was then proposed by Coifi, that Paulinus should fully explain to them the nature of the new religion, which they were called upon to receive. When the prelate had concluded his discourse, the Chief Priest exclaimed, that he had long understood the vanity of their old worship, because the more he sought to discover its truth, the less he found; he proposed, therefore, that the altars and temples of the idols, and the sacred inclosures in which they stood, should be overthrown and burnt. The King demanded of him who ought to set the example of violating them, and the Priest himself offered to begin. He asked the King accordingly for arms and for a horse; girt a sword to his side, mounted, and took a lance in his hand. When the people beheld him, they thought that he was seized with madness, because in bearing arms, and riding on a horse, he broke through the prohibitions attached among them to the sacerdotal office. He, however, rode resolutely towards the temple, and at once desecrated it, by throwing his lance within the inclosure; his companions then, as he exhorted them, set fire to it. The scene of this memorable event was a little east of York, upon the river Derwent, at a place then called Godmunddingaham, the home of the protection of the gods. The village which now stands upon the site, retains the name, with no other change than that of a convenient abbreviation from five syllables to three, Godmundham.

The new converts acted with indiscreet zeal in thus destroying what appears to have been the most noted place of heathen worship in Northumbria. It had been the wise advice of Gregory to Mellitus, that the Anglo-Saxon temples should not be demolished; but that he and his fellow-missionaries should cast out and consume the idols, and then purify the buildings themselves with holy water; and erect altars and place relics there, in order that the people might be better disposed to receive the new religion, seeing its rites performed in the fanes which they were wont to frequent. Godmunddingaham having been destroyed, a wooden oratory was hastily erected in York, for the ceremony of the King's baptism, which was performed there on Easter-day, A.D. 627. A church, of stone, was immediately commenced upon the same spot, inclosing the oratory. It was conferred upon Paulinus, as his See, and he superintended the building. The King's example was readily followed by the people; and Paulinus is said to have been employed six-and-thirty days, from morning till evening, in baptizing the multitudes who flocked to him at Yevering. Oratories had not yet been built, nor baptisteries constructed; the converts, therefore, were baptized in rivers, by immersion, according to the practice of those ages. The ceremony was performed in the river Glen in Bernicia; and in Deira, where he usually resided with the court, in the Swale, near Catterick.

The influence of Edwin's example was not confined to his own dominions. By his persuasions, Eorpwald, the son and successor of Redwald, established Christianity in East-Anglia. But, after having obtained an acknowledged ascendency over all the Anglo-Saxon kingdoms, Kent alone excepted,... after subduing great part of Wales, and the isles of Man and Anglesey,... Edwin, while he maintained order through his dominions by means of a vigilant police, and endeavoured to civilize, as well as to convert, his subjects,...unhappily fell in battle against the combined Kings, Cadwallon of Gwynedd, and Penda, who had erected a new Anglo-Saxon kingdom in Mercia. Penda was still a Heathen; but the British King was the more ferocious of the two: he boasted, now that he had defeated the most powerful of the invaders, that he would exterminate the whole race from Britain; and, in pursuance of this threat, his army spared neither sex nor age; the common religion which the Northumbrians possessed, had no effect in mitigating the inhumanity of the conquerors; and the enormous cruelties which they perpetrated were long remembered with horror. Deira and Bernicia were now again divided, and Paganism was restored in both, by the two sons of Ethelfrith, who ventured to assert a claim to their perilous thrones. Both were slain by the terrible Cadwallon. The Britons now fondly believed that the predictions of their bards were about to be fulfilled, in the recovery of their country by a hero who had been victorious in fourteen great battles and sixty skirmishes, but the last reasonable hope of that fulfilment was destroyed when Cadwallon and the flower of his army were cut off by the Bernicians under Oswald, third son of that Ethelfrith whom Edwin had slain.

During Edwin's reign Oswald and his brothers had found protection in Scotland, where Christianity was flourishing, the island of Hy, or Iona, which appears to have been the chief seat of the Druidical superstition in those parts, being then famous for its monastery of Icolmkill, in which many of the arts, and all the learning of that age, were cultivated. The three brothers became Christians during their exile. Oswald was the only sincere convert; he erected the Cross for his standard before the battle in which Cadwallon was slain; and, after the victory, sending for a monk from Icolmkill, he re-established the religion which his brethren had suppressed, and gave him the isle of Lindisfarn for his episcopal seat. By his influence also Cynegils, the King of Wessex, was induced to receive baptism, and set up the new religion in his dominions. Oswald fell in battle against Penda, and his brother Oswy succeeded to the throne. Penda's son Peada visited the new King, became enamoured of his daughter Alhfleda, and embraced Christianity that he might obtain her for his wife. Through this marriage it was introduced among the Mercians during Penda's life, with his connivance, and established there after his death. By Oswy's interference it was restored in Essex, where it had been supplanted by the old idolatry. Sussex was now the only unconverted kingdom; there it was introduced through the influence of Mercia; and thus, in the course of eighty-two years from the arrival of Augustine and his fellow-missionaries in Kent, Christianity became the religion of all the Anglo-Saxon states.

CHAPTER IV.

CAUSES WHICH PROMOTED THE SUCCESS OF CHRISTIANITY AMONG THE ANGLO-SAXONS.

In regarding the triumph of Christianity among the Anglo-Saxons, a natural inquiry rises why it should have been so easily established, and with so little struggle, seeing that its introduction into heathen countries has in later centuries been found so exceedingly difficult, as at one time to be generally considered hopeless, and almost impossible without a miracle. This striking difference is to be explained by the very different circumstances under which all recent attempts had been undertaken, and the different character of the false faiths against which they were directed.

The paganism of our Saxon ancestors was not rooted in their history, nor intimately connected with their institutions and manners; it had no hold upon the reason, the imagination, or the feelings of the people. It appealed to no records, or inspired founders: in its forms it was poor and unimpressive; there was nothing useful or consolatory in its tenets; and whatever strength it derived from local superstitions was lost by transplantation ; for the conquerors, when they settled in Britain, were cut off from those sacred places in their native land which they had regarded with hereditary reverence. Such a religion, without pomp and without pretensions, had nothing which could be opposed to Christianity. On the other hand, the Christian missionaries came with the loftiest claims, and with no mean display of worldly dignity. They appeared not as unprotected, humble, and indigent adventurers, whose sole reliance was upon the compassion of those whom they offered to instruct; but as members of that body by which arts and learning were exclusively possessed,...a body enjoying the highest consideration and the highest influence throughout all the Christian kingdoms: they came as accredited messengers from the head of that body, and from that city, which, though no longer the seat of empire, was still the heart of the European world ; for wheresoever the Christian religion had extended itself in the west, Rome was already a more sacred name than it had ever been in the height of its power.

The missionaries therefore appeared with a character of superiority, their claim to which was not to be disputed. They spake as men having authority. They appealed to their books for the history of the faith which they taught: and for the truth of its great doctrines they appealed to that inward evidence which the heart of man bears in the sense of its own frailties, and infirmities, and wants. They offered an universal instead of a local religion; a clear and coherent system instead of a mass of unconnected fancies; an assured and unquestionable faith for vague and unsettled notions, which had neither foundation nor support. The errors and fables with which Romish Christianity was debased, in no degree impeded its effect: gross as they were, it is even probable that they rendered it more acceptable to a rude and ignorant people, ... a people standing as much in need of rites and ceremonies, of tangible forms, and a visible dispensation, as the Jews themselves when the law was promulgated. The missionaries also possessed in themselves a strength beyond what they derived from their cause, and from the adventitious circumstances that favoured them. They were the prime spirits of the age, trained in the most perfect school of discipline, steady in purpose, politic in contrivance, little scrupulous concerning the measures which they employed, because they were persuaded that any measures were justifiable if they conduced to bring about the good end which was their aim. This principle led to abominable consequences among their successors, but they themselves had no sinister views; they were men of the loftiest minds, and ennobled by the highest and holiest motives; their sole object in life was to increase the number of the blessed, and extend the kingdom of their Saviour, by communicating to their fellow-creatures the appointed means of salvation; and elevated as they were above all worldly hopes and fears, they were ready to lay down their lives in the performance of this duty, sure by that sacrifice of obtaining crowns in heaven, and altars upon earth, as their reward.

Thus excellently qualified for their undertaking, and with these great advantages, the missionaries began their work; not rashly and unadvisedly, but upon a well-concerted system. They addressed themselves to the Kings of the Heptarchy, and when the King was converted, the conversion of the chiefs and of the people followed, as a matter of course. Every thing favoured them in this attempt. The princes who accepted the new faith were thereby qualified to contract matrimonial alliances with the Kings of France, then divided into many kingdoms; an asylum for themselves or their families was thus obtained, in case of those reverses which in such a stage of society are so frequent; and they plainly felt themselves advanced in dignity by professing a religion which at that time distinguished the civilized from the barbarous parts of Europe. If they desired to improve their subjects, to meliorate the state of their kingdoms, and to embellish their courts and capitals, it was by means of the Christian clergy alone that these good ends could be effected. The chiefs perceived their interest in promoting a faith which inculcated upon their dependents, the duties of obedience and fidelity; and it could not but be acceptable to the inferior classes, because, while it taught them to expect equal and retributive justice beyond the grave, it required from their lords the practice of humanity and beneficence among the works, by aid of which they were to obtain a place in heaven. It is probable, indeed, that the servile part of the population may have been favourably inclined to Christianity, and in some degree prepared for it: for slavery prevailed in the island when the North-men invaded it, and in a conquest, as in a purchase, the slaves would be transferred with the soil to which they were attached. But the conquerors cared too little about their own idolatry, to interfere with the worship of their slaves. It is likely, therefore, that these persons remembered the religion of their forefathers with some degree of reverential respect; perhaps, some of its forms may have been preserved among them, and, in consequence, an inclination to assist the Britons in the efforts which, from time to time, were made for recovering their country. It is, therefore, not unlikely, that the Anglo-Saxons perceived some political advantage in a change which bound the labouring part of the people to their lords by a religious tie, and broke the bond between them and their enemies. The Heathen priests seem not, in any instance, to have opposed a determined resistance. Probably, the rank and influence which they possessed was inconsiderable; and they no where acted as a body. The Jutes, and the Angles, and the Saxons, may have cared little for each other's gods, or have regarded them as inimical; and each may have beheld with satisfaction, the overthrow of rival, or of hostile, altars.

The change was beneficial in every way. Hitherto, there had been no other field of enterprise than what was offered by war: the church now opened to aspiring minds, a surer way to a higher, and more enviable, and more lasting, distinction. The finest and noblest of the human faculties had hitherto lain dormant: they were quickened and developed now, and spirits which would else have been extinguished in inaction, and have past away from the earth unconscious of their own strength, shone forth in their proper sphere. Whatever knowledge and whatever arts had survived the decay and fall of the Roman empire, were transplanted hither, with the religion to which they owed their preservation. The inhabitants of Britain were no longer divided from the whole world; they became a part of Christendom. The intellectual intercommunion of nations, such as it was, became in consequence greater at that time than it is now; and it is probable that more English, in proportion to the population of the country, went into Italy in those ages for the purposes of devotion, than have ever in any subsequent age been led thither by curiosity, and fashion, and the desire of improvement.

The Anglo-Saxons were indebted to the missionaries probably for the use of letters, certainly for their first written laws. These were promulgated by Ethelbert, the first Christian King, with the consent of his nobles, and, differing in this respect from the laws of all the other Gothic nations, in the vernacular tongue. In the continental kingdoms the laws were given in Latin, because it was the language of the great body of the population, and continued to be that of the law; here the Saxon was preferred, upon the same clear principle that the laws which all were bound to obey, ought to be intelligible to all. Latin, however, was made the language of religion; there had been the same reason for this in Italy, and Spain, and France, as for making it the language of the laws; and in England also there was a reason, which, though different, was not less valid. A common language was necessary for the clergy, who considered themselves as belonging less to the particular country in which they happened individually to be born, or stationed, than to their order, and to Christendom; for in those ages Christendom was regarded as something more than a mere name. No modern language was as yet fixed, or reduced to rules, or regarded as a written tongue: of necessity, therefore, Latin, in which the Western Clergy read the Scriptures, and in which the Fathers of the Western Church had composed their works, and the Councils had issued their decrees, was every where retained as the natural and professional language of the ministers of religion. They preached, and catechized, and confessed in the common speech of the country; and that the church service was not verbally intelligible to the congregation was, upon their principles, no inconvenience. It was a sacrifice which was offered for the people, not a service, in which they were required to join with the lips, and the understanding, and the heart. They understood its general purport; the spectacle impressed them; and the reverent and awful sense of devotion, which was thus produced, was deemed enough.

But if in this respect there was no real disadvantage in the use of a foreign tongue, in other respects many and most important advantages arose from it. The clergy became of necessity a learned body; and to their humble and patient labours we owe the whole history of the middle ages, and the preservation of those works of antiquity, which, for the instruction of all after-ages, have been preserved. The students at Canterbury, in Bede's time, were as well skilled, both in Latin and Greek, as in their native speech; and Bede himself (worthy to be called Venerable, if ever that epithet was worthily applied) had acquired all that could possibly be learnt from books, and was master of what was then the whole circle of human knowledge. Nor were the clergy the teachers of letters only; from them the ornamental and the useful arts were derived. Church music was introduced at Canterbury, and from thence into the other kingdoms. Churches, which at first, like those at that time existing in Scotland, were constructed of timber, and thatched with reeds, were, in imitation of the continental temples, built with stone, and covered with lead; glass for their windows was introduced; and church architecture, in the course of a few generations, attained a perfection and a magnificence, which in ancient times have never been surpassed, and which modern ages, with all their wealth, cannot afford to vie with.

The seed had not fallen among thorns, nor upon a hard and sterile soil; and though some tares were sown with it, the harvests, nevertheless, were for a while abundant. Wherever Christianity has been preached among heathen or barbarous nations, women and old men have been the readiest believers; the former, because their importance in society and their happiness are so materially promoted by its domestic institutions;...the latter, because needing its hopes and consolations, and desiring to pass their latter days in tranquillity, they feel the value of a religion which was announced with Peace on Earth, and which, while its kingdom is delayed, imparts to the mind of every individual by whom it is faithfully received, that peace which passeth all understanding. All ranks received the new religion with enthusiasm. Many Kings, weary of the cares and dangers of royalty, or struck with remorse for the crimes by which they had acquired or abused their rank, abdicated their thrones, and retired into monasteries to pass the remainder of their days in tranquillity or in penance. Widowed Queens were thankful to find a like asylum. The daughters of royal or noble houses, preferring the hopes of a better world to the precarious enjoyments of this, found in the convent comforts and security, which in those turbulent ages were hardly to be obtained elsewhere: and youths of royal blood, whose enterprising tempers might otherwise have contributed to the misery of their own and of the neighbouring states, embraced a religious life, and went forth as missionaries to convert and civilize the barbarians of Germany and of the North. To the servile part of the community the gospel was indeed tidings of great joy: frequently they were emancipated, either in the first fervour of their owner's conversion, or as an act of atonement and meritorious charity at death. The people in the north of England are described as going out in joyful procession to meet the itinerant priest when they knew of his approach, bending to receive his blessing, and crowding to hear his instructions. The churches were frequented; he who preached at a cross in the open air never wanted an attentive congregation; and the zeal of the clergy, for as yet they were neither corrupted by wealth, nor tainted by ambition, was rewarded by general respect and love.

They well deserved their popularity. Wherever monasteries were founded marshes were drained, or woods cleared, and wastes brought into cultivation; the means of subsistence were increased by improved agriculture, and by improved horticulture new comforts were added to life. The humblest as well as the highest pursuits were followed in these great and most beneficial establishments. While part of the members were studying the most inscrutable points of theology, and indulging themselves in logical subtleties of psychological research which foster the presumption of the human mind, instead of convincing it of its weakness,...others were employed in teaching babes and children the rudiments of useful knowledge; others as copyists, limners, carvers, workers in wood, and in stone, and in metal, and in trades and manufactures of every kind, which the community required.

The enmity between the Britons and Anglo-Saxons was not diminished by the conversion of the latter nation, because that conversion was not, as among the other northern conquerors, derived from the conquered people. It rather, for a time, aggravated the hostile feeling with which the Britons, or Welsh, as they must now be called, regarded the invaders of their country. The Saxons received Christianity with its latest ceremonial additions and doctrinal corruptions*. The Welsh were possessed of a purer faith; and, it is said, that though they had not scrupled to eat and drink with the Pagan Saxons, they refused to hold this communion with them after they became Christians, on the score of their idolatrous religion. In return, they were regarded as having fallen into schism, during the two centuries which had elapsed since the wreck of Roman civilization in the island. They had, in reality, become more barbarous, because of the unsuccessful wars which, with few intervals, they waged against the now-established conquerors, and the almost continual divisions among themselves;

* Upon this point, Fuller touches with his characteristic felicity. Taking his "farewell of Augustine," this delightful writer says, "he found here a plain religion (simplicity is the badge of antiquity,) practised by the Britons; living some of them in the contempt, and many more in the ignorance, of worldly vanities. He brought in a religion, spun with a coarser thread, though guarded with a finer trimming; made luscious to the senses with pleasing ceremonies, so that many who could not judge of the goodness, were courted with the gaudiness, thereof. We are indebted to God his goodness in moving Gregory; Gregory's carefulness in sending Augustine; Augustine's forwardness in preaching here; but above all, let us bless God's exceeding great favour, that that doctrine which Augustine planted here but impure, and his successors made worse with watering, is since, by the happy reformation, cleared and refined to the purity of the scriptures."

while, on the other hand, the Saxons, from the time of their conversion, had been progressive in arts and comforts. The Welsh clergy may not, perhaps, have felt their inferiority to their neighbours in learning; but they were aware of the strength which their order derived from union under one head; and though there is reason to believe that the Britons had been more connected with the Eastern than the Western Church, they acknowledged, at length, the supremacy of the See of Rome, for the sake of its protection; conformed to its ceremonies, and gradually received its corruptions.

CHAPTER V.

RELIGION OF THE DANES—THEIR CONVERSION.

Many years had not elapsed after the full establishment of Christianity throughout the island, before the Danes began their invasions, which they continued from time to time, sometimes being defeated, but more frequently with success; till, after a long and dreadful contest, they possessed themselves, partly by treaty, partly by conquest, first of a considerable part of the ill-united Anglo-Saxon kingdoms, and ultimately of the throne.

The Danes were of the same race as their northern predecessors in England, but they were far more ferocious than those tribes who conquered the country from the Romans and the Britons; and their insatiable appetite for war and carnage was inflamed by a wild and fierce mythology. This mythology was founded on the traditionary belief of their predecessors; but upon that foundation an extraordinary system of fable had been constructed by the Scalds, or poets, who wrought in the old Scandinavian faith a change similar to that which was effected in Jewish theology by the Rabbis, and in the Romish belief by Monks and Friars. Perhaps, like the Bards among the Keltic tribes, the Scalds may have originally belonged to the sacerdotal class. It was their office to record in verse the actions of kings and heroes; no other histories were preserved by these nations; for though they possessed an alphabet, their state of ignorance was such that they scarcely applied it to any other use than the imaginary purposes of magic. These historical poems were recited at public ceremonies and at feasts; they served as war-songs also. This custom, according with other circumstances, made their chiefs beyond all other men ambitious of military renown; and the Scalds were liberally requited with gifts and honours for that portion of fame which it was in their power, and in theirs only, to award. The authority which they derived from their office, as historians, may not improbably account for the belief that their mythological fables obtained. Whatever the cause may have been, those fables became the belief of the people, as the theogony of Hesiod and the machinery of the Homeric poems were accredited in Greece.

The accounts which have reached us of their system are of undoubted authenticity; and they are more complete than those of any other barbarous superstition. It acknowledged the patriarchal truth that one Almighty God hath existed for ever, by whom all things were made. Alfader, the universal parent, was the name by which he was known. Long before the earth was made, he formed Nifleheim, or Evil-Vome, the abode of the wicked, in the remotest north. Opposite to this, in the remotest south, there existed a fiery region called Muspelsheim, the dominion of a dreadful being, by name Surtur, which is to say, the Black, who held in his hand a burning sword. Between the world of fire and Nifleheim there was a great abyss, into which rivers of venom, rising from a fountain in the middle of hell, rolled and concreted, filling that side of the abyss with incrusted poison and ice and cold vapours; beneath which, in the interior, there were whirlwinds and tempests. On the other side, sparks and lightnings continually proceeded from the world of Surtur. Thus, there breathed always an icy wind from the north, and a fiery one from the south; in the middle of the abyss, beyond the influence of either, it was light and serene. To the north of this clear calm region the work of creation began. A breath of life went forth, and warmed the cold vapours; they resolved into drops; and by the power of him who governed, the giant Ymir was produced. A male and female sprung from under his arm during his sleep, and a son from his feet, and these begat the race of the Giants of the frost, who multiplied, and were all wicked like Ymir, their father. At the same time that Ymir was produced, the same liquefaction give birth to the cow Oedumla, by whose milk, which flowed in rivers, the giant Ymir was fed. From the cow there sprung a man gifted with beauty and power; he was the father of Bore; and Bore, marrying the daughter of a giant, begat Odin and his two brethren, between whom and Ymir there was enmity.

These brethren were gods; they slew Ymir, and the blood which issued from his wounds drowned all the giants of the frost, except one wise giant and his family, who escaped in a bark, and perpetuated the race of the giants. The three brethren then dragged the body of Ymir into the midst of the abyss, and of it they made the heaven and the earth. They made the water and the sea of his blood, the mountains of his bones, and the rocks of his teeth; the firmament they made of his scull, and placed four dwarfs, called East, West, North, and South, to support it at the four corners where it rested upon the earth; they tost into the air his brains, which became clouds, and from his hair they made the herbs of the field. Then they seized fires from Muspelsheim, and placed them in the upper and lower parts of the sky, to enlighten the earth. The earth which they made was round ; round about it was the deep sea, and the shores were given to the giants; but they raised a fortress, called Midgard, against the giants, which, with its circumference, surrounds the world; and in the middle of the earth they built Asgard, which is the court of the gods. There Odin had his palace called Lidskialf, the Terror of the Nations, from whence he beheld all places and all things. He and his brethren one day, as they were walking upon the shore, found two pieces of wood floating upon the waves, and taking them they made of the one a man, and a woman of the other ; the man they named Aske, and the woman Emla, and these were the parents of the human race.

But Odin took Frigga, who is the earth, his daughter, to wife, and from that marriage the Ases, that is to say, the Gods, proceeded. Their sacred city is in heaven, under the ash Ydrasil, which is the greatest of all trees, for its roots cover Nifleheim, and its branches spread over the whole earth, and reach above the heavens. The way from heaven to earth is by a bridge, which is the rainbow ; and at the end of that bridge Heimdall, the sentinel of the gods, hath his station to watch the giants. He sees an hundred leagues round him by night as well as by day; his hearing is so acute that he hears the wool grow on the sheep's back; and when he sounds his trumpet it is heard throughout all worlds. The souls of all who were slain in battle were received in heaven, in the palace of Odin, called Valhalla, which had five hundred and forty gates. There they passed their lives in continual enjoyment, fighting and cutting each other to pieces every morning, then returning whole to dine upon the boar Serimner, who was hunted and eaten every day, and restored to life every night that he might be ready for the morrow; their drink was ale out of the sculls of their enemies, or mead, which a she-goat produced every day instead of milk, in quantity sufficient to inebriate them all. But this life of perfect enjoyment was not to endure for ever; for, mighty as the Gods of Valhalla were, they had enemies mighty as themselves, and who were destined to prevail over them at last.

The most remarkable of these was Loke; he was of the race of the giants: handsome in his person, of extraordinary ability and cunning, but wicked and malicious, and of so inconstant a temper, that he often associated with the Gods, and on many occasions extricated them from great dangers. This Loke had three dreadful offspring by a giantess. The wolf Fenris was one, the Great Serpent was the second, and Hela, or Death, the third. The Gods knew from many oracles what evils would be brought upon them by this accursed progeny, and to defer a destiny which was not to be averted, Odin sent for them from the country of the Giants. Hela he placed in Nifleheim, and appointed her to govern the nine dolorous worlds, to which all who die of sickness or old age are fated. Grief is her hall, and Famine her table; Hunger her knife, Delay and Slackness her servants, Faintness her porch, and Precipice her gate; Cursing and Howling are her tent, and her bed is Sickness and Pain. The Great Serpent he threw into the middle of the ocean, but there the monster grew till with his length he encompassed the whole globe of the earth. The wolf Fenris they bred up for a while among them, and then by treachery bound him in an enchanted chain, fastened it to a rock, and sunk him deep into the earth. The Gods also imprisoned Loke in a cavern, and suspended a snake over his head, whose venom fell drop by drop upon his face. The deceit and cruelty which the Gods used against this race, could not, however, change that order of events which the oracles had foretold. That dreadful time, which is called the Twilight of the Gods, must at length arise; Loke and the wolf Fenris will then break loose, and, with the Great Serpent, and the Giants of the frost, and Surtur with his fiery sword, and all the powers of Muspelheim, pass over the bridge of heaven, which will break beneath them. The Gods, and all the heroes of Valhalla, will give them battle. Thor, the strongest of the race of Odin, will slay the Great Serpent, but be himself suffocated by the floods of poison which the monster vomits forth. Loke and Heimdall will kill each other. The wolf Fenris, after devouring the Sun, will devour Odin also, and himself be rent in pieces by Vidar, the son of Odin; and Surtur, with his fires, will consume the whole world, Gods, heroes, and men perishing in the conflagration. Another and better earth will afterwards arise, another Sun, other Gods, and a happier race of men.

Such is the brief outline of that mythology which is detailed in the Edda. It had grown up in the interval between the Saxon conquest and the first Danish invasions. The deified progenitors of the Anglo-Saxon kings were here converted into beings, wholly mythological; and, except in their names, there appears to have existed little or no resemblance between the earlier and later religion of these kindred nations. How much of the fabulous superstructure was intended to be believed by those who framed it, or how much was actually believed, cannot, at this distance of time, be determined. Possibly, as among the Greeks, and as perhaps was the case with many Monkish legends, tales which were invented in mere sport of fancy, obtained a credit that had neither been designed nor foreseen, but which was allowed to prevail by those who found advantage in its prevalence. There were some daring spirits who disbelieved such Gods, and openly defied them; but such darings arose from the excess of that ferocious spirit which the system itself produced and fostered; for, monstrous as the mythology is, it had a dreadful effect upon the national character.

The nations by which the kingdoms of the Heptarchy were founded, were not more cruel in war than the Greeks and Romans in their best ages; but the Danes equalled in cruelty the worst barbarians of Asia or Africa. Under the name of Danes, our old historians include the people of Sweden and Norway, as well as of Zealand and Jutland. Those countries were then divided into numberless petty kingdoms; the population was confined to the coasts and the rivers; the habits of the people were wholly piratical, and their institutions were founded upon a system of piracy. For the prevention of civil war, it was their custom that, on the death of a king, one of his sons should be chosen to succeed him, and the rest provided with ships, that they might assume the title of Sea-Kings, and conquer a territory for themselves, or live as freebooters upon the ocean. The Land-Kings themselves made piracy their sport during the summer; and all persons who were able to fit out ships, carried it on under the inferior title of Vikingr. It was their boast that they never slept under a smoky roof, nor drank over a hearth; and they who had accumulated wealth in this course of life, ordered it to be buried with them, that their sons might not be tempted to desist from the only pursuit which was accounted honourable.

These habits of piracy were rendered more ferocious by the character of their dreadful superstition. To a people who were taught that all who died of age or sickness were doomed to an abode of misery in the world to come, the greatest of all calamities was to die in peace. Men threw themselves from precipices to avoid this evil. A bay in Sweden, surrounded with high rocks, which was one of the places frequented for this purpose, is still called the Hall of Odin, that name having been given it when it was believed to be the entrance to his palace, for those who sought it by a voluntary death. And as their notions of future reward were not less preposterous than those which they entertained of future punishment, they were even more injurious in effect. When the Vikingr spent the day in carnage, and refreshed themselves by drinking ale and mead out of human sculls, they fancied that they were establishing their claim to the joys of Valhalla, by taking this foretaste of its happiness on earth.

But among men, as among wild beasts, the taste of blood creates the appetite for it, and the appetite for it is strengthened by indulgence. Men who had learnt to delight in the death of their enemies, were not contented with inflicting mere death; they craved for the sight of torments. The Spread Eagle of heraldry is derived from one of their inhuman practices toward their prisoners. This subject is too horrible to be pursued. Suffice it to record the name of Olver, the Norwegian, who, because he abolished in his company of pirates the custom which was common among them, of tossing infants upon pikes, obtained the name of Barnakall, or the Preserver of Children, an appellation more truly honourable than was ever conferred upon a conqueror.

In societies of the profligate and wicked there are always some whose miserable ambition it is to distinguish themselves by being pre-eminently bad. There were among these atrocious people a set of men calling themselves Berserkir, whose practice it was, before they went into battle, to madden themselves with rage, and then act like wild beasts in their fury. This state of mind they produced, not by intoxicating drugs (like the Malays, when they are preparing to *run a muck*,) but by the effort of a strong will, directed to a desperate purpose, over the willing body. Odin is said to have been the first who practised it. The men who affected it were at one time held in honour; but either they were found dangerous to their companions, or the voluntary paroxysm induced such effects of real insanity, and permanent injury to the overwrought frame, that it was at length prohibited.

It may well be supposed that the rites of such a people partook the character of their ferocious faith. Some of their ceremonies were obscene, others were bloody. They sacrificed human victims, whose bodies were suspended in the sacred groves. In that at Upsal seventy-two victims were counted at one time. When we consider the real nature of every Pagan idolatry, the loathsome obscenities and revolting cruelties which are found in all, and the direct tendency of all to corrupt and harden the heart, we shall not wonder that the early Christians ascribed to them a diabolical origin, and believed the Gods of the Heathen to be not mere creatures of perverted fancy, but actual Devils, who delighted in thus deluding mankind, and disinheriting them of that eternal happiness whereof they were created capable.

The Danes who settled in England became Christians by position and contact. Alfred, with that wisdom which appeared in all his actions, compelled those whom he subdued to receive baptism. They who established themselves afterwards by conquest in the island, found it politic to receive the religion of the country. The change was no doubt accelerated by propagandists from the Anglo-Saxon Church; but if there had been great zeal or great success in their endeavours, some record of it would have been preserved. The missionaries of that church were more usefully employed in medicating the bitter waters at their spring. They sowed the seed of Christianity throughout the Scandinavian kingdoms, and many of them watered it with their blood. Their holy efforts were assisted by political events. Charlemagne and Otho the Great provided for the introduction of their religion wherever they extended their conquests. They built abbeys, and established bishopricks, well knowing that by no other means could the improvement of the country, the civilization of the people, and the security of their states, be so materially promoted. By this policy, by the steady system of the Popes, the admirable zeal of the

Benedictines, and by the blessing of God, which crowned all, the whole of the Scandinavian nations were converted about the time of the Norman conquest; and thus an end was put to those religions which made war their principle, and sanctifying the most atrocious and accursed actions, had the misery of mankind for their end. It was from a clear and certain knowledge of this tendency that, by the laws of Wihtræd, a sacrifice to the idols was to be punished with confiscation of property, and the pillory; and by the laws of our great Alfred with death.

CHAPTER VI.

THE ANGLO-SAXON CHURCH—ST. DUNSTAN.

The church government established in this island by Augustine and his fellow-labourers was that episcopal form which had prevailed among the Britons, and which was derived from the Apostles in uninterrupted descent. The dioceses were originally of the same extent as the respective kingdoms of the Heptarchy; the clergy resided with the Bishop, and itinerated through the diocese, preaching at a cross in the open air. There was no public provision for erecting churches and endowing them; these things might in those ages safely be left to individual munificence and piety. Cathedrals and monasteries were built, and lands settled upon them, by royal founders and benefactors: and their estates were augmented by private grants, often given as an atonement for crimes, but unquestionably far more often from the pure impulse of devotion. Beside these endowments, tithes, the institution of which was regarded not as merely political and temporary, but as of moral and perpetual obligation, were paid by those who became Christians, the converts taking upon themselves, with the other obligations of their new religion, this payment, which was universal throughout Christendom. The full predial tithe was intended; the smaller ones were at first voluntary oblations, and the whole was received into a common fund, for the fourfold purpose of supporting the clergy, repairing the church, relieving the poor, and entertaining the pilgrim and the stranger. The distribution was left to the Bishop and his assistants. Such was the practice of the Anglo-Saxon, as it seems to have been of the British, Church.

Long before the kingdoms of the Heptarchy were united, a perfect union of their churches had been effected, and perfect uniformity established, under the primacy of Canterbury, by the exertions of its seventh Archbishop, Theodore, a native, like St. Paul, of Tarsus, in Cilicia. This extraordinary man, whose name ought to be held among us in grateful and respectful remembrance, was appointed to his high station by Pope Vitalian, when, in the sixty-sixth year of his age, he was residing as a lay-brother in a monastery at Rome. He was chosen because he was well acquainted with France, having twice been employed there, and given proof of his singular abilities; and his advanced age was not considered to be an objection, because his undecayed vigour, and the youthfulness of his spirit, seemed to promise many years of activity and usefulness ; an expectation which was well fulfilled, for Theodore lived to be fourscore and eight. He brought with him what was then a large and truly an invaluable library of Greek and Latin books ; the works of Homer were among them. He founded a school at Canterbury, the students of which are said by Bede to have been in his time as well versed in Latin and Greek as in their mother tongue ; arithmetic, astronomy, and the art of Latin versification were taught there. The fine chanting, which before had been peculiar to Canterbury, was by him introduced into all our churches. He restricted the bishops and secular clergy to their own dioceses, the monks to their own monasteries ; thus establishing due subordination and order, and forbidding that practice of roving which led to the neglect of discipline and the relaxation of morals. He prohibited divorce for any other cause than the one which is allowed by the Gospel ; and he procured the first legislative provision for the clergy in these kingdoms, in the form of a kirk-scot, or tax of one Saxon penny upon every house which was worth thirty pence of yearly rent. The payment of tithes had at first been voluntary, though it was considered as a religious obligation. King Ethelwolph, the father of Alfred, subjected the whole kingdom to it by a legislative act. No institution was ever more admirably adapted to its end. It relieved the clergy from the distraction of temporal concerns. It exempted the tenth part of all property from the ordinary course of descent, set it apart, and sanctified it for the support of a body of men, who were not a distinct tribe, like the Levites, but were chosen from all ranks of the community for their moral and intellectual qualifications.

The cathedral was at first the only, and long continued to be the Mother Church, so called because there it was that believers received their second birth in baptism, the rights of baptism and burial appertaining to the Cathedral alone. The first subordinate houses of worship were Chapels, or Oratories, as humble as the means of the founder, erected by the itinerant clergy, in situations where the numbers and piety of the people, and their distance from the Cathedral, made it desirable that they should be provided with a place for assembling, in a climate where field-worship could not be performed during the greater part of the year. Parochial churches were subsequently founded by those who desired the benefit of a resident Priest for their vassals and themselves; and thus the limits of the estate became those of the parish. These churches were at first regarded as chapels of ease to the Cathedral, and the officiating minister as being the Bishop's Curate, was appointed by him, and removable at his pleasure; this dependence was gradually loosened, till at length the Priest was held to possess a legal right in his benefice; and Theodore, to encourage the building of churches, vested the patronage of them in the founder and his heirs. The tithes of the parish were then naturally appropriated to its own church. A certain portion of glebe was added, enough to supply the incumbent with those necessaries of life which were not to be purchased in those times, and could not conveniently be received from his parishioners in kind, but not enough to engage him in the business of agriculture; his pursuits, it was justly deemed, ought to be of a higher nature, and his time more worthily employed for himself and others. Without the allotment of a house and glebe, no church could be legally consecrated. The endowment of a full tenth was liberal, but not too large; the greater part of the country was then in forest and waste land, and the quantity of produce no where more than was consumed in the immediate vicinity, for agriculture was no where pursued in the spirit of trade.

The parochial Priest kept a register of his poor parishioners, which he called over at the church door from time to time, and distributed relief to them according to his means and their individual necessities. But in that stage of society the poor were not numerous, except after some visitation of war, in which the minister suffered with his flock; while villanage and domestic slavery existed, pauperism, except from the consequences of hostile inroads, must have been almost unknown. The cost of hospitality was far greater than that of relieving the poor. The manse, like the monastery, was placed beside the highway, or on the edge of some wide common, for the convenience of the pilgrim and the stranger.

The ecclesiastical government was modelled in many respects upon the established forms of civil policy; and, as among the Anglo-Saxons, the tithing men exercised a salutary superintendence over every ten *friborgs*, so, in the Church, Deans, who were called Urban, or Rural, according as their jurisdiction lay in the city or country, were appointed to superintend a certain number of parishes. At first they were elected by the clergy of the district, subject to the Bishop's approval: the Bishops subsequently assumed the power of appointing and removing them, and sometimes delegated to them an episcopal jurisdiction, in which case they were denominated *Chorepiscopi*, or Rural Bishops. They held monthly Chapters, corresponding to the Courts-Baron, and quarterly ones, which were more fully attended. The clergy of the deanery were bound to attend, and present all irregularities committed in their re pective parishes, as also to answer any complaints which might be brought against themselves. At these Chapters, all business which now belongs to the Ecclesiastical Courts was originally transacted, personal suits were adjusted, and wholesome discipline enforced, by suspending the offending clergy from their functions, the laymen from the sacraments. But as society became more complicated, and the hierarchy more ambitious, these ancient and most useful courts were discountenanced, and finally disused.

The attainments of the clergy, in the first ages of the Anglo-Saxon Church, were very considerable. King Ina sent for Greek masters from Athens; Aldhelm, Bishop of Sherburn, was versed in Hebrew; and Charlemagne was advised by Alcuin to send students from Tours to improve themselves at York. But a great and total degeneracy took place during the latter years of the Heptarchy, and for two generations after the union of its kingdoms. It began from natural causes. In the beginning none but the best and finest spirits engaged in the clerical profession; men who were actuated by the desire of intellectual and spiritual advancement, .. by the love of God and of their fellow-creatures. But the way of life which they had thus chosen was taken up by their successors for very different motives. Mere worldly views assuredly operated upon a great proportion of them; no other way of life offered so fair a prospect of power to the ambitious, of security to the prudent, of tranquillity and ease to the easy-minded. Moreover, in the beginning the vital truths of Christianity were in full action, because the clergy were labouring to establish a religion essentially true; after they had succeeded, the gross corruptions with which it was mingled began to work.

These causes of deterioration were inevitable in the order of events; moreover the location of the parochial clergy upon their cures tended to the dissolution of manners and decay of learning; they were thus removed from superintendence, from the opportunities of learning and improvement, and in great measure from professional restraint. But the Danes brought on a swifter ruin. Their fury fell always upon the monasteries, whither they were attracted by the certainty of finding large booty, and little or no resistance; perhaps also by hatred of a religion so strongly opposed in all things to their own ferocious faith and abominable manners. There they found not only the church-plate, and the abundant stores of the community, but the moveable wealth of all the surrounding country, brought thither in vain hope of miraculous protection. The annals of those disastrous times record nothing so minutely as the destruction of these extensive edifices, and the slaughter of their unoffending inhabitants. Scholars and teachers, for the monasteries were then the only schools, were indiscriminately massacred; books which were then so rare as to be almost above all price, were consumed in the same flames with the building: and this cause, were there no other, would be sufficient to explain the total loss of learning in the Anglo-Saxon Church.

When Alfred succeeded to the throne, there was not a single priest, south of the Thames, who understood Latin enough to construe his daily prayers, and very few in other parts of the kingdom. The monastic establishments throughout the island had been broken up. As the best means of restoring them he sent for a colony of Monks from France, and their pupils with them, who were training for the same profession. It was not, however, till many years after his death that monachism again began to flourish, through the growing ascendency of the Benedictine order, and the exertions of Dunstan, one of the most ambitious and least ambiguous characters in ecclesiastical history. The spirit of that corrupt church, which enrolled him among her Saints, is manifested no less in the course of his undoubted actions, than in the falsehoods wherewith they have been embellished and set forth; there is, therefore, no individual in English history whose life more clearly illustrates the age of monastic imposture.

Dunstan was born near Glastonbury, in the reign of Edward the Elder; one of his uncles was Primate, another Bishop of Winchester, and he was remotely allied to the royal family. A short time before his birth, his parents, Heorstan and Cynethryth, were at church on the festival of the Purification, known in this country by the name of Candlemas, because all who attended it carried lighted candles, with which they walked in procession after the service. In the midst of mass, the lamps and tapers were suddenly extinguished; the church, though at mid-day, was filled with a preternatural darkness; and while the whole congregation, in fear and trembling, wondered what this might portend, a fire descended from heaven, and kindled the taper in Cynethryth's hand, thus miraculously foreshewing how great a light should from her be born into the world.

To this church Dunstan, while yet a child, was taken by his father, to pass the vigil of some great holyday in devotional exercises; and falling asleep, he saw in a vision a venerable old man, with a heavenly countenance, in garments white as snow, who, telling him that building must be enlarged and elevated, led him over it, and measuring the ground with a line, impressed upon his mind ineffaceably the plan and dimensions of the work which he was appointed to accomplish. Glastonbury was a spot which real history might even then have sanctified to every feeling and imaginative mind; but churches and monasteries had begun to vie with each other in promoting a gainful superstition, by all the arts of falsehood. The probable and undisputed belief that the first church which had been consecrated in Britain was upon this site was not sufficient: already it was established as a traditionary truth, that the edifice had not been built by human hands, but that Joseph of Arimathea found it miraculously placed there to receive him: and after a lapse of nine centuries, the church itself, though composed of no firmer materials than basket-work, was shewn as still existing. St. Patrick had chosen it for a place of retirement, and had learnt, from a writing miraculously discovered there, that whosoever should visit the near Tor in honour of St. Michael, would obtain thirty years' indulgence, in confirmation of which his left arm was withered, till he made it known that our Lord had chosen that eminence for a place where men might acceptably invoke the Archangel. St. David came to Glastonbury with the intent of consecrating its church to the Holy Virgin; but our Lord appeared to him in a vision, and told him the ceremony must not be profaned by any man's repeating it, for he himself had long ago performed it to the honour of his Blessed Mother: and then perforating the Bishop's hand with his finger, in proof of the reality of the vision, left him, with an assurance that during mass on the ensuing day the wound should be closed as suddenly as it was inflicted, a promise which did not fail to be fulfilled. The monastery had been founded by King Ina, whose memory was deservedly honoured in Wessex. A stone oratory had been added, which was dedicated to Christ and St. Peter; and St. David, because of the increasing number of visitants, built a chapel to the Virgin. There were cemeteries in Ireland which were believed to ensure the salvation of all whose bodies were deposited there; this was too much for common English credulity; nevertheless it was asserted that one who was buried in the sacred ground of Glastonbury could hardly be condemned. It was the undoubted burial-place of Arthur, the hero of British romance, whose monument was respected by a brave enemy; and there was a tradition that Joseph of Arimathea was interred in some unknown spot, deep under the hill, where, according to his own desire, two vessels filled with the real blood of our Saviour were placed in the sepulchre with him; in the fulness of time these precious relics would be discovered, and such numerous and splendid miracles would then be wrought by them, that the whole world would repair thither for devotion.

The Anglo-Saxon monasteries had never been under any uniform discipline; each followed its own rule, independent of all others. Glastonbury at this time was mostly filled with monks from Ireland; it was favourite ground with them for St. Patrick's sake, and as they had no large endowments, they contributed to their own support by educating the children of the nobles. Dunstan was one of their pupils. In such a school local associations would produce and foster ardent enthusiasm, or audacious craft, according to the disposition of the individual. A feeble body and a commanding intellect predisposed him for both in turn. He was of diminutive size from his birth, and by severe application to study brought on a disease, in which, after having been delirious for many days, he was thought to be at the point of death. But feeling at night a sudden excitement as if health were restored, he rose from his bed, and ran toward the church to return thanks for his recovery. The doors were closed, but he found a ladder left there by workmen, who had been repairing the roof; by this he ascended, and in the morning was found asleep in the church, unconscious how he had come there. They who larded the history of his life with miracles, assert that as he was going there the Devil beset him with a pack of fiendish dogs, and was driven away by his strenuous exertions; and that Angels had borne him down where it was not possible for him to have descended without supernatural assistance. Divested of such machinery, the fact appears to be, that, in an access of delirium, or perhaps in his sleep, he had got into the church, by some perilous mode of descent, which he would not have attempted in his senses; he himself at the time might easily believe this to be miraculous, and from thenceforth he was regarded as a youth of whom something extraordinary was to be expected.

As soon as he had attained the requisite age, he entered into minor orders, in conformity to the desire of his parents, and took the clerical habit in the monastery wherein he had been educated. He was now equally remarkable for diligence in his studies, for his various accomplishments, and for manual dexterity; he composed music, he played upon the harp, organ, and cymbals, wrought metals, worked as an artist in wax, wood, ivory, silver and gold, and excelled in design, in painting, and in calligraphy. The Archbishop, his uncle, introduced him to the palace, where he soon became a favourite with King Athelstan, whom he delighted by his skill in music, and who sometimes employed him in hearing and adjudging causes. There were, however, persons who accused him of studying the historical songs and magical verses of their heathen forefathers, a charge almost as serious as that of heresy in succeeding ages; and an instance of that art which he afterwards practised more successfully was brought against him in proof of the accusation. A noble woman, who intended to embroider some rich vestments as a present for the church, requested Dunstan to trace the pattern for her; he hung his harp upon the wall, while he was thus employed, and the tune and words of a well-known anthem were heard distinctly to proceed from it, although no human hand was near. The matron and her maidens ran out, exclaiming that he was wiser than he ought to be; ventriloquism was not suspected, and as his life was not yet such as might entitle him to perform miracles, the premature trick was ascribed to magic. He was banished from the court, and men who, for some unexplained cause hated him, pursued and overtook him, bound him hand and foot, trampled upon him, and threw him into a marsh, leaving him there, as they thought, to perish.

Escaping, however, from this danger, he went to his uncle Elphege, Bishop of Winchester, who advised him to become a monk. Dunstan inclined to prefer a married life; the Prelate upon this is said to have prayed that God would please to correct in him this error, and the young man being soon afflicted with a dangerous disease, took upon himself the obligations of monachism, under the influence of severe pain and the fear of death. He now returned to Glastonbury, and there built for himself a miserable cell against the wall of the monastery, more like a grave than the habitation of a living man. It was five feet long, two and a half wide, and not above four in height, above the ground; but the ground was excavated, so that he could stand upright in it, though it was impossible for him to lie there at full length. The door filled up one side, and the window was in the door. This was his forge and workshop, as well as his dwelling-place, and this was the scene of the most notorious miracle in the monastic history of England; for here it was that the Devil, who annoyed him sometimes in the shape of a bear, sometimes of a dog, a serpent, or a fox, came one night in a human form to molest him, while he was working at the forge, and looking in at the window, began to tempt him with wanton conversation. Dunstan, who had not at first recognised his visitor, bore it till he had heated his tongs sufficiently, and then with the red-hot instrument seized him by the nose. So he is said to have declared to the neighbours, who came in the morning to ask what those horrible cries had been which had startled them from their sleep; and the miraculous story obtained for him the credit which he sought.

A widow of the royal family, who had retired to a cell adjoining the monastery, was advised in her last illness by Dunstan to divest herself of all her property before she died, that the prince of this world when she was departing might find upon her nothing of his own. She bestowed the whole upon him; the personals he distributed among the poor, and settled the estates upon the church of Glastonbury, transferring to it also his own ample patrimony which had now devolved upon him. When Edmund succeeded his brother Athelstan, Dunstan was recalled to court, but was again dismissed to his convent, through the influence of those who dreaded his overweening ambition, or disliked his views. The King, narrowly escaping from death in a stag-hunt, in the moment of his danger and deliverance, repented of his conduct towards him; and as this was attended by an immediate profusion of miracles, made him Abbot of Glastonbury, where he then introduced the Benedictine rule, being the first abbot of that order in England. Edmund also confirmed and enlarged the privileges which former kings, from the days of Cuthred and Ina, had conferred upon this most ancient church, making the town of Glastonbury more free than other places, and granting to its abbot power as well in causes known as unknown, in small and in great, above and under the earth, on dry land and in the water, in woods and in plains, and inhibiting under God's curse any one, either Bishop, Duke, Prince, or their servants, from entering to exercise authority there. This privilege was written in letters of gold, in a splendid book of the Gospels, which he presented to the church.

After Edmund's death, Dunstan retained the same favour with Edred his successor, who deposited part of the royal deeds and treasures in his monastery, and would have made him Bishop of Crediton. Dunstan in opposition to the King's wishes, and the entreaties of the Queen-mother, declined this promotion, and recommended another person to the see. The motives for his conduct are explained by a vision which he related to the King on the following morning. St. Peter, St. Paul, and St. Andrew, he said, had appeared to him in the night, and chastised him for having refused to be of their fellowship; they warned him not to commit that sin a second time, nor to refuse the primacy when it should be offered him, and they told him that he must one day travel to Rome. He had resolved upon reforming, or rather re-modelling, the Anglo-Saxon Church, a task for which he was qualified by his rank, his connections, his influence at court, his great and versatile talents, and more than all, it must be added, by his daring ambition, which scrupled at nothing for the furtherance of its purpose.

Dunstan would in any age or station have been a remarkable man, but no times could have suited him so well as the dark age of priestcraft in which he flourished. In the decay and dissolution to which human societies and institutions are subject, civilized nations become barbarous, and barbarous ones sink into so savage a state that all remembrance of their former civilization is lost, scarcely a wreck remaining. This utter degradation is prevented by priestcraft there only where the prevalent superstition is connected with learning and the arts. Christianity, in the days of Dunstan, was as much a system of priestcraft as that which at this day prevails in Hindostan or Tibet; but with this mighty difference, that whereas inquiry can only shew the priest of a false religion, how every thing which he teaches and professes to believe is mere imposture or delusion, the Christian minister even in the darkest times of Popery might ascertain by strict investigation that the history of his religion is true, and that the divinity of its precepts is proved by their purity, and their perfect adaptation to the nature of man, in its strength and in its weakness. Such as the Romish Church then was, however defiled, it was the salt of the earth, the sole conservative principle by which Europe was saved from the lowest and most brutal barbarism; and they who exerted themselves to strengthen its power, may have easily believed that they were acting meritoriously, even when their motives were most selfish, and the means to which they resorted, most nefarious.

The strength of the Church depended upon its unity, and that upon the supremacy of Rome. To establish and support that supremacy the Popes were in those times encouraging the regular in opposition to the secular clergy; and to effect this they took advantage of a revolution in monachism of which St. Benedict, an Italian peasant, had been unconsciously the author. Benedict had formed a rule for the monks under his direction, which because it was milder and less unreasonable than the manner of life prescribed in any former institutions of the kind, prevailed gradually to the extinction of all others in the western Church. His monasteries were awhile independent of each other; but they soon found the convenience of associating for the better defence of their privileges; and this was favoured by provincial Councils, because the object of preserving discipline was promoted by it, till the Benedictines throughout Christendom, became at length members of one body, under one General. Wise Princes encouraged them as the only instructors of youth, and the best promoters of civilization. The Popes had a further object in view: the tendency of national churches was to continue independent of the papal power; but the Regulars belonged to their Order, not to their country, and owing their exemption from episcopal jurisdiction to the Popes, they for their own sake supported the Roman see in all its usurpations.

Another great object of the Popes at this time was that of compelling the clergy to celibacy.

Nothing in ecclesiastical history is more certain than that no such obligation was imposed during the three first centuries. After that time it was gradually introduced, first by requiring that no person should marry after ordination, then by insisting that married men, when they were ordained, should separate from their wives. This prohibition, for which Scripture affords not the slightest pretext, was long resisted, and was held by the clergy of this country in general disregard when Dunstan undertook the task of reforming the Anglo-Saxon Church. It needed reformation in many respects: the clergy were grossly ignorant, and partook the coarse dissolute manners of their countrymen, which of late years had been greatly worsened by communication with the Danes. Dunstan was supported in his intentions by Odo the Primate. This prelate, who was the son of a Dane, had been a warrior, and even after he was made a Bishop, fought by the side of King Athelstan. When the primacy was offered him, he would not accept it, till he had professed among the Benedictines; and accordingly he went for that purpose to Fleury, then the most celebrated seat and nursery of the order, whither the body of Benedict had been translated. Such Christianity as Odo's had done little to mitigate the stern and unfeeling temper which he derived from his Danish blood: the interests of his order took place with him of the duties of his profession, and he therefore with all his authority assisted Dunstan in the enterprise which he had undertaken. Their object was to make the clergy put away their wives, to establish the Benedictine rule in all the monasteries, expel those secular priests who according to the old custom resided with their respective Bishops, and introduce monks in their stead. They proceeded in this with the favour of Edmund, and of his successor Edred, who because he suffered under a slow and wasting disease, was the more easily governed by these ambitious and haughty churchmen. But a plan which went directly to alter the constitution of the national church, called forth a strong and well-grounded opposition, and their opponents obtained a temporary triumph after Edred's early death. Edwy the son of Edmund succeeded his uncle at the age of sixteen. He was married to Elgiva, so prematurely were marriages contracted in those times; but as his wife was related to him in what the Romish Church had thought proper in its crooked policy to call a prohibited degree, the followers of that church who admired the conduct of Dunstan, have represented her as his concubine. Her well-known story is one of the most deeply

tragic tales in British history. On the coronation-day, the young King after dinner rose from table, and leaving his guests over their cups, went into an inner apartment to his wife and her mother. Such an act of disrespect to his nobles might have been excused in one so young, especially when through the contagion of Danish manners, a fashion of gross excess in drinking had become so general that it prevailed even at episcopal tables. It gave offence, however; Odo desired that some persons would go and bring the King back to his guests; and Dunstan with a Bishop his kinsman was chosen to execute this rude commission which none of the nobles, displeased as they were, and heated perhaps with drink were willing to undertake. Instead of persuading him to return by fatherly advice, mildly and prudently offered, they dragged him into the hall by force. Their insolence provoked the spirit which it was intended to subdue. Incensed at it, and by the language which Dunstan had addressed to Elgiva, Edwy deprived him of his honours, confiscated his property and banished him; and it is said that unless he had embarked in all haste, messengers would have overtaken him, with orders to put out his eyes.

The contemporary author of Dunstan's life, an eye-witness of many of his actions and probably an instrument in them, has related that on this occasion when the King's officers were making an inventory of his goods at Glastonbury, the Devil was heard laughing and rejoicing, and that the Saint knowing his voice told him not to exult too much, for upon a change of affairs he would be as much cast down. If Dunstan threatened vengeance at his departure, it was in the spirit of a conspirator, not of a prophet. While he retired to Flanders, and found an asylum in the monastery of St. Peter's at Ghent, the party which he left in England attacked the young King first with spiritual arms, never more flagitiously employed, then with open rebellion. The Primate Odo pronounced against him sentence of divorce, sent armed men into the palace to seize Elgiva, branded her face with a red-hot iron for the double purpose of destroying her beauty, and marking her for infamy, and banished her to Ireland. The ministers in this execrable act were less inhuman than their employers; they performed their orders so imperfectly, that when the wounds healed no deformity remained, and Elgiva escaping from banishment, returned to England to rejoin her husband. She was overtaken at Gloucester by Odo's people, and hamstrung to prevent the possibility of a second escape: the monsters who perpetrated this accursed deed are called the servants of God by the monkish biographer, and the crime itself has been recorded as a meritorious action. The beautiful Elgiva's sufferings were soon terminated by death; and Edwy was prevented from taking vengeance by the revolt of the Northumbrians and Mercians, who under Odo's sanction set up his brother Edgar, a boy of thirteen, as King. Dunstan was then recalled, and whatever share he may have had in the previous measures, it is certain that he now contracted the guilt of a full participation in them.

His return was like a triumph. The first promotion which he obtained was to the see of Worcester, and the craft of the monastic party was strikingly exhibited at his consecration. When Odo performed the ceremony he consecrated him Archbishop of Canterbury instead of Bishop of Worcester. One of the by-standers, who was not in the secret, reproved the Primate for this, saying, that it was against the canons to have two Archbishops for the same see at one time; and that he had no authority thus to elect his own successor. But Odo audaciously replied, that what he had done was not his own act; he had spoken under the immediate influence of the Holy Ghost, Dunstan being destined to succeed him in the primacy as the most redoubted champion against the prince of this world. There seemed sufficient likelihood that this impudent prediction would bring about its fulfilment, the obvious purpose for which it was intended. Edwy, after struggling three years against the competitor, whom these ambitious churchmen had set up, was removed from the contest by a violent death. Nor was it enough for his flagitious enemies to have deprived him of his wife, driven him from his throne, and brought both these illustrious victims to an untimely and miserable end; still farther to blacken the memory of this most injured prince, they affirmed that Dunstan had seen a host of Devils rejoicing over his soul as their allotted prey, and that the saint, by his intercession had rescued him from that everlasting damnation to which he must otherwise have been condemned.

The dominant faction expected now to accomplish all their measures; and as a proof of the ascendency which they possessed over the king, Dunstan was made Bishop of London, and permitted to hold the see of Worcester at the same time. But upon Odo's death the secular clergy exerted themselves to oppose the farther advancement of this intolerant monk; and Elfin of Winchester was by their means promoted to the primacy. They are accused of having effected this by bribes. Elfin had but a short enjoyment of his promotion. On his way to Rome, there to receive his pall, he was lost in the snow in attempting to cross the Alps at a dangerous season; and the monks with their usual spirit represented this fate as a judgment upon him, for having intruded into a see which it had been revealed that Dunstan should succeed to. The seculars were still powerful enough to prevent the promotion of their dreaded enemy, and Byrthelm, Bishop of Dorchester, was appointed to the vacant diocese. But they could not support him there. Complaints were raised against him that he was remiss in the correction of offences; a phrase, whereby is meant, that he did not compel the clergy to put away their wives. Upon this charge, he was sent back to his former see with some disgrace, and Dunstan was then elevated to the authority which he had so long desired over the English church. He went to Rome according to the then prevailing custom, and received his pall from the hands of Pope John XII.

The new Archbishop was not sparing of miracles to overawe the people, and prepare them for submitting to his measures with devout obedience. While he was performing his first mass, a dove alighted upon him, and remained during the whole ceremony; in those days the impious assertion was safely made, that this was the same dove which had appeared when our Saviour was baptized in the river Jordan. He said of himself that, whether sleeping or waking, his spirit was alway intent upon spiritual things. He affirmed also, that he saw in a dream his own mother solemnly espoused to the King of Heaven, that all the choirs of Heaven joined in hymns of joy, and that an angel had taught him an anthem upon the occasion; and he made one of his clerks write down this anthem, and had it performed in his church, as a divine composition. The dream was said to be symbolical, and the mother of Dunstan to typify the church as by him reformed. So long as Edgar lived, such easy frauds were sufficient for their purpose. That King was wholly in the hands of the monastic party; they engaged to defend him from the Devil and his angels, and he bound himself to protect them against their earthly opponents. On his part the contract was faithfully performed; the clergy were driven out, and the Benedictines established every where in their stead.

But upon Edgar's death, a vigorous resistance was made. The widowed Queen took part with the clergy; they were restored by violence in many parts of the kingdom, and in like manner again ejected by Dunstan, who had got possession of the young King Edward. But the wily and unscrupulous Primate perceived that force alone was not to be relied on: a synod therefore was convened at Winchester; and when the advocates of the Secular Clergy appealed to the King, and entreated that they might be restored to their rightful possessions, a voice proceeded from a crucifix against the wall, saying, "Let it not be! let it not be! you have done well, and would do ill to change it." The Saint's antagonists were not so ignorant of the miraculous craft as to be put to silence by a defeat thus brought about. A second council was assembled, without effecting any thing. Dunstan took care that the third, which was held at Calne, should prove decisive. The nobles, as well as the heads of both parties, attended. The King was kept away because of his youth, though he had been present at the former meetings. Beornelm, a Scotch Bishop, pleaded the cause of the clergy with great ability; alleging scripture in their behalf, and custom; and arguing upon the morality and reason of the case, against the celibacy to which, by these new laws, they were to be compelled. His speech produced a great effect, and Dunstan did not attempt to answer it; he had laid aside, says his biographer, all means, excepting prayer. "You endeavour," said he, "to overcome me, who am now growing old, and disposed to silence rather than contention. I confess that I am unwilling to be overcome; and I commit the cause of his church to Christ himself, as judge!" No sooner had these words been spoken than the beams and rafters gave way: that part of the floor upon which the clergy and their friends were arranged fell with them, many being killed in the fall, and others grievously hurt; but the part, where Dunstan and his party had taken their seats, remained firm.

The arch miracle-monger lived ten years to enjoy his victory and carry into effect his proposed alterations in the Church. His end was worthy of his life; for during those juggling ages, when the chief performers in the Romish church were no longer able or willing to act wonders for themselves, ready instruments were always at hand to carry on the system of deceit to the last. When his death was approaching, a Priest, who, on the eve of Ascension-day, had been keeping vigils in the church, declared he had seen Dunstan seated on his archiepiscopal throne, and dictating laws to the clergy; when, behold, a multitude of Cherubim and Seraphim entered at all the doors, attired in glittering white garments, and wearing crowns of gold. And here, says a Benedictine historian, the greatness of his sanctity must be observed; they were not any Angels who came to escort him, but those only of the highest orders in the hierarchy of Heaven, even Cherubim and Seraphim themselves. They arranged themselves in order before the Saint, and addressed him, saying, "Hail, our Dunstan! if thou art ready, come, and enter into our fellowship!" But the Saint made answer, "Holy spirits, ye know that upon this day Christ ascended into heaven: it is my duty to refresh the people of God both with words and with the sacrament at this time; and therefore I cannot come to-day." In condescension to his wishes, a farther respite than he required was granted, and they promised to return for him on the Saturday.

Accordingly, on Ascension-day, St. Dunstan officiated for the last time; he preached upon the mysteries of religion as he had never preached before, such was the fervour with which the prospect of his near glorification inspired him; and when he gave the people his blessing, his countenance became like that of an angel, and was suffused with a splendour, wherein it was apparent that the Holy Spirit was pleased to make its presence visible. He then exhorted them to remember him and his exhortations, for the time of his departure was at hand, and he must no longer abide among them. At this, such lamentations were set up as if the world were at an end, and the day of judgment had begun; and the priest, who hitherto had doubted whether what he had beheld during the night were a vision, or an actual appearance, knew now that it was real, and with tears and groans related before the congregation all that he had seen and heard. The Saint, after taking his last meal, re-entered the church, and fixed upon the place for his grave. He then went to his bed; and as he lay there, surrounded by his monks, he and the bed whereon he was lying, were thrice, by some unseen power, elevated from the floor to the ceiling, and gently lowered again, while the attendants, as if terrified at the prodigy, and believing that their Saint, like Elijah, was to be translated in the body, started from the bed-side, and clung to the walls and door-posts. Saturday came, and the Cherubim and Seraphim, according to their promise, descended to escort him: they were not, indeed, visible to others, but he saw them, and as the monks knew this, the people believed it. "See," says one of his biographers, "how he hath been honoured whom God thought worthy of honour!

see in what manner he hath entered into the joy of his Lord, who was found faithful over the talents of doctrine committed to his charge!" The multitude, as they attended his funeral, beat themselves with open hands, and lacerated their faces, a ceremony of heathen mourning which had not yet been abrogated; and the Saint was deposited in the cathedral over which he had presided, there to work miracles, and attract pilgrims and devotees to his shrine.

The life of Dunstan is thus given at length, because a more complete exemplar of the monkish character, in its worst form, could not be found: because there is scarcely any other miraculous biography in which the machinery is so apparent; and because it rests upon such testimony, that the Romanists can neither by any subtlety rid themselves of the facts, nor escape from the inevitable inference. The most atrocious parts, are matter of authentic history; others, which, though less notorious, authenticate themselves by their consistency, are related by a contemporary monk, who declares that he had witnessed much of what he records, and heard the rest from the disciples of the Saint. The miracles at his death are not described by this author, because the manuscript from which his work was printed was imperfect, and broke off at that point: they are found in a writer of the next century, who was Precentor of the church at Canterbury, and enjoyed the friendship and confidence of Lanfranc, the first Norman Archbishop. Whether, therefore, those miracles were actually performed by the monks, or only averred by them as having been wrought, either in their own sight, or in that of their predecessors, there is the same fraudulent purpose, the same audacity of imposture; and they remain irrefragable proofs of that system of deceit which the Romish Church carried on every where till the time of the reformation, and still pursues wherever it retains its temporal power or its influence.

CHAPTER VII.

CORRUPTION OF MANNERS AMONG THE ANGLO SAXONS.—FOREIGN CLERGY INTRODUCED BY THE NORMAN CONQUEST.—PROGRESS OF THE PAPAL USURPATIONS.

If Dunstan had been succeeded by men of similar talents and temper, and England had remained undisturbed by invasions, the priesthood might have obtained as complete an ascendency as in ancient Egypt, or in Tibet, founded upon deceit, and upheld by uncommunicated knowledge, and unrelenting severity. There might have been some immediate good in the triumph of cunning over force, inasmuch as such a system would have tamed the barbarians whom it subdued; but it would have rendered them as unprogressive as the Chinese, and at a lower stage in civilization. Time was not allowed for this. The Danes renewed their ravages: the monasteries underwent a second spoliation: Dunstan's immediate successor at Canterbury was put to death by these inhuman invaders; the learning which he had revived was extinguished, and the yoke of his ecclesiastical discipline was thrown off.

The Danes, during their short dominion, conformed to the religion of the country, and the conversion of their native land was completed in consequence. This good arose from a conquest which, in other respects, degraded the English nation. Indeed, they had shewn an unhappy readiness at receiving any imported vices. From the Saxons who frequented England during times of peace, they are said to have learnt manners more ferocious than their own; habits of dissolute effeminacy from the Flemings; and now, from the Danes, excessive gluttony and drunkenness. Such was the general depravity, that the Norman conquest, if considered in its immediate evils, may appear as much a dispensation of divine justice upon an abandoned people, as it proved to be of mercy in its results. Even the forms of Christianity were in danger of being lost through the criminal ignorance of the clergy, who could scarcely stammer out a service which they did not understand: one who had any knowledge of the Latin grammar was regarded as a prodigy of learning. Dunstan would have established an order of things in which the monks, by directing the consciences of the great, should have possessed and exercised the real power; a state not less pernicious had ensued, in which the clergy became the abject menials of the chiefs, and were, consequently, held in contempt. Such was their degradation, and such the irreverence with which the half-converted barbarians conformed to the religious usages of the age, that the nobles, instead of attending at church, would have matins and mass performed in the chambers where they were in bed with their wives or concubines. The condition of the country accorded in other respects with this sample of its manners. A horrid tyranny was exercised over the peasants; the Lords, for the sake of supplying their own prodigal excesses, seized their goods, and sold their persons to foreign slave-dealers. Girls were kidnapped for this abominable traffic; and it was common for these petty tyrants to sell their female vassals for prostitution at home, or to foreign traders, even though they were pregnant by themselves. When such actions were so frequent as to become a national reproach, no heavier afflictions could fall upon the nation than its offences deserved.

After the battle of Hastings William obtained easy possession of the crown. The nobles for the sake of present safety or advantage, submitted to a foreign Prince, whom, had there been a head to unite them, they might have successfully opposed; engaging afterwards, as the yoke galled them, in partial insurrections, they were destroyed piecemeal, and their domains transferred to the Norman Chiefs. The Clergy opposed him with a more determined spirit of resistance; and the Conqueror found their enmity so inveterate, that he made an ordinance for excluding the native monks and priests from all dignities in the Church. So strictly was it observed, and so extensive was the compulsory transfer of property which ensued upon the conquest, that in the course of the next generation, among all the Bishops, Abbots and Earls of the realm, not one was to be found of English birth. To accelerate this object William deprived many prelates of their sees, and appointed foreigners in their stead. Some fled into Scotland, deeming their persons in danger; and matter of accusation was easily found against others, in the part which they had taken, or in the relaxed morals which had infected all ranks during the late distempered times. Stigand the Primate was one of those who were thus deposed; the real cause of his removal was that he had refused to crown the Conqueror, and had taken an honourable part in exciting the men of Kent to demand and obtain a confirmation of their customs. Lanfranc, Abbot of

St. Stephen's at Caen, an Italian by birth, was the person whom William selected to succeed him. A man more eminent for talents and learning could not have been found; but being either unwilling to remove to a turbulent country, or apprehensive that he might be called upon to contend with a prince who was resolute in his purposes as well as politic, he pleaded his ignorance of the language and of the barbarous people as a reason for wishing to decline the promotion. Yielding, however, to the king's wishes, he at length accepted it; and one of his first measures was to give the farther sanction of the Church to the new government, by imposing, at a council held under his directions, certain penances upon those who had killed or wounded any of William's men at the battle of Hastings; the archers were enjoined to fast three Lents, because as none could tell what execution had been done by his arrows, it behoved all to consider themselves guilty; but a commutation was permitted in money, oı by building or repairing churches.

In further condescension to William's system, he proceeded to deprive Wulstan, Bishop of Worcester, for insufficiency in learning, and for his ignorance of the French tongue; for even this, in the insolence of iniquitous power, was deemed a sufficient cause. Wulstan was a man who had escaped the contagion of those dissolute times. His habits were simple, his life exemplary, his character decided; and on this urgent occasion he was not wanting to himself. The synod before which he was summoned was held in Westminster Abbey, and Lanfranc there called upon him to deliver up his pastoral staff. Upon this the old man rose, and holding the crosier firmly in his hand replied, "I know, my Lord Archbishop, that of a truth I am not worthy of this dignity, nor sufficient for its duties. I knew it when the clergy elected, when the Prelates compelled, when my master summoned me to the office. He, by authority of the apostolic see, laid this burthen upon my shoulders, and with this staff ordered me to be invested with the episcopal degree. You now require from me the pastoral staff which you did not deliver, and take from me the office which you did not confer: and I, who am not ignorant of my own insufficiency, obeying the decree of this holy Synod, resign them, not to you, but to him by whose authority I received them!" So saying, he advanced to the tomb of King Edward the Confessor, and addressed himself to the dead: "Master," said he, "thou knowest how unwillingly I took upon myself this charge, forced to it by thee! for although neither the choice of the brethren, nor the desire of the people, nor the consent of the prelates, nor the favour of the nobles, was wanting; thy pleasure predominated more than all, and especially compelled me. Behold a new King, a new law, a new Primate! they decree new rights, and promulgate new statutes. Thee they accuse of error in having so commanded; me of presumption in having obeyed. Then indeed thou wert liable to error, being mortal; but now, being with God, thou canst not err! Not therefore to these, who require what they did not give, and who, as men, may deceive and be deceived, but to thee who hast given, and who art beyond the reach of error or ignorance, I render up my staff! to thee I resign the care of those whom thou hast committed to my charge!" With that he laid his crosier upon the tomb, and took his seat as a simple monk among the monks.

The solemnity of such an appeal, from a venerable old man, might well induce the Synod to desist from its injurious purpose: but it is affirmed, that where he deposited the crosier there it remained, fast imbedded in the stone, and that in deference to this miraculous manifestation, he was permitted to retain his see. If the miracle were reported at the time, it was probably used by Lanfranc as a means for inducing William to let the proceedings cease, and saving him from the appearance of being foiled in his intent. Like most churchmen of those ages, Lanfranc though a great, and in many respects a meritorious, man, was not scrupulous in the use of such arts. There were other things wherein he conformed to the spirit of his church in the worst parts of that audacious system which was about his time matured. He promoted its favourite object of imposing celibacy upon the clergy, by procuring a decree that no priest should take a wife, nor any married man be ordained; more than this could not then be effected, and the married clergy were still numerous and powerful enough to avert the separation which the Pope would fain have enforced. He was also a zealous advocate for transubstantiation, which prodigious dogma had hardly been heard of in this island before his time.

Under a weak prince Lanfranc might have borne a distinguished part, in furthering the usurpations of the Romish see; he had to deal with one who was able and resolute, as well as violent, and their knowledge of each other served as a salutary restraint upon both. With the view of strengthening an invalid title to the succession, William had solicited the Pope's approbation of his claim, and had displayed a consecrated banner at the battle of Hastings. But when Gregory VII., (the memorable Hildebrand) afterwards required in return that he should do fealty for the crown of England, and take better care for the payment of the money which his predecessors were wont to send to Rome, he promised to remit the arrears, but refused the fealty, because he had never engaged to perform it, nor had it ever been done by the Kings of England before him. Amid all the difficulties and dangers that beset his throne, William would not abate one jot of his rights in deference even to the imperious Hildebrand. He forbade the clergy to go out of the kingdom, or to acknowledge a Pope, or to excommunicate a noble without his permission, or to publish any letters from Rome till he should have approved them. He separated the ecclesiastical from the civil courts, with which they had hitherto been conjoined. And he deprived the clergy of many of their lands, and subjected the rest to military service.

These measures, some of which were in themselves injurious, and all in direct opposition to the pretensions of the papacy, could not easily be brooked by the Primate; and at one time Lanfranc felt so severely the difficulties wherewith he had to contend, that he entreated the Pope to release him from a situation which made his life a burthen.. By yielding however sometimes where resistance would have been vain, he was enabled at others to defend the rights of the clergy, and of the people; and when William's half brother Odo usurped and annexed to his own possessions five and twenty manors belonging to the Church of Canterbury, Lanfranc appealed to the laws, and after a public trial, on Pinnendon Heath, recovered them to the great joy and benefit of the tenants, who thus continued under the easiest and most liberal of all tenures. William had that high respect for his integrity, that when he went beyond sea he left him sole Justiciary of the kingdom. The favour which he possessed had not been acquired by servile acquiescence to the King's will, nor any other unworthy means. One day when a minstrel exclaimed, as William sate at table in his court in a dress resplendent with gold and jewels, that he beheld a visible God, Lanfranc called upon the King not to permit such blasphemous adulation, and the flatterer accordingly was punished with stripes instead of receiving the reward which he expected.

Lanfranc rebuilt Canterbury Cathedral with stone from the fine quarries near Caen; he founded also two hospices without the city walls, and erected stone mansions for himself on most of his estates. His revenues enabled him to make this princely expenditure, while he annually bestowed in alms £500, a sum equivalent to full twelve times the amount in these days. His benevolence toward the monks of his own Church extended to their relations, none of whom he suffered to be distressed by want. Under his primacy no promotion in the Church was to be obtained by purchase, neither was any unfit person raised to the episcopal rank. And by his influence with the King, the trade in slaves, who were sold to Ireland, was prohibited ; for though good old Wulstan was the first who raised his voice against this iniquity, the King would hardly have relinquished the great profit which accrued to him from it, without Lanfranc's interference.

Two objects of considerable importance were effected during this primacy. One was the removal of episcopal sees from those places which had fallen to decay, into prosperous and growing towns: the other was the establishment of one liturgy throughout the kingdom. This uniformity was brought about in consequence of a scandalous fray at Glastonbury. Thurstan the Norman Abbot chose to introduce a service there which the monks opposed; he brought armed men to support his authority; the monks defended themselves with whatever was at hand, forms, candlesticks, even the crucifix itself, till eight were wounded, and two killed upon the steps of the high altar. Both parties having been culpable in this unpardonable transaction, the Abbot was sent back to Normandy, and the monks distributed in different convents; and that no farther disputes might arise from the same cause, a service was compiled by Osmund Bishop of Salisbury, and introduced into all the churches.

It is to be regretted that Lanfranc, to whom England is beholden for the restoration of letters, and who was indeed the light of his age, should so far have partaken the spirit of the Romish church, as to abet its fraudulent arts, if not actually to practise them himself. When his cathedral was rebuilt, he removed the body of Dunstan with all solemnity; it was a becoming act; but he ordered Osbern, the lying biographer of that arch-deceiver, to preach upon his miracles; and the more to honour the translation, a devil was cast out of a possessed monk, with as many plain circumstances of imposture, as ever were apparent in any such exhibition. An artifice, proceeding from the same system of deceit, was either devised or encouraged by him, to bring about the election of one, whom he approved for his successor. Anselm, Abbot of Bec, in Normandy, the person whom he thought best fitted to uphold the interests of the church, had come to visit Lanfranc; returning to rest one night after matins, he found a gold ring in the bed, and suspecting, it is said, at first, that the Devil might have some concern in putting it there, he made a cross upon it before he ventured to take it up. No one in the monastery owned the ring, and Anselm therefore ordered it to be sold for the benefit of the house; but Lanfranc, when the circumstance was told him, remarked, that Anselm was certainly destined to succeed him in the primacy.

The pretensions of the Roman Church had at this time been carried to their highest pitch by Gregory VII., one of those restless spirits who obtain an opprobrious renown in history, for disturbing the age in which they live. The Romanists themselves acknowledge now the inordinate ambition of this haughty Pontiff, who may be deemed the founder of the papal dominion; but during many centuries, he was held up as an object of admiration to the christian world, and still holds his place as a saint in the Romish Calendar. His sanctity, the legends of that church relate, was pre-figured in childhood, by sparks proceeding from his garments, and by a lambent light which appeared to issue from his head. He himself affirmed, that in a dream, there went forth fire from his mouth, and set the world in flames; and his enemies, who vilified him as a sorcerer, admitted, that such a vision was appropriate to one, who was indeed a firebrand. Another of his dreams was, that he saw St. Paul clearing out dung from his church, wherein cattle had taken shelter, and calling upon him to assist him in the work; andcertain persons who were keeping vigils in St. Peter's Church, beheld, in a waking vision, St. Peter and Hildebrand labouring at the same task. By such artifices his reputation for sanctity was established among the people, while he obtained promotion for his activity and talents; till at length, rather by intrigue and popular outcry, than by canonical election, he was chosen Pope. Hitherto, the Popes had recognised the supremacy of the Emperors, by notifying to them their election before they were consecrated, and having that ceremony performed in the presence of an imperial envoy. Hildebrand conformed to this, being conscious that his elevation was informal, and glad to have it thus ratified. The use he made of the power which he had thus obtained, was to throw off all dependence upon the temporal authority, and establish a system, whereby Rome should again become the mistress of the world. A grander scheme never was devised by human ambition; and wild as it may appear, it was, at that time, in many points so beneficial, that the most upright men might conscientiously have laboured to advance it. Whether the desire of benefiting mankind had any place among the early impulses of Hildebrand, may well be doubted, upon the most impartial consideration of his conduct; but in preparing the way for an intolerable tyranny, and for the worst of all abuses, he began by reforming abuses, and vindicating legal rights.

Throughout Christendom the church had been so liberally endowed, that its wealth at once endangered and corrupted it. Monasteries and Cathedrals were frequently despoiled of their lands. Lanfranc had successfully resisted an usurpation of this kind; and Hildebrand boldly began by threatening the King of France with ecclesiastical censures, if such injustice were not redressed in that kingdom. Sees were kept vacant, that the Kings might enjoy their revenues; they were disposed of by purchase so commonly, that simony became the characteristic sin of the age: in all such cases, they passed into unworthy hands; and even when they were not sold, equal, or greater evil resulted, if they were given, for favour or consanguinity, to subjects who disgraced the profession by their ignorance and their habits of life. To prevent such abuses, Hildebrand claimed the right of investiture, which Princes had hitherto exercised as their undisputed prerogative. In the first of these measures, he was clearly justified. The second was a questionable point; yet, on the whole, it may appear that the power might best be intrusted to the spiritual head of Christendom. But when he proceeded to anathematize all who should receive investiture from lay-hands, and all lay-men who should confer it, that measure manifested an assumption of temporal authority, which, if it were once established, must render all Sovereigns dependant upon the Pope. And this conclusion, the intrepid Hildebrand loudly proclaimed. His language was, that if Kings presumed to disobey the edicts of the apostolic See, they were cut off from participating in the body and blood of Christ, and forfeited their dignities. For if that See had power to determine and judge in things celestial and spiritual, how much more in things earthly and secular? The Church, he affirmed, had power to give or take away all empires, kingdoms, duchies, principalities, marquisates, counties, and possessions of all men whatsoever.

Had the authority, which the Pope thus arrogated, appeared as monstrous then as it does now, the claim could not have been advanced with any likelihood of establishing it. But what is now understood by constitutional rights, had no existence in those days. A power unlimited by any laws, was every where vested in the Sovereigns, and the Pontiff only arrogated over them, by a pretended right divine, that authority which they exercised over others originally by right of the sword. Were it, indeed, as possible to realize the fair ideal of a Christian Pope, as of a patriot King, such authority might more beneficially be trusted to a spiritual than to a secular autocrat. But the system of the Papal Church was any thing rather than Christianity; and the papal court at the time when it advanced its loftiest pretensions, was the most scandalous in Christendom. The usurpation was resisted for awhile as boldly as it was attempted. Even among the clergy themselves, a strong party was found, who, for motives worthy and unworthy, sided with the Emperor in the struggle; many for the sake of retaining the preferment which they had obtained by simoniacal means, the great body because the determination of compelling them to celibacy was now rigorously pursued. On the other hand, Hildebrand found partisans in the Empire. The dreadful war between the Guelphs and Ghibellines, by which Germany and Italy were so long convulsed, was thus begun. A rival Pope was set up on one side, a rival Emperor on the other: both parties proceeded with equal violence and with alternate success. But the papal party acted upon a matured system, which a succession of men, raised for their abilities and devoted to the cause, steadily carried on; there was neither weakness nor vacillation in their councils, and they profited by every opportunity which feeble or rash princes afforded them.

The struggle between the spiritual and temporal authorities, did not extend to England during the life of William the Conqueror: Hildebrand was wholly occupied in his contest with the Emperor, and Lanfranc best promoted the interests of the church, by avoiding all disputes with a King of his decided temper. The same conciliatory prudence enabled him to live upon fair terms with William Rufus, and even to exercise a controlling influence over his irregular mind. But upon Lanfranc's death, the Red King restrained himself no longer: to supply the expenditure of his excesses, as Abbacies and Prelacies fell, he kept them vacant, and by a system like that of rack-rent, drew from the helpless tenants all that it was possible to extort. The ample revenues of Canterbury were thus perverted for nearly five years, nor would the repeated entreaties of the clergy then have prevailed upon him to nominate a primate, if a dangerous illness had not awakened in him some fear of what might follow after death. Under that fear he appointed Anselm, partly perhaps in deference to what had been Lanfranc's wish, and partly as thinking him a person who would not offer any determined opposition to his will. Anselm, like his predecessor, would have refused the undesirable promotion; "the Church of England," he said, "was a plough which ought to be drawn by two oxen of equal strength; would they then yoke him to it, an old feeble sheep with a wild bull?" He characterized himself untruly; for whatever his individual disposition might have been, his conduct was in full conformity with the aspiring views of his church.

There were at this time two Popes, each excommunicating the other with all his adherents. England had not yet made its choice between them; but Anselm, in defiance or in ignorance of the late king's law, had acknowledged Hildebrand's successor, and now demanded leave to go and receive the pall from him at Rome. Rufus, already exasperated by the proper firmness, with which the Archbishop had called upon him to fill up the vacant benefices, took advantage of this, and accused him before the Great Council of having broken his fealty and disobeyed the laws. The case was plain, and the Bishops declared that unless he retracted his submission to Pope Urban, they would not obey him as their Primate. Obedience was not to be obtained from Anselm, and the Bishops, when Rufus called upon them to depose him, replied, that it was beyond their power. The proceedings, therefore, were suspended; and as the King soon afterwards thought proper to recognise the same Pope, that cause of dispute was removed, and the pall was sent to Anselm. But the reconciliation was of short continuance. The manner in which Rufus continued to wrong the church, called for interference on the Primate's part, and this again provoked the irascible King; and when Anselm, after having been twice refused, persisted in requesting leave to visit Rome, he was told, that if he went, his possessions should be sequestered, and he should never be allowed to return.

To Rome, however, he went, and was received with all the honours due to a Confessor in the church's cause. The Pope lodged him in his own palace, and ordered that the English who came to that city, should kiss his toe. He wrote also to William, commanding him to restore the Archbishop's property; but the resolute King had no sooner been informed that the bearer of this letter was one of Anselm's servants, than he swore that he would pull out his eyes if he did not immediately leave England. The matter was laid before the Council of Bari, at that time assembled; and the Pope represented to them the irreligious life of the Tyrant, as he styled him, according to the complaints against him which had repeatedly been preferred; exhortations and menaces, he said, had often been tried, but with what effect might be seen in the expulsion of a man like Anselm; what then remained to be done? The Council replied that he should be smitten with an anathema by the sword of St. Peter; and the Pope would instantly have fulminated the sentence, if Anselm had not on his knees interposed, and prevailed upon him yet a little longer to refrain.

But though in this instance Anselm moderated the proceedings of the Council, he entered heartily into the feelings of that assembly when the question of investiture was brought forward; and excommunication was denounced by acclamation against all who should do homage to a layman for ecclesiastical honours. It was too execrable, they said, that hands which could create the Creator, and offer him to the Father as a redeeming sacrifice, should become the servants of those which were continually polluted with impure contacts, with rapine, and with blood. Rufus, who like his father was a man of strong intellect and dauntless resolution, cared little for this, while it excited no opposition to him at home. He perceived the impolicy of quarrelling with a power, which was not to be met in the field and opposed with arms: at the same time he was determined not to yield to it, by inviting Anselm back. A middle course suited the views of one who cared so little for the future; and he negotiated a sort of suspension with the Pope, which left the matter as it stood during the remainder of his reign.

Rufus had succeeded to the English throne, in exclusion of an elder brother, upon the ground of his father's appointment. Henry, who obtained possession of it now, had no such plea; he found it expedient, therefore, to conciliate the clergy as well as the people. And in the charter of liberties with which he began his reign, he promised neither to sell, let or retain benefices, and to restore its old immunities to the Church. The Primate was of course invited back, and was received with every mark of respect and honour. But when he was required to do homage for the possessions of his see, he declared that the late canons rendered this impossible, and that if the King persisted in demanding it, he must again quit the kingdom. Upon this Henry, who at that time could ill dispense with the services of so important a personage, proposed that the matter should be referred to the Pope: Anselm unwillingly consented to a measure which he well knew could only create delay; but in Henry's situation delay was of great moment... The messengers returned with an answer, in which the Pope insisted on his point, and supported it by the strangest distortion of Scripture: "I am the door; by me if any man enter in he shall be saved." "He that entereth not by the door into the sheep-fold, but climbeth up some other way, the same is a thief and a robber." "If Kings," said the Pope, "take upon themselves to be the door of the Church, whosoever enter by them become thieves and robbers, not shepherds. Palaces belong to the Emperor, Churches to the Priest; and it is written 'Render unto Cæsar the things that are Cæsar's and to God the things that are God's.' How shameful is it for the Mother to be polluted in adultery by her sons! If therefore, O King, thou art a son of the Church, as every Catholic Christian is, allow thy Mother a lawful marriage, that the Church may be wedded to a legitimate husband, not by man, but by Christ...It is monstrous for a son to beget his father, a man to create his God: and that Priests are called Gods, as being the Vicars of Christ, is manifest in Scripture."

Such arguments were more likely to incense than satisfy a prince of Henry Beauclerc's understanding. He commanded Anselm either to do homage or leave the kingdom, and Anselm with equal firmness replied that he would do neither. A second reference to Rome ensued: two monks were deputed thither by the Primate, three Bishops by the King. The Pope upon this occasion acted with consummate duplicity, for which the motive is not apparent. To the Bishops he said that as their King was in other respects so excellent a Prince, he would consent to his granting investitures; but he would not send him a written concession, lest it might come to the knowledge of other Princes, and they should thereby be encouraged to despise the papal authority. By the monks he sent letters to Anselm, exhorting him to persist in his refusal. Both parties made their report before the Great Council of the realm; the Prelates solemnly asseverating that they faithfully repeated what had passed between them and the Pope, the monks producing their letters. On the one part, it was contended that oral testimony might not be admitted against written documents; on the other, that the solemn declaration of three Prelates ought to outweigh the word of two monks and a sheet of sheep's skin with a leaden seal...

To this it was replied, that the Gospel itself was contained in skins of parchment. If, however, it was not easy to determine what had been the real decision of the Pontiff, his double dealing was palpable; and Anselm may have been influenced by a proper feeling of indignation, when he so far conceded to the King as no longer to refuse communion with those Bishops who had received investiture from his hands. At length, by Henry's desire, Anselm went to Rome to negotiate there in person; and the matter ended in a compromise, that no layman should invest by delivery of the ring and crosier, but that Prelates should perform homage for their temporalities.

During these disputes no Council had been held in England, and therefore a great decay of discipline was complained of. The marriage of the Clergy was what Anselm regarded as the most intolerable of all abuses. This real abuse had grown out of it, that the son succeeded by inheritance to his father's church, a custom which, if it had taken root, would have formed the clergy into a separate cast. This, therefore, was justly prohibited; but it was found necessary to dispense with a canon which forbade the ordination or promotion of the sons of priests, because it appeared that the best qualified and greater part of the clergy were in that predicament. Canons, each severer than the last, were now enacted for the purpose of compelling them to celibacy. Married priests were required immediately to put away their wives, and never to see or speak to them, except in cases of urgent necessity and in the presence of witnesses. They who disobeyed were to be excommunicated, their goods forfeited, and their wives reduced to servitude, as slaves to the Bishop of the diocese. The wife of a priest was to be banished from the parish in which her husband resided, and condemned to slavery if she ever held any intercourse with him: and no woman might dwell with a clergyman, except she were his sister or his aunt, or of an age to which no suspicion could attach. Scripture was perverted with the grossest absurdity to justify these injurious laws, and prodigies were fabricated in default of truth and reason for their support. It was affirmed that when married priests were administering the communion, the cup had been torn from their hands by a vehement wind, and the bread portentously snatched away: and that many of their wives had perished, under a divine judgement, by suicide, or by sudden death, and their bodies had been cast out of the grave by the evil spirits who had possession of their souls. Cardinal

Crema came over as Legate to promote this favourite object of the Papacy. It happened that having in the morning delivered a discourse upon the wickedness of marriage in the Clergy, he was discovered at night in bed with an harlot. This flagrant example was not necessary to prove the unfitness of such canons. The general feeling was strongly against them: and Henry, instead of enforcing laws so exceptionable, or resisting them as he ought to have done, turned them to his own advantage, by allowing the clergy to retain their wives upon payment of a certain tax.

The efforts which Anselm had made in this cause, and for promoting the sovereignty of the Roman See, entitled him to canonization; and miracles enough for establishing his claim were adduced. His biographer, the historian Eadmer, asserts, that a precious balsam intended for embalming his body having been spilt, with the little which remained, Baldwin, the master of his household, wished to anoint the face of the deceased Primate, and that right hand wherewith so many holy treatises had been written. It was so little that it scarcely moistened the end of a finger when put into the vessel; Eadmer, however, was directed to hold his hand for the last drop, and the balsam flowed from the empty vessel in such profusion, that there was enough to anoint the whole body again and again. Nor was this the only miracle which Eadmer witnessed. The stone coffin had been made too shallow, and while the assistants lamenting this mistake knew not how to remedy it, the Bishop of Rochester drew his crosier across the body, and immediately the corpse contracted itself to the desired dimensions. Such is the character of ecclesiastical biography in that age, and in this spirit of deliberate and systematic falsehood are the lives of the Romish Saints composed.

The struggle between the papal and royal authorities did not impede the progress of those improvements which the Norman Clergy introduced. A surprising revival of literature had been effected by Lanfranc and Anselm; it extended beyond the monasteries, where learning had hitherto been confined; and the schools at Cambridge are believed to have been first established at this time. The rigour with which Henry I., during a reign of five and thirty years, maintained tranquillity at home, allowing of no oppression except that which was exercised by his own officers, favoured the improvement of the nation. The original Saxon Churches, as they fell to decay, were now generally supplied by more elaborate structures; and the introduction of painted glass, by making larger windows necessary, led to the perfection of church architecture.

The ensuing reign was as disgraceful to the hierarchy, as it was disastrous to the realm. Stephen had every requisite for the throne, except the first and most indispensable, a lawful title; the Bishops who had sworn allegiance to the rightful successor, violated their oath and supported him, the Legate approved his coronation, and the Pope sent him letters of confirmation, because he promised a reverent obedience to St. Peter. The court of Rome, which was never withheld by any inconvenient scruples from taking whatever advantage political events might offer, gained by this usurpation more than it had lost during the schism; whatever the Prelates asked, or Rome required, Stephen was ready to grant, and when Henry, the first of the Plantagenet kings, succeeded to the crown, the securities which his ancestors had provided against ecclesiastical encroachments, had all been swept away.

CHAPTER VIII.

HENRY II., THOMAS À BECKET.

WITH many weaknesses, and some vices, Henry II. was an able Prince. He found his kingdom in a state of frightful anarchy. During his predecessor's turbulent reign, castles had been built in all parts of the land, each being the strong hold of some petty tyrant, who, having a band of ruffians in his service, exercised the most grievous oppression as far as his power extended, and inflicted torments upon all who fell into his hands for the purpose of extorting money. This multiplied tyranny, which rendered the state of England worse than it had been during the ravages of the Danes, was put down with a strong hand; and the King having thus deserved the blessings of the people, applied himself with equal determination to suppress the abuses of the ecclesiastical power.

The most crying of these abuses was the exemption from all secular jurisdiction which the clergy had established for themselves. This was an evil, which had imperceptibly arisen. The higher clergy at first interfered in disputes for the christian purpose of reconciling the parties; gradually they became judges instead of mediators and arbitrators; and in this, too, there was an evident propriety, because in those rude ages, no other persons were so well qualified for the judicial office; because it might be presumed, that they would temper justice with mercy, and because a religious sanction accompanied their decisions. Under the Saxon Kings, the Bishop sat with the sheriff in the County Court, and the Conqueror when he separated their jurisdictions, did not foresee the consequences which resulted. The Ecclesiastical courts followed the Canon law, parts of which had been forged for the purpose of withdrawing the dignified clergy from the ordinary tribunals, and placing them under the Pope's immediate authority, that is to say, his protection. By these laws, no clergyman might be condemned to death; stripes were the severest punishment that might be inflicted. Every one who had received the tonsure came under the privilege of the Canons; in that age, the number of those who were ordained, and had no benefice was very great, and these persons existing in idleness and poverty, stood in need of their privilege often enough to prove that such immunities were incompatible with the general good. But it was not from the conduct of such persons only, that this inference was drawn; in the age when the pretensions of the Church were highest, the corruption of its members was also at its height. A contemporary monk has acknowledged, that the Prelates were more intent on maintaining the privileges, than correcting the vices, of the clergy, who, because of the impunity which they possessed, stood in no awe either of God or man. A legend of that age marks the opinion which was entertained of their general depravity. It was related in history, not as a fable, but as a fact, that Satan and the company of infernal spirits sent their thanks in writing, by a lost soul from hell, to the whole ecclesiastical body, for denying themselves no one gratification, and for sending more of their flock thither, through their negligence, than had ever arrived in any formeı time.

While Henry was pursuing the great object of securing the public peace by a vigorous administration of justice, the judges represented to him the evil consequences of the immunity from all secular punishment which the clergy claimed and enjoyed, instancing, that because of these privileges, there had been already committed during his reign, more than an hundred acts of homicide, which were not cognizable by the laws. Well aware how difficult it would be to correct this abuse, and reduce the ecclesiastical power within those bounds to which the Conqueror and his sons had confined it, Henry thought that the surest mode of facilitating this object, would be to select for the primacy, a person in whom he could confide. He chose, therefore, the Chancellor Thomas à Becket, the most confidential, as well as the ablest, of his servants, and the most intimate of his friends; a man who had hitherto resembled Wolsey in the favour which he enjoyed, and in the boundless magnificence of his life; but his character was compounded of stronger elements, and his mind of a higher class.

Though Becket already held several lucrative appointments in the Church, he was only in Deacons' orders, and had imbibed little of the spirit of his profession. Hitherto he had been soldier, courtier, statesman, any thing rather than churchman; the boon companion of the King, his confidential counsellor, and the faithful minister of his will. If he desired this farther elevation, he dreaded it also; but the apprehension of difficulty and undefined danger, operates as an incentive to ambitious zeal, especially in a mind like his. To his friends he said, that he must either lose the

King's favour, or sacrifice to it the service of his God ; and to Henry himself, he expressed a like anticipation ; but it was said with a smile, so that, whether intentionally or not, the manner conveyed a meaning which invalidated the words. Henry, indeed, believed that in raising Becket to the primacy, he promoted one, who knowing and approving his views, would continue to further them ; and under that persuasion he issued a peremptory mandate for his appointment, in opposition to the advice of the Empress Queen his mother, the opinion of the nation, and of the clergy,..the very men in whom the ostensible right of election resided, opposing it as strongly as they could, and declaring it was indecent that a man, who was rather a soldier than a priest, and who spent his time in hunting and hawking, should be made an Archbishop. They, as well as Henry, mistook the character of the man.

Becket on one day was ordained Priest, and consecrated Archbishop on the next. From that hour he devoted himself to the cause of the Church, the sense of duty being perfectly in accord with his ambitious disposition. To all outward appearance, the change in his life which ensued, was not less total and immediate than that which the grace of God effects in a repentant sinner ; but the inner man remained unchanged. The costliest splendour was still displayed in his apparel; beneath his canonical dress he wore the Benedictine habit; under that, sackcloth well stocked with vermin, (for vermin were among the accompaniments of monastic sanctity;) and within were the daring spirit, the fiery temper, and the haughty heart. Every part of his conduct now indicated the aspirant saint; his food was of the coarsest kind; bitter herbs were boiled in water to render his drink nauseous; he flogged himself; he washed the feet of the poor; he visited the sick; and the large sum which his predecessor had annually disbursed in alms, was doubled by his munificent charity. His determination to oppose the King was intimated by sending back the seals of office, and desiring that he would provide himself with another Chancellor, for he could hardly suffice, he said, to the duties of one office, far less of two. Upon this, the King called upon him to surrender also the archdeaconry of his own see, an office much more incompatible with his new dignity than the Chancellorship; it was the richest benefice in England, under a bishopric, and Becket withheld his resignation till it was forced from him. He must have acted undoubtedly upon some imagined right; covetousness could have no place in a mind like his.

Henry had made an impolitic choice between the rival Popes, in acknowledging Alexander III., who had assisted in compiling the Decretals, and had been chosen by the Guelph party as a fit person to support the loftiest pretensions of the papacy. That Pontiff held a council at Tours, in which the reformation of abuses, or the suppression of errors, was less the object than to assist and strengthen what were called the liberties of the Church. Becket, who obtained permission to attend, presented to the council a book of the life and miracles of Anselm, composed by his directions, as the miraculous life of Dunstan had been in like manner by Lanfranc's orders; and upon the ground that Anselm's sanctity was established by the miracles fabricated for the purpose, solicited canonization for him. As Anselm's chief merit consisted in the firmness with which he had supported the papal against the kingly power, this proposal for canonizing him, carried with it a sort of defiance to the King. The Pope not deeming it prudent to disgust Henry by an act in itself gratuitously offensive, referred it to the decision of a Synod in England; but Becket soon found himself too deeply engaged in other disputes to pursue this point, and more than two centuries elapsed before Anselm was enrolled in the Kalendar.

Immediately on his return from the Council, he instituted proceedings for the recovery of church-lands, in pursuance of a canon passed there against all persons by whom such property was either usurped or detained. Had he proceeded temperately like Lanfranc, the laws and public feeling would in like manner have supported him. But he asserted the maxim of the canon law, that no grant and no length of possession can hold against the claims of the Church; and, upon that ground, sought to recover castles, towns, honours and manors from the barons, and even from the crown itself, which had devolved to them in the regular course of descent; although such claims, may, in themselves, have been well-founded, it is to be presumed, that unless there had been strong reasons for waiving them, they would not have been left dormant by his predecessors. He insisted also, that it was his right to present to all benefices in the manors of his tenants, and in maintenance of the assumed right, excommunicated a lord who refused to let possession be taken by a clergyman thus appointed. This lord held also under the King, and Henry in support of an acknowledged prerogative, ordered Becket to withdraw the sentence. A haughty answer was returned, that it was not for the King to command who should be absolved or who excommunicated; but the law was explicit in this case, and Becket yielded after a warm contention, which served only to shew a spirit of aggression on his part, and thereby increased the King's displeasure.

Undeceived when too late in the character of his former minister and friend, Henry in pursuing his plans of salutary reform, had to encounter opposition where he had reckoned upon assistance. Plain reason, however, and evident justice, and public opinion, were on his side, and he had a strong case to begin with. A priest had debauched the daughter of a respectable man, and then murdered the father that he might not be disturbed in his guilty intercourse with her. The King demanded that this atrocious criminal should be brought before a civil tribunal, and suffer condign punishment upon conviction; but Becket placed the culprit under custody of his diocesan, that he might not be delivered to the King's justice. Upon this Henry summoned the Bishops to attend him. He complained to them of the corruption of their courts, and of the practice of commuting all punishments for money, whereby, he said, they levied in a year more money from the people than he did. He observed that a clerical offender, instead of being screened from punishment by his sacred character ought to be more severely punished because he had abused that character. And he required that in future ecclesiastical persons accused of heinous crimes should be delivered into the hands of the Bishop, and if by him found guilty, be degraded, and then transferred to the civil power for punishment.

The Prelates would have assented to this considerate and equitable proposal, which saved the honour of the Church, while it vindicated the rights of the law. But Becket conferred with them apart, and in deference to him they returned for answer, that no clergyman ought to suffer death, or loss of limb for any crime whatsoever; nor to be judged in a secular court. The reason which they assigned was compounded of legal subtilty and ecclesiastical pride; it was a maxim, they said, that no one ought to be punished twice for the same offence; but ecclesiastical censures were a punishment, and of all punishments the most grievous, because they touched the soul. The only concession they made was to admit that a clergyman, who had been degraded, became amenable to the common law for any offence committed after his degradation. Henry had inherited the irritable temper of the Norman Kings. Provoked at such a reply, he demanded of them whether they would obey the ancient customs of the realm? Becket replied, "saving the privileges of his order:" and the other Prelates, all but one, returned the same answer; upon which the King remarked that there was venom in the exception, and that he saw they were drawn up against him in battle array. The dispute, for it was no longer a council, continued all day; and Henry at last left the hall in anger. The following morning he manifested his strong displeasure against the Primate by depriving him of the castles which had been intrusted to him as Chancellor; and which he had continued to hold after his resignation of that office.

But the Prelates re-considered the matter when they were no longer awed by Becket's presence, nor under the control of his commanding spirit... They felt the justice of the King's pretensions, and perceiving that he was bent upon effecting what he had undertaken, they represented to the Primate the propriety of making some concession. His answer was, that if an Angel were to descend from Heaven, and advise him to make the acknowledgment which the King required, without that saving clause, he would anathematize the Angel. Yet he was prevailed upon to relax this haughty resolution by the representations of his friends, and by the Pope's almoner, who affirmed that he had instructions from Rome to persuade him to submission...The King, they said, had no intention of touching the immunities of the Church: a nominal concession was all that he required; it was only a point of honour on his part that was at stake. Becket could hardly have believed this, acquainted as he well was both with the temper and the settled purpose of the King. Howbeit he yielded, waited on him at Woodstock, and told him he would observe the royal customs. Henry received him, not with the cordial affability of former times,...that was impossible,...but as one who was gladly disposed to accept the proffered conciliation; he expressed his satisfaction at the promise, and only required that Becket should repeat it before the Great Council of the realm.

Three months afterwards the Great Council was assembled at Clarendon, a palace not far from Salisbury, which is supposed to have derived its name from a fortification there erected by Constantine Chlorus, and from which, in after years, one of the best and wisest of British statesmen and historians took his title. During the interval they who had acted as mediators with Becket supposed their work was done, and he had been left to take counsel with his own ambitious heart. To act in concert with Henry, and to promote the general good by the surrender of usurped immunities which were neither consistent with justice nor with decency, was a part less congenial to his temper than to stand forward, like Anselm, in the face of Europe, and brave the King as champion for the Church's privileges. When, therefore, the Parliament met, and Henry called upon the Bishops for that unqualified promise of observing the customs, which it had been understood they were to make, Becket again required that it should be made with the saving clause. It was not likely that the King should render justice to the sense of ecclesiastical duty which was thus manifested by a breach of faith; however Becket may have stood self-justified, he had deceived the King; and in resentment at the deception practised upon him, Henry gave loose to the natural violence of his disposition. The threats which he uttered of banishment, and even of death, if they did not make the Primate tremble for himself, made others tremble for him. The Bishops entreated him, even with tears, to submit. The Earls of Leicester and Cornwall told him they were ordered to use force if he persisted in his refusal, and they implored him not to urge on a catastrophe, which, if it took place, would be calamitous and disgraceful to them all. Two Knights Templars, men of great ability and in the King's favour, were desired to use their influence; and they weeping supplicated him on their knees to have some regard to himself, and some pity for his clergy. It was manifest that Henry, exasperated as he was, was now determined upon carrying his point, by whatever means; for the clash of arms was heard, and men were seen in the adjoining apartments brandishing swords and battle-axes, ready at a word to have used them. Becket's heart was not susceptible of fear: but in this case the generous anxiety concerning him which was expressed, and an apprehension that if the signal for violence were given, the blow might fall on others as well as on himself, moved him; and yielding a second time, he promised on the word of truth that he would observe the ancient customs of the realm. The other Prelates followed his example. It was then ordered that such of the assembly as knew the customs best, should put them in writing: a list of the elders was made out to whom this task was assigned; and at Becket's motion the business was prorogued till the morrow.

The customs which were now reduced to writing were called the Constitutions of Clarendon; the most important articles which they contained relating to ecclesiastical matters, were, that disputes concerning the advowsons and presentations of churches, should be tried and determined in the King's courts. That ecclesiastics should answer in the secular courts for matters there cognizable, and in the spiritual ones for cases within the spiritual jurisdiction; so that the King's justiciary should send to the court of holy Church to see in what manner the cause might be tried there; and if a clerk were convicted, or confessed his guilt, the Church should not protect him. No prelate or dignified clergyman might leave the realm without the King's license, and when they went the King might demand security that they would not procure any evil or damage to the King or kingdom. No tenant or officer of the King might be excommunicated, nor his land laid under an interdict, unless the King or his justiciary had been apprized of the proceedings. Appeals were to proceed from the Archdeacon to the Bishop, and from the Bishop to the Archbishop; if he failed in doing justice, the cause was to be brought to the King, and by his precept determined in the Archbishop's court, so that it might not be carried farther without the King's consent. If there were any dispute concerning a tenement which on the one part was pretended to be held in frank-almoigne, and on the other as a lay-fee, the question was to be first determined before the King's Chief Justice, by the verdict of twelve lawful men, and the cause then referred to its proper court. An inhabitant of the King's demesne, refusing to appear if he were cited by the ecclesiastical authorities, might be put under an interdict, but not excommunicated until the King's chief officer of the place should have been required to compel him by course of law to answer: if the officer failed in this duty, he should be at the mercy of the King, and the Bishop might in that case compel the accused person by ecclesiastical censures. Bishoprics and monasteries of royal foundation should be in the hands of the King while vacant, as his own demesne; the elections were to be made in the King's chapel, with his assent, and the advice of such prelates as he might convoke; and the person elected should do homage saving his order, before he was consecrated.

If these constitutions were in direct opposition to the system of Hildebrand and his successors, and at once removed all those encroachments, which the hierarchy had made in this kingdom during Stephen's contested reign, it should be remembered, that they were not new edicts enacted in a spirit of hostility to the Church, but a declaration and * recognition of the existing laws.

* *Recordatio vel recognitio cujusdam partis consuetudinum, et libertatum, et dignitatum antecessorum suorum, videlicet*

They were laid before Parliament on the following day, and the Prelates were then required to set their seals to the record. Becket alone demurred. He had pledged his word to observe the customs, and his name was inserted in the preamble among those who recognised and consented to them; his declaration, therefore, that he had not engaged to confirm them by setting his seal, was curiously inconsistent, showing at the same time how lax were his notions of a moral obligation, and how strong his conscientous adherence to the papal cause. He asked time for consideration, and it was granted. Three transcripts of the record were made, one for the royal archives, one for the Archbishop of York, the third was delivered to Becket, and the Parliament then broke up. Whether he afterwards sealed to it, has not been stated. It may be presumed that he did, because when the King some time after sent to the Pope, requesting him to confirm the ancient customs of the kingdom by authority of the apostolical see, Becket joined with the Archbishop of York in writing to support the request. In so doing, he acted with a deceitfulness, for which an excuse can be found only in the convenient casuistry of his own church. For as if he had

regis Henrici, avi sui, et aliorum, quæ observari et teneri debent in regno. These are the words of the preamble.

committed a sin in consenting to these customs, he imposed upon himself the penance of abstaining from the service of the altar forty days. The Pope absolved him from that sin, in consideration of his intentions, and of the compulsion under which he had acted; but he counselled him to be moderate. Difficult as it was for Becket to learn this lesson, it was probably in obedience to the advice, that he repaired to the King's residence at Woodstock, and solicited audience. But Henry had been informed that Becket had spoken contemptuously of his infirm and irritable temper, and as if to prove that he could be steady in a just resentment, he refused to see him.

Such marked displeasure afforded Becket a pretext for taking the course which was most in unison with his own feelings. He sent an agent to the French King, that he might secure for himself a powerful protector, and going by night to the port of Romney, embarked for France. But though he, who had the example of Anselm before his eyes, set at nought the laws which he had pledged his word to observe, the sailors would not expose themselves to danger by carrying him, and he was therefore fain to return to Canterbury. His motions had been watched, and he was just in time to prevent the King's officers who had been sent to seize his possessions.

Henry was alarmed at this attempt, well knowing what embarrassment his former minister might create for him if he were admitted to the counsels of the French King; and when Becket presented himself again at Woodstock, he received him mildly: the only expression of his real feeling was a question, put as it were in sport, whether the reason why he had wished to withdraw from the kingdom, was, because the same land could not contain them both? Each at this time appears to have judged of the other's heart, by the rankling at his own: and interested spirits were not wanting on both sides to exasperate their mutual suspicions and ill-will. The Court of Rome expected by an open contest to increase its power, as hitherto it had uniformly done; and there were men about Henry, who, if any confiscation of church property could be brought about, looked for a share in the spoils.

Becket, on returning from the interview, said to his friends that he must either yield with shame or combat manfully. When such appeared to be the alternative, the choice which such a man would make could not be doubtful. He began to act boldly in defiance of the Constitutions of Clarendon, protecting churchmen upon the ground of their assumed immunities, as if no such statutes had existed. Henry was warned by some of his counsellors to take heed, or it would be seen that he whom the Clergy should elect would be King, and reign no longer than it pleased the Primate. The Great Council was summoned at Northampton; and when Becket repaired thither, the King was inaccessible to him the first day, and on the second refused to receive from him the customary kiss of peace. Indeed he could not with propriety have accepted it, for Becket had been cited there to answer for his conduct as an offender, and defaulter. The first accusation was, that he had refused justice to a great officer of the household; and that having, upon complaint made to the King, been ordered to appear before him, his answer had been, that he would not obey the summons. A charge of high-treason was founded upon this, such were the notions of feudal obligation! and being held guilty, his goods and chattels were declared to be at the King's mercy. In cases of such forfeiture, a commutation was usually accepted which custom had rendered fixed, and in Kent at the moderate sum of forty shillings; but from the Archbishop five hundred pounds were exacted: a vindictive sentence, neither to be justified by the offence, nor by the disproportion between his property and that of the poorest freeman who could have become amenable to the same law.

He gave sureties for the payment, and thus ended the business of the first day.

If the King had acted as became him, he would have rested his dispute with Becket upon the Customs, and arraigned him for disregarding the Constitutions of Clarendon. Instead of this he sought to break his spirit, and ruin his fortune by a series of demands not less unjust than ungenerous...On the following day he called upon him for three hundred pounds, which he had received as warden of the King's castles, while he held that trust. He replied that he had expended more than that sum upon them, as the repairs themselves might prove; but he would pay it, for money should be no ground of quarrel between him and the King. Such an answer might have disarmed Henry's resentment had his better mind prevailed: in his then temper it mortified him, and increased his irritation. The next demand was for five hundred pounds, which Henry affirmed he had lent him: Becket answered it had been given to him, not lent: his affirmation was not allowed to balance the King's, and for this also he gave surety. There can be little doubt that he had received it as a gift, and that as such it was intended at the time, though the intention may not have been expressed. But Henry's determination to crush the man whom he now regarded as his mortal enemy, was more fully displayed on the third day, when he called upon him for an account of all the monies which he had received during his Chancellorship, and demanded payment of the balance. Becket's conduct at Clarendon was more excusable than Henry's at Northampton: his vacillation and retractations, and the degree of duplicity with which he had acted, arose from a sense of duty, always honourable in itself, even when as in his case, erroneous both in principle and action: but the King acted tortuously, in the spirit of hatred and vengeance. The answer was that he had not been questioned for these monies before his consecration, but on the contrary, Prince Henry, the King's eldest son, and Leicester his Justiciary, had discharged him from all such demands, and as so discharged, the Church received him. To this charge therefore he was not bound to plead: but it had come upon him unexpectedly, and he asked leave to consult with the Bishops, with whom accordingly he retired into a separate apartment.

Whether Becket after the manner in which he had been discharged from this demand, were still liable to it in strict law, may be a questionable point; but that in honour and equity he stood discharged is evident; and free judges, could such have been found, would have pronounced his acquittal with as little hesitation then, as an unbiassed judgment can feel upon the question now. The sum claimed was the enormous one of forty-four thousand marks of silver. He was advised to compound, and offered two thousand which were of course refused. The legal question, however, seems not to have been debated by the Bishops: they saw the demand in its true light, and perfectly understood what was the King's purpose: but they were no friends to Becket; they knew he had provoked a dispute which might well have been avoided, and in which if it continued, they must unwillingly be implicated; and they stood in fear of Henry, who, like his Norman predecessors, was of a temper to make men tremble. The Bishop of London advised him to resign the primacy, which if he did, the King, he observed, might then be moved to reinstate him in his possessions. One Prelate agreed in this counsel, because it appeared to him that Becket had only to choose between surrendering his see or losing his life; another, because it was better for the Church that one man should suffer than all; a third, because it was expedient to submit for a time. The Bishop of Worcester said he would not belie his conscience by saying that the cure of souls might be resigned for the sake of pleasing a prince, or of appeasing him; neither would he deliver a contrary opinion which might draw upon him the King's displeasure. The only person who supported Becket was the late King's brother, Henry of Winchester, a man of great ability and courage: he declared that the advice which had been given was pernicious, and that the rights of the clergy would be overthrown, if the primate were to set an example of relinquishing his charge at the will or menace of his sovereign. Perceiving how little help or counsel he was likely to find in his brethren, Becket desired to speak with the Earls of Leicester and Cornwall; and saying that the persons best acquainted with his affairs were not present, requested on that ground a respite till Monday, (the morrow being Sunday,) when he promised to make his answer to the demand, as God should inspire him.

Becket was one of those men whose true greatness is seen only in times of difficulty and danger, when they are deprived of all adventitious aid and left wholly to themselves. The large retinue of knights and other followers, who had attended him to Parliament, forsook him in his disgrace. His contempt as well as his indignation was roused by this ungrateful and cowardly desertion, and turning it to account, he sent his servants out to collect the poor and the maimed, the halt and the blind, from the streets and lanes of the town, and from the highways and hedges, and invite them to his table; with such an army, he said, he should more easily obtain the victory, than with those who had shamefully forsaken him in the hour of danger. This was in the spirit of the age, and of the man. His heart was never stronger; but the body gave way, and agitation of mind brought on a severe fit of a disease to which he was subject; so that when Monday came he was unable to leave his bed. The illness was said to be feigned, and two earls were deputed to cite him before the Parliament. They saw what detained him, he said, but with God's help he would appear before them on the morrow, even if he were carried in a litter. The respite was granted; but it was intimated to him, probably with the intention of instigating him to flight, that if he appeared, his destruction, or at least, his imprisonment, was resolved on.

Feeling himself in the situation of an injured man as the Primate now did, and looking to Heaven for that protection, which seemed to be denied him on earth; the religious feeling which such circumstances induce, softened his heart as well as elevated it, and at one time he had almost resolved to go barefoot to the palace, throw himself at the King's feet, and adjure him to be reconciled by the remembrance of their former friendship. But then a conscientious attachment to the cause which had drawn on him this persecution came in aid of his native pride; and, finally, his determination was made to connect his own cause with that of the Church, and to act or suffer in that spirit. On the Monday at an early hour many of the Bishops came to exhort him to submission, for the peace of the Church, and for his own safety; otherwise, they told him, he would be charged with perjury and treason, for breaking the customs which he had so lately sworn to observe. To this he replied, that he had been inexcusable before God, in swearing to observe them; but it was better to repent than perish. David had sworn rashly, and repented; Herod kept his oath, and perished. He enjoined them therefore to reject what he rejected, and annul these customs, which if they continued in force would overthrow the Church. Assuming then a loftier tone, he told them it was a detestable proceeding that in this affair they should not only have forsaken him, their spiritual father, but have sat in judgement upon him with the Barons. He forbade them to be present at any further proceedings against him, in virtue of the obedience which they owed him, and at the peril of their order; and he declared that he appealed to their mother, the Church of Rome, the refuge of all who were oppressed. He commanded them to thunder out the ecclesiastical censures, should the secular power presume to lay hands on him, their father and metropolitan; and he concluded by assuring them that, even though his body should be burnt, he would neither shamefully yield, nor wickedly forsake the flock committed to his charge.

As soon as the bishops left him, he went into the Church, and there at St. Stephen's altar performed the mass appointed for that martyr's day, beginning with these words, "Princes sate and spake against me;" and as if this did not sufficiently manifest his readiness to endure martyrdom, he caused a verse of the psalms to be sung, which could not be mistaken as to its intended application; "the Kings of the earth stand up, and the rulers take counsel together against the Lord, and against his anointed." Then having secretly provided himself with a consecrated wafer, he proceeded to the Great Council, and at the door took the silver cross from the chaplain, who according to custom was bearing it before him. The Bishops came out to meet him; they knew that this unusual conduct could not be intended to mollify the King, nor to indicate a wish for conciliation: and the Bishop of Hereford putting forth his hand said, Let me be your cross-bearer, as becomes me! But Becket answered, No: the cross was his safeguard, and would denote under what Prince he was combating. The Archbishop of York reproved him for coming thus, as it were armed, in defiance of his sovereign; and Gilbert of London observed, that if the King saw him enter with such arms, he would unsheathe his own, which were of greater force. Becket replied that the King's weapon could indeed kill the body, but his could destroy the soul. Then passing on, he entered the assembly, and took his seat in silence, holding the cross before him.

If Becket at this time actually thought his life in danger, the fate which he afterwards met, may prove that the apprehension was not so unreasonable as it might otherwise be deemed. Whether he entertained such fear or not, it was plainly his intention to act as if he did; should he provoke the blow which he seemed to expect, he was ready to meet it with becoming dignity and characteristic courage; in the more likely case that the unusual manner of his appearance would confuse the King's counsels, something might occur of which he might take advantage. Considering, therefore, Becket's temper and opinions, the measure was as judicious as it was bold. Henry was no sooner informed in what attitude the primate was approaching, than he rose hastily from his seat, and retired into an inner room, whither he summoned all the other lords, spiritual and temporal, and complained to them of this act of defiance. The Great Council, as well as the King, regarded it as a deliberate insult, studied for the purpose of throwing upon them the imputation of some treacherous purpose. Henry's violent temper was exasperated to such a pitch, that the Archbishop of York trembled for Becket's life, and departed with his chaplains, dreading to behold what might ensue. The Bishop of Exeter hastened fearfully to the primate and besought him to have pity upon himself, and his brethren, who were all in danger of perishing on his account. Becket, eyeing him with stern contempt, replied, "Fly then! thou canst not understand the things which are of God!" And he remained unmoved, holding the cross, and awaiting what might befal.

His part was not difficult after it had once been taken: the straight path is always easy. But Henry was thoroughly perplexed. The general sense of the Great Council was, that the Primate's present conduct was an affront to the King and the peers; that Henry had drawn it on himself, by elevating such a person to that high and unmerited station; and that for ingratitude and breach of fealty, Becket ought to be impeached of perjury and of high treason. Not from moderation, but with the hope of avoiding the embarrassments which he foresaw in that mode of proceeding, Henry rejected their opinion, and reverting to his pecuniary charges, sent to demand of the Primate whether upon that matter he would stand to the judgement of the court. Becket preremptorily refused, and it was then again proposed to attaint him. But the Bishops dared not proceed to this, because he had appealed to the Pope; and they knew the power of the Roman see too well, not to be fearful of offending it. They besought the King that he would let them appeal to Rome, against the Primate, on the score of his perjury; promising that if they might be excused from concurring with the temporal lords in the sentence which was about to be past, they would use their utmost endeavours for persuading the Pope to depose him from the primacy. The King unwarily consented: upon which they repaired to Becket, and pronouncing him guilty of perjury, as having broken his fealty, they renounced their obedience to him, placed themselves under the Pope's protection against him, and cited him before the Pope to answer the accusation. His only reply was, "I hear what you say!" He could not have heard any thing more conformable to his own views and wishes. The prelates then took their seats on the opposite side of the hall.

Meantime the temporal peers pronounced him guilty of perjury and treason; and leaving the inner chamber where their resolution had been passed, came to notify it to the accused. The alternative, however, of rendering his accounts, and discharging the balance was still to be allowed him, and Leicester, as Chief Justiciary, called upon him to come before the King and do this, otherwise, said he, hear your sentence!... "My sentence!" exclaimed Becket, rising from his seat; "nay, Sir Earl, hear you first! You are not ignorant, how faithfully, according to the things of this world, I served my Lord the King, in consideration of which service it pleased him to raise me to the primacy; God knows against my will! for I knew my own unfitness, and rather for love of him than of God, consented, which is this day sufficiently made evident, seeing that God withdraws from me both himself, and the King also. It was asked at my election, in presence of Prince Henry, unto whom that charge had been committed, in what manner I was given to the Church? And the answer was, Free and discharged from all bonds of the court. Being, therefore, thus free and discharged, I am not bound to answer concerning these things; nor will I."

The Earl here observed that this reply was very different from what had before been given. "Listen, my son! Becket pursued. In as much as the soul is of more worth than the body, by so much more are you bound to obey God and me, rather than an earthly King. Neither by law or reason is it allowed that children should judge or condemn their father. Wherefore I disclaim the King's judgement, and yours, and all the other peers', being only to be judged under God by our Lord the Pope, to whom I here appeal before you all, committing the church of Canterbury, my order and dignity, with all thereunto appertaining, to God's protection and to his. In like manner, my brethren, and fellow-bishops, you who have chosen to obey man rather than God, I cite you before the presence of our Lord the Pope! And thus, relying on the authority of the Catholic Church, and of the Apostolic See, I depart hence." As he was leaving the hall a clamour was raised against him, and some there were who reproached him as a perjured traitor: upon which he looked fiercely round, and said with a loud voice, that were it not forbidden by his holy orders, he would defend himself by arms against those who dared thus to accuse him. Anger for the moment overcame him, and he who had hitherto displayed such perfect dignity throughout this trying scene, forgot himself so far as to revile in foul and inhuman language two of the persons who were, indecently indeed, expressing their disapprobation of his conduct. No attempt at detaining him was made. The beggars, with the populace, and the poorer clergy, followed him in crowds, and were entertained as his guests, in the monastery where he was lodged. His next measure was to request permission to leave the kingdom. Henry replied he would advise with his council the next day; but Becket deeming it imprudent to await the decision, left Northampton privily in the night; and eluding pursuit by a circuitous course, effected his escape at length to the coast of Flanders.

However incensed the King may have been at Becket's flight, and apprehensive as he certainly was of its injurious consequences, he was careful not to prejudice his own case by hastily proceeding to extremities; and therefore forbore from seizing his temporalities, or visiting his offence upon those who were related to him, as the barbarous customs of that age authorized. Without delay he despatched ambassadors to the King of France and to the Pope, the two persons whose good will it most behoved him to conciliate. But the French King, who, from many circumstances personal and political, was inimically disposed towards Henry, had assured Becket when that prelate, meditating such a retreat, had sent over an agent to secure his reception, that he would receive him not as a Bishop or Archbishop, but as a partner in his kingdom. In this he was actuated by principle not less than passion, for he was devout by nature, thoroughly imbued with the superstition of the age, and believed the cause of the hierarchy to be that of religion. When, therefore, the ambassadors presented their letters requesting that he would not admit into his territories the late Archbishop of Canterbury, who had fled from England like a traitor; he took up the unadvised expression, and repeating "late Archbishop!" demanded who had deposed him? They were embarrassed by the question. "I," he pursued, "am a king as well as my brother of England; yet I would not have deprived the lowest clerk in my dominions, nor do I think I have power to do so. I knew this Thomas when he was chancellor: he served your King long and faithfully, and this is his reward, that his master having driven him from England, would also drive him out of France!" So warmly indeed did Louis take up the Primate's cause, that he despatched his almoner to the Pope, exhorting him as he regarded the honour of the Church, and the weal of the French kingdom, to support Thomas, Archbishop of Canterbury, against the English tyrant.

The ambassadors proceeded to Sens, where Alexander III. at that time resided, Rome being in possession of the antipope. They consisted of the Archbishop of York, four other bishops, and four barons,—showing what importance Henry attached to the cause. Higher persons, they said, the King could find none in his kingdom; if he could, he would have sent them to show his reverence toward the holy Father and the sacred Roman Church. What they solicited was, that his Holiness would send the Archbishop back to England, and appoint legates to judge him there. Some cardinals were of opinion it was expedient to do this in conformity to the King's desire, lest Henry should be driven to espouse the cause of the rival pope. But the papal court was not now to learn that the boldest policy is the best. Legates, Alexander said, they should have; but when it was asked of him that they might have powers for deciding the cause without appeal, "That," he replied, "is my glory, which I will not give to another; and certainly when the Archbishop is judged it shall be by ourselves. It is not reasonable that we should remand him to England, there to be judged by his adversaries, and in the midst of his enemies." The bent of his mind was so apparent in all this, that the Earl of Arundel, who was the head-piece of the embassy, hinted to him such conduct might perhaps provoke the King to seek for better treatment from his competitor; and the ambassadors left Sens without asking his blessing.

Becket, who had obtained a liberal allowance for himself and his followers from Louis, arrived at Sens soon afterwards. The Cardinals received him coldly, as one who was likely to weaken their cause by the contest in which he was involving them; but the Pope gave him public audience, seated him at his right hand, and as a farther mark of honour, bade him keep his seat while he spake. The Primate rested his case upon that point which was sure to interest the persons to whom he appealed. Leaving the pecuniary demand which had been the occasion of the breach unnoticed, he produced the constitutions of Clarendon, and called upon the assembly to judge whether, without destroying his own soul, he could consent that such laws against the liberty of the Church should be brought into action? Hitherto there had been an evident leaning towards Henry on the part of the Cardinals; but now the whole council resolved with one accord, that in Becket's person the cause of the universal Catholic Church should be supported. They then examined the constitutions, and the Pope tolerating six of them, not, he said, as good, but as less evil than the rest, condemned the other ten; thus sitting in judgement upon the acts of an English parliament, and the laws of England. The Pope upon this occasion informed the assembly, that Becket had applied to him before he left England to be pardoned for the sin of consenting to these constitutions; his repentance, he said, the sacrifices which he had made, and the sufferings he had endured, entitled him to indulgence.

But Becket was conscious that his own appointment to the primacy had been a greater violation of the rights of the Church than any of those which he had thus brought under the Pope's cognizance; and that Alexander, by deposing him upon that plea, might not only satisfy the King of England, without compromising the papal cause, but establish a strong precedent upon one of the most important points disputed between the civil and ecclesiastical powers. On the following day, he appeared before the Pope and the Cardinals in a more private room, and acknowledged that these troubles had been brought upon the Church of England, through his miserable offence; for he had ascended into the fold of

Christ, not by the true door, not having been called thither by a canonical election, but obtruded by the terror of secular power: what wonder then that he should have succeeded so ill? Had he, however, surrendered his see through fear of the King's menaces, when his brethren advised him so to do, that would have been leaving a pernicious example. Therefore he had deferred it till the present hour; but now, acknowledging the unlawfulness of his entrance, and fearing a worse exit; perceiving also that his strength was unequal to the burthen, and lest the flock whose unworthy pastor he had been made should perish, he resigned his see into the holy Father's hands. Accordingly, taking off his episcopal ring, he delivered it to the Pope, desired him to provide a proper pastor for the Church, which was now vacant, and then left the room. There were some of opinion that a happier means of terminating the dispute could not be devised, that the resignation ought to be accepted, and Becket provided for at some future opportunity. But Alexander, who as a statesman was worthy of his station, maintained, that if Becket were permitted to fall a sacrifice, all other bishops would fall with him; no ecclesiastic after such an example would venture to resist the will of his sovereign; the fabric of the Church would thus be shaken, and the papal authority perish. Becket was now called in, and the Pope told him that whatever fault there had been in his promotion, was cancelled by the manner in which he had acknowledged it, and by his resignation; that he now restored him to his functions, and would never desert him while he lived, viewing him as a pattern for imitation, dear to God and men, dear to himself, and to the Catholic Church. But as hitherto he had lived in affluence, it was now time that he should learn the lessons which poverty alone could teach; and for that end he commended him to the abbot of Pontigny, there present, one of the poor of Christ, in whose monastery he might live as became a banished man, and a champion of our Lord. He then gave him his blessing, and sent him, in compliance with his own request, a Cistertian habit. Becket was thus enrolled in that order, and observed at Pontigny the monastic rule of life, according to the strictest form which was at that time prevailing.

The conduct of the Pope irritated Henry, and he gave orders for stopping the payment of that annual contribution known by the name of Peter's-pence. Had Wicliffe then been living, or had there been among the English bishops another man endowed with the same talents and intrepidity as Becket, it is more than likely that the Church of England would then have separated from that of Rome, and that a reformation would have commenced, not less honourable in its origin than beneficial in its consequences. But Henry had no counsellor equal to the crisis. He sequestered the Primate's estates, ordered the Bishops to suspend the revenues of every clergyman who followed him into France, or took part in his behalf, declared all correspondence with him criminal, and forbade his name to be mentioned in the public prayers. But acting under the impulse of passion, he went beyond the bounds of policy and justice in his resentment, banishing, by one sweeping sentence, all the kinsmen, friends, and dependants of Becket, to the number of nearly four hundred persons, without exception of sex or age; their goods were confiscated, and they were compelled to take an oath, that they would repair to Becket wherever he might be, the King's intention being to distress him by the sight of their sufferings, and burthen him with their support. This inhuman act was in the spirit of feudal tyranny and of the times. When Henry had determined upon raising his favourite to the primacy, the Bishops of the province were threatened, that they and all their relations should be banished, if they refused to elect him, and this had been done certainly with Becket's knowledge, probably with his consent. The conduct which cannot be justified, may thus be explained: it admits of no palliation;...and indeed, next to the guilt of those who commit wicked actions, is that of the historian who glosses them over or excuses them.

This inhumanity, which on other occasions would only have excited the compassion of a few obscure individuals, called forth an outcry of indignation, and produced a display of ostentatious charity toward the sufferers. Some of them made their way to Pontigny; others were absolved from the observance of their oath; and they were liberally maintained by those powerful persons who supported the papal cause, especially the King of France: some were even invited by the Queen of Sicily, and went to partake her bounty, so widely did the interest which was excited by this dispute extend. Nor was this the only unworthy act into which Henry was hurried by his anger. He had resolved, with the advice of his Barons and the consent of his clergy, to send ambassadors to the Pope, requiring him so to rid him of the traitor Becket, as that he might establish another Primate in his stead, and to engage, that he and his successors would, as far as in them lay, maintain to the Kings of England the customs of Henry I., otherwise he and his clergy would no longer obey Pope Alexander,...so near was the Church of England to a separation at that time! The resolution was becoming, if it had been adhered to steadily: and Henry's ambassadors at the Diet of Wittenberg so far pledged him, that the Emperor in his letters-patent announced the adherence of England to the Ghibelline Pope. But their act was disavowed in a manner which evinced a want of firmness in the King, perhaps of veracity. His own mind appears to have been subdued by the superstition of the age, and he stood in awe both of the Pope, and of the man whom he hated.

A conference between Henry and the Pope had been proposed, to which the King consented, upon the reasonable condition that Becket should not be present. But Becket dreaded the effect of such an interview, and entreated Alexander not to agree to it on that condition, saying, that without the assistance of an interpreter as competent as himself, he would be in danger of being deceived by the King's subtlety. Circumstances at this time enabled Alexander to return to Rome; and this good fortune encouraged him to answer the King in a manner which might justly be deemed dignified, if it were justified by the occasion. It had never, he said, been heard that the Roman Church had driven any person out of her train at the command of Princes, especially one who was banished for the cause of justice. To succour the exiled and oppressed of all nations against the violence of their sovereigns, was a privilege and authority granted from above to the apostolic see. In the same temper he appointed Becket his legate for England, thus arming him with full powers for proceeding to extremities against his sovereign, an act not less flagrantly improper than it was gratuitously offensive to the King.

With such powers in his own cause no man ought to have been invested, least of all men one so vehement as Becket. Already, from his retirement at Pontigny, he had addressed epistles monitory and comminatory to the King, wherein he bade him remember that Sovereigns received their authority from the Church, and that Priests were the fathers and masters of Kings, Princes, and of all the faithful: it was madness then if a son should attempt to hold his father in subjection, or a pupil his master, and reduce under his power that person by whom he may be bound or loosed, not only on earth, but in heaven. To pass sentence upon a priest was not within the sphere of human laws: it was not for Kings to judge Bishops, but to bow their heads before them; and he reminded Henry that Kings and Emperors had been excommunicated. To the Clergy he said that in his person Christ had been judged again before an earthly tribunal. "Arise! why sleep ye? unsheathe the sword of Peter! Avenge the injuries of the Church! cry aloud! cease not!" That he was preparing to draw that sword himself was apparent from these preliminaries, and from his suspending the Bishop of Salisbury for having admitted a Dean into that cathedral, during the absence of certain canons who had followed him into exile. And so apprehensive was Henry of what was to ensue, that summoning his counsellors, he complained to them with tears and violent emotion, saying, Becket tore his body and soul, and they were all traitors for using no endeavours to deliver him from that man's annoyance! One of the Norman Bishops advised him to appeal to the Pope, as the sole means which could avert the impending sentence; and to this, inconsistent as it was with the dignity of the Crown, and with the very principles for which he was contending, he consented. The truth is, that at heart he was a superstitious man: in times of vexation or low spirits he used to talk of retiring into a convent; and the course of his private life made absolution so convenient and necessary to his comfort, that the thought of lying under the censures of the Church was more than he could bear. Accordingly two Bishops were deputed to notify the appeal to Becket.

Before they arrived, Becket had commenced the spiritual war in a manner not less characterestic of the man, than of the age. The body of St. Drauscio was venerated at Soissons, where he had been bishop; and there prevailed an opinion that any person about to engage * in battle, would be rendered invincible by keeping a vigil before his shrine. Persons came even from Italy, and other distant countries under this persuasion; and the success of Robert de Montfort, in a judicial combat, after performing this devotion, had recently given it great credit in England. To Soissons therefore Becket went, and watched one night before the body, as one who was prepared to enter the lists, and needed his heavenly assistance; a second vigil he kept before the shrine of St. Gregory the Great, the founder of the Anglo-Saxon Church, whose relics also were

* How St. Drauscio, an inoffensive man, whose life is one of the most uneventful in hagiology, should have become the Patron Saint in such cases, does not appear. The most notable thing recorded of him is, that after he had been dead and buried three years, he not only permitted his devotees to cut his hair and his nails for relics, but even allowed them to draw one of his teeth, though the operation produced an effusion of blood, as if it had been performed upon a living subject!

deposited at Soissons; and a third before the altar of his own patroness the Virgin. Thus armed for the conflict, he prepared on the ensuing Whitsunday, to thunder out his censures against the King in the Church at Vizelay, near his convent. A message from the King of France, announcing that Henry was dangerously ill, and on that account advising him to defer the sentence, withheld him from this last extremity; but to every thing short of it he proceeded. On the appointed day a great concourse of people assembled at the Church; Becket preached, in what strain we know not, in what temper is but too plain. At the end an awful pause ensued, the bells tolled, the crosses were inverted, and the assistant priests, twelve in number, stood round him, holding torches, which were presently with dreadful execrations to be extinguished. He then pronounced the impious form of excommunication against John of Oxford, for associating with schismatics, and for what he styled his intrusion into the deanery of Salisbury; against the Archdeacon of Poitiers, for holding communion with the Archbishop of Cologne, who adhered to the Ghibelline Pope; against three persons to whom part of his sequestered goods had been granted, and against all who should dare lay hands on the property of his Church: finally, against Joceline de Baliol, and the Chief Justiciary, as favourers of the King's tyranny, and contrivers of those heretical pravities, the constitutions of Clarendon. The execrations were concluded by dashing down the torches and extinguishing them, as the prelate, in the words of this execrable ceremony pronounced an authoritative wish, that the souls of those whom he had delivered to perdition, might in like manner be quenched in hell. This was not all: he read the constitutions, and condemned the whole of them; excommunicated all who should abet, enforce, or observe them; annulled the statute whereby they were enacted, and absolved the bishops from the oath which they had taken to obey them. Then naming the King, and mentioning the admonitions which he had sent him, he there in public called upon him to repent and atone for the wrongs which he had offered to the Church, otherwise, a sentence, such as that which they had just heard pronounced, should fall upon his head.

Excommunication had been one means whereby the Druids maintained their hierocracy; and it has been thought, that among nations of Keltic origin, the clergy, as succeeding to their influence, established more easily the portentous tyranny which they exercised, not over the minds of men alone, but in all temporal concerns. Every community must possess the right of expelling those members who will not conform to its regulations: the Church, therefore, must have power to excommunicate a refractory member, as the State has to outlaw a bad subject, who will not answer to the laws. But there is reason to believe that no heathen priests ever abused this power so prodigiously, as the Roman clergy; nor even if the ceremonies were borrowed, as is not improbable from heathen superstition, could they originally have been so revolting, so horrible, as when a christian minister called upon the Redeemer of mankind, to fulfil execrations which the Devil himself might seem to have inspired. In the forms of malediction appointed for this blasphemous service, a curse was pronounced against the obnoxious persons in soul and body, and in all their limbs and joints and members, every part being specified with a bitterness which seemed to delight in dwelling on the sufferings that it imprecated. They were curst with pleonastic specification, at home and abroad, in their goings out and their comings in, in towns and in castles, in fields and in meadows, in streets and in public ways, by land and by water, sleeping and waking, standing and sitting and lying, eating and drinking, in their food and in their excrement, speaking or holding their peace, by day and by night, and every hour, in all places and at all times, every where and always. The heavens were adjured to be as brass to them, and the earth as iron; the one to reject their bodies, and the other their souls. God was invoked, in this accursed service, to afflict them with hunger and thirst, with poverty and want, with cold and with fever, with scabs and ulcers and itch, with blindness and madness,...to eject them from their homes, and consume their substance,...to make their wives widows, and their children orphans and beggars; all things belonging to them were cursed, the dog which guarded them, and the cock which wakened them. None was to compassionate their sufferings, nor to relieve or visit them in sickness. Prayers and benedictions, instead of availing them, were to operate as farther curses. Finally, their dead bodies were to be cast aside for dogs and wolves, and their souls to be eternally tormented with Korah, Dathan and Abiram, Judas and Pilate, Ananias and Sapphira, Nero and Decius, and Herod, and Julian, and Simon Magus, in fire everlasting.

This was the sentence with which Becket threatened the King, and which he actually pronounced against persons who had acted in obedience to the King and to the laws of their country. If the individual, upon whom such curses were imprecated, felt only an apprehension that it was possible they might be efficient, the mere thought of such a possibility might have brought about one of the maledictions, by driving him mad. But the reasonable doubt which the subject himself must have entertained, and endeavoured to strengthen, was opposed by the general belief, and by the conduct of all about him; for whosoever associated with one thus marked for perdition, and delivered over judicially to the Devil and his angels, placed himself thereby under the same tremendous penalties. The condition of a leper was more tolerable than that of an excommunicated person. The leper, though excluded from the community, was still within the pale of the Church and of human charity: they who avoided his dangerous presence, assisted him with alms; and he had companions enough in affliction to form a society of their own,...a miserable one indeed, but still a society, in which the sense of suffering was alleviated by resignation, the comforts of religion, and the prospect of death and of the life to come. But the excommunicated man was cut off from consolation and hope; it remained for him only to despair and die, or to obtain absolution by entire submission to the Church; and in the present case it must be remembered that submission implied the sacrifice of the points in dispute, that is, the sacrifice of principle and justice, of national interests, of kingly and individual honour. There were some parts of Europe, where if a person remained one year under ecclesiastical censures, all his possessions of whatever kind were forfeited. This was not the law in England, where indeed the usurpations of the Romish Church had been resisted longer and more steadily than on the continent. But the next step after excommunicating the King, might be to pronounce sentence of deposition against him; and that sentence, while it endangered him in England, would, in all likelihood, deprive him of his continental territories, which the king of France, who continually instigated Becket against him, was eager to invade.

But there was another measure, even more to be dreaded in its consequences, of which Henry stood in fear. Supported as he was in the grounds of this dispute both by his barons and by the nation, and by the bishops also in the personal contest with Becket, a sentence of excommunication and deposition might have failed to shake the allegiance of his subjects. An interdict would do this by bringing the evil home to them, for the effect of an interdict was to suspend all religious forms, usages and sacraments, save only that baptism was allowed to infants, and confession to those who were at the point of death. The churches were closed, no priest might officiate either in public or private; the dead were deprived of christian burial, and the living could contract no marriages. Of all the devices of the papal church this was the most effectual for breaking the bonds of loyalty, and compelling subjects to rise against their sovereign. Expecting that Becket would have recourse to it, Henry took measures of the severest precaution : he gave instructions that the ports should be closely watched, and ordered that if an ecclesiastic were detected bringing over letters of interdict, he should be punished with mutilation of members; if a layman, with death: and that if such letters reached the country and were promulgated, any priest, who in obedience refused to perform service should be castrated. In such a spirit was one tyranny opposed by another during those ages of inhumanity and superstition! Exasperated with the Cistercians of Pontigny for having received the Primate into their convent, he announced that if they continued to harbour him, he would expel their order from his dominions. This angry act gave Becket an opportunity of shewing his generosity by withdrawing, and enabled Louis to wound his enemy's feelings, by despatching an escort to attend him, and inviting him to choose an asylum in any part of his dominions. He fixed upon the convent of St. Columba by the city of Sens, and was received there with public honours.

This was one of the many unworthy acts committed by Henry under the influence of anger, during this long and acrimonious struggle. He acted with more prudence by his ministers, and prosecuted with sufficient policy the appeal which it had been impolitic to make. While a paper war was carried on with bitterness between Becket, and the English Bishops, his messengers at Rome were employing golden arguments with a court, which in Becket's own words, was prostituted like a harlot for hire. The excommunicated John of Oxford was one of these ministers; for him to have undertaken such a commission implied a confidence in his own dexterity which was not belied by the event. He obtained absolution for himself; resigned his deanery to the Pope, and received it again from his appointment; and persuaded Alexander to depute two Cardinals as his legates in the King's continental territories, with full powers to hear and determine the cause, and to absolve the excommunicated persons; thus revoking the legatine power which had been granted to Becket, and annulling all that he had done at Vezelay. The Pope, who had previously ratified those acts, was so conscious of his inconsistency, that when he notified these concessions to the King, he strictly enjoined him to keep the letter secret, and not le tit be seen, except in case of necessity. This was not all; the messengers brought back with them the letters which Becket and his friends had written to the Pope, and some of these proved to be from persons of the King's household who had never before been suspected. In these letters Becket had called Henry a malicious tyrant; but no new discovery could now imbitter Henry's feelings toward him.

When the Primate was apprized of this unexpected change in the conduct of the papal court, he said, that if it were true, the Pope had not only strangled him, but the English and Gallican Churches also. Its effect was immediately perceived in the treatment of his unhappy kinsmen and dependants who had been driven into banishment for his sake. It was now seen to what motives the liberality with which some of the French Nobles and Bishops had hitherto supported them, was owing; for now, when Becket was deemed to be forsaken by the Pope, their aid was inhumanly withdarwn;—some of these poor people were left in such utter destitution that they died of cold and hunger, and Becket, who in this emergency neither abandoned himself nor them, implored Alexander to take means for preserving the rest from the same fate. His spirit was one of those which difficulties and dangers seem only to exalt; the same temper, which in prosperity made him violent and imperious, assuming under adverse fortune the character of heroic fortitude. Still being more statesman than saint by habit as well as inclination, he exerted now in his own behalf those talents to which he owed his elevation, and which qualified him better for the Chancellorship than the Primacy; he represented to Alexander that Henry's policy was to gain time by prolonging the business till the Papacy should become vacant, and then to make a recognition of the obnoxious customs, the terms upon which he would acknowledge his successor. If he succeeded in this, other princes would extort the like emancipation from the Church, her liberty and jurisdiction would be destroyed, and there would be none to restrain the wickedness of tyrants: and addressing to the Pope phrases of supplication which, in Scripture, are appropriated to the Almighty, Rise, Lord, he said, and delay no longer! Let the light of thy countenance shine upon me, and do unto me and my wretched friends according to thy mercy! Save us, for we perish! And he called upon him to clear up his own honour, which was now obscured, though till now, it had remained singly inviolate, when all else was lost.

These representations were strongly aided by the King of France, Louis VII. being equally sincere in his enmity towards Henry and his devotion to the Church; and Alexander, emboldened also at this time by a fortunate change in his own contest with the Emperor, restricted the power of his legates, whom he now deputed rather as mediators than as judges. Their task was the more difficult because Henry was persuaded that Becket had had no small share in instigating the King of France and the Earl of Flanders to make war upon him. Becket made oath that he was innocent:—of directly instigating them, no doubt, he was clear; but it is as little to be doubted, that he had exasperated the ill-will of the one prince, and that both had been encouraged by the advantages which they expected to derive from the embarrassment in which Henry was thus involved. From Becket's disposition even less was to be hoped than from the King's: he cautioned them to place no confidence in those Balaams, the English bishops, and expressed his trust that they would cure the royal Syrian of his leprosy, but inflict merited punishment upon the Gehazis of his train. To the Pope he wrote, "It is by forbearance on our side that the powers of the world grow insolent, and Kings become tyrants, so as to believe that no rights, no privileges are to be left the Church, unless at their pleasure. But blessed is he who takes and dashes their little ones against the stones! For if Judah does not, according to the command of the law, root out the Canaanite, he will grow up against him to be perpetually his enemy and his scourge." In vain did the legates recommend to him moderation and humility, and exhort him to give way for the peace of the Church. He would neither concede the slightest point, nor consent to abide by their judgement; whereas Henry offered to give them any security they should ask, that he would submit to it in every point, if they would render him that justice which the lowest of men had a right to demand. While one party was so intractable, nothing could be done by mediation; their powers did not extend farther, and Henry was so offended at being thus paltered with, that in their hearing he wished he might never again see the face of a Cardinal. He came, however, to a better understanding with them before they departed, and when they took their leave shed tears, as he begged them to use their intercession with the Pope, for ridding him of Becket.

Becket was at this time elated by a brief, wherein the Pope, by virtue of his apostolical powers, annulled the decree of the Great Council at Northampton, confiscating the primate's goods for contumacy. But this mark of favour was heavily counterbalanced when he received a prohibition from excommunicating any person in England, or interdicting that realm, till the affair should have been brought before the Pope. Henry was incautious enough to say that he had now got the Pope and all the Cardinals in his purse, and even to state in his own family what bribes he had given, and how they had been applied. It is not to be believed that Alexander himself, was accessible by such means; infamously venal as the court of Rome had become, this was a case in which he had too much at stake, even if his personal character were such as might otherwise warrant the imputation. He would willingly have reconciled the parties; and inclining to one party or the other, asBecket's vehemence and the urgent interference of the French King, or the fair statements and able negotiations of Henry's ministers, prevailed, his own wishes were indicated in the exhortations to humility and moderation, which be repeatedly but vainly addressed to the

Primate. The King had said to the Legates he would be content with those customs which it could be proved that his ancestors had enjoyed, by the oaths of an hundred Englishmen, an hundred Normans, and an hundred men of his other continental dominions. If this would not satisfy Becket, he would abide by the arbitration of three English and three Norman bishops: and if this offer also were rejected, he would submit to the Pope's judgement, provided only that his act should not prejudice the rights of his successors. The Legates conceived a hope that Henry would concede the customs, if by so doing he could rid himself of Becket, and that for the sake of succeeding in this point, Becket would resign his archbishoprick; but when this proposal was made to him, he replied the concessions were not equal; the King was bound in duty and for the good of his soul, to renounce the customs, but he could not surrender the primacy without betraying the Church. And he assured the Pope that he would rather be put to death, than suffer himself to be torn while living from his mother, the Church of Canterbury, which had nursed him and reared him to what he was; ...rather perish by the cruellest death, than shamefully live, while the King was permitted to act as he did, without receiving condign punishment.

At length peace having been made between the two Kings, it was arranged that at the interview between them, Henry and Becket should meet. The latter was difficultly persuaded to this; and though to satisfy Louis, he knelt to humble himself before his sovereign, it was with an unbending spirit. His language was so qualified as to shew that he yielded not a tittle of the disputed points; and when Henry declared all he asked was that he would then promise, without fraud or fallacy, to keep all the laws which his predecessors had kept in former reigns, and which he himself had formerly promised to keep, the answer still contained the same fatal condition of saving his order:.. to regain the King's favour he would do all he could without prejudice to the honour of God. Henry did not refrain from reproaching Becket with ingratitude and pride; but subduing this emotion of anger he addressed himself to Louis, in a manner which if that monarch had been less blindly devoted to the papal court must have wrought a change in his disposition toward the contending parties. Mark! said he, my liege! whatever displeases him he says is against the honour of God: and with this plea he would dispossess me of all my rights! But that I may not be thought to require any thing contrary to that honour, I make him this offer.

There have been many Kings of England before me, some who had greater power than I, others who had less. There have been many Archbishops of Canterbury before him, great and holy men. What the greatest and holiest of his predecessors did for the least of mine, let him do that for me, and I shall be satisfied. The whole assembly with one accord declared that the King had condescended sufficiently; even Louis felt, for the time, the fairness of such a proposal, and turning to Becket who continued silent, asked him, if he would be greater and wiser than all those holy men? and wherefore he hesitated when peace was at hand? The inflexible primate replied, It is true, many of my predecessors were greater and better than I. Each of them in his time cut off some abuses, but not all; if they had, I should not now be exposed to this fiery trial; a trial whereby being proved as they have been, I also may be found worthy of their praise and reward. If any one of them was too cool in his zeal, or too intemperate in it, I am not bound to follow his example, one way or the other. I would willingly return to my church if it were possessed of that liberty which in the days of my predecessors it enjoyed; but admit customs which are contrary to the decrees of the holy Fathers I will not: nor give up the honour of Christ, for the sake of recovering the favour of man.

Becket's own friends were, on this occasion, so sensible of the imprudence .. if not the unreasonableness and unrelenting obstinacy of his conduct, that they prevented him from proceeding, and drew him forcibly away. The opinion that he no longer deserved protection, when it was now plainly seen that his arrogance was the only obstacle to peace, was loudly expressed; and when the interview ended, it was thought that he had irrecoverably forfeited the King of France's favour. So it appeared from Louis's demeanour, who neither visited him that night, nor sent him food as before from his own kitchen, nor saw him on the ensuing day, before his departure. His followers were in despair, expecting to be banished from the French territories. But that conduct which Louis had seen in its true light when Becket was in the presence of his King, and the candour of the one was contrasted with the stubborn pride of the other, assumed a different colour when he reflected upon it in solitude, under the influence of unmitigated enmity towards Henry, and unbounded devotion to the Church. Regarding the Primate then as the heroic and saintly champion of a sacred cause, he sent for him, fell at his feet, entreated with tears forgiveness for having advised him to prefer the favour of man before the honour of God, recommended his kingdom to God and him, .. as to a tutelary being, and promised never to desert him and his followers. And when Henry, by his messengers, expressed his wonder that he should continue to abet the Primate after what he had himself witnessed at the interview ; tell your King, was his reply, that he will not give up certain customs because they appertain to his royal dignity, neither will I give up the hereditary privilege of my crown, which is to protect the unfortunate and the victims of injustice. There was magnanimity as well as error in this conduct; and perhaps Louis himself was not aware how greatly the satisfaction which he felt, in performing a generous part, was enhanced by knowing that it was the surest way to mortify and injure a rival whom he hated.

In this long contention, for five years had now elapsed since Becket withdrew from England, each party had committed acts as unwarrantable as the other could have desired, giving thus just cause of indignation on both sides. The question concerning Becket's accounts as chancellor was altogether slighted by him, as a demand, which but for the constitutions of Clarendon, would never have been brought forward: nor did Henry press a point, which, whatever he might deem of its legality, he knew to be substantially unjust. But there was a demand upon Henry, in which the Church was too much interested ever to relax its pursuit; ... it was for restitution,... even to the last farthing, of all that had been taken from the Primate and those who had either followed, or been driven after him into exile. Henry had declared that he would make no restitution, and had even sworn that all the property which had been seized on this account, he had bestowed upon poor churches. But Becket ceased not to call upon the Pope to use the rigour of justice; and Alexander, whose letters of admonition produced no effect, sent letters of commination, now, bidding the King not to imagine that the Lord, who now slept, might not be awakened, nor that the sword of St. Peter was rusted in the scabbard and had lost its edge; and warning him that if restitution were not made before the beginning of Lent, the Primate should no longer be restrained as he had thus long been.

Becket waited till the term prescribed, and then without informing the Pope of his intentions, thundered out his censures against so many of the King's household, that Henry was surrounded by excommunicated persons, and had scarcely one among his chaplains, from whom he could receive the kiss of peace. The Bishops of London and of Salisbury, who were among these persons, appealed to the Pope; and Henry, declaring that he resented this audacious act not less than if Becket had vomited out his poison upon his own person, wrote to Alexander, complaining that he seemed to have abandoned him to the malice of his enemy, and requesting him to annul these injurious proceedings. His desire now was that Becket might be appointed to some foreign see, and thereby removed from France; such a termination of the dispute Henry would have purchased at any price; if Alexander would do this, he promised to procure for him a peace with the Emperor, to buy over all the Roman nobles of the Ghibelline party, to give him 10,000 marks, and allow him to appoint whom he pleased to Canterbury, and to all the other sees then vacant. He made presents to the Roman barons of Alexander's party, for their interest: and promised large sums to several Italian cities if they could effect it by their interference. The Sicilian court, whose friendship was of the utmost importance to Alexander at this time, was induced earnestly to second these solicitations, and this long contest created hardly less trouble and anxiety to the Pope than to Henry himself. Gladly would he have reconciled the parties, and to his honour it must be said that though dexterously availing himself of every opportunity to strengthen and extend the papal power, he acted throughout in a spirit of mediation. But Becket's inflexible temper frustrated all his conciliatory plans. Though Alexander exhorted, entreated and admonished him to suspend the censures which he had past, till it should be seen what a new legation might effect with the King, and though he requested it particularly on the Bishop of Salisbury's behalf, on the score of his own long intimacy with that prelate, who moreover had acted not from inclination, but under fear of the King, through the natural infirmity of old age, Becket equally disregarded the advice and the solicitations of the Pontiff,.. his opinions and his feelings, relying so confidently upon the support of the French King and the system of the Papal Court, that he ventured to treat with this disrespect the Pope himself.

The censures indeed produced in England the effect which the intrepid Primate looked for. For the other prelates, though they had hitherto acted in concert with their excommunicated brethren, refused to hold communion with them now, and even in direct defiance of the King's orders, enjoined all men in their respective dioceses to avoid them, in obedience to the sentence. Becket announced his intention not to spare the King's person, if repentance and satisfaction were delayed, and ordered his Clergy to stop the celebration of divine service after the Purification, if the King should continue contumacious till that time. However Henry, he said, might affect to threaten, in reality he trembled with fear, seeing the accomplices of his iniquity thus delivered over to Satan. Nothing but punishment could recall him; and when they were crushed, he might be more easily subdued! In this language did he speak of his sovereign; and so nearly was he considered in the light of an independent power engaged in hostilities with him upon equal terms, that the common expression which the Pope as well as he himself used for the proposed accommodation, was that of concluding peace between them. The two Nuncios who were now charged with this negotiation required Henry, for the love of God and the remission of his sins, to restore Becket and take him sincerely into favour: till this should be done, they refused to absolve the excommunicated persons. Growing angry in the debate which ensued, Henry turned away, swearing that if the Pope would not grant any thing which he requested, he would take other courses. "Sir," said one of the Nuncios, "do not threaten! we fear no threats, for we are of a court that has been accustomed to give laws to Emperors and Kings."

After long disputation concerning a written form of reconciliation, in which the King insisted upon saving the dignity of his Kingdom, and Becket upon saving the honour of the Church; all mention of the accounts was waived on one part, and of the customs on the other. Upon the point of restitution, Becket would have accepted half the amount of the estimated claim; with regard to the rest, he told his agents, he was willing to shew a patient forbearance, because it was expedient that the Church should have something in her power to keep the King in awe with, and to bring out against him, if he should begin new disturbances and seditions. Every thing seemed at last to be accorded, when the negotiation was broken off, because Henry would not consent to perform the customary form of giving the kiss of peace; this he said he could not do, though willing to have done it, because in his anger he had publicly sworn that he would never give it to Becket; but he protested that he would bear no rancour against him. The Primate was not satisfied with this; the French King who desired the continuance of a contest so harassing to his enemy, encouraged him not to accede to any terms, without this form; and the Nuncio admonished Henry to comply with what was required of him, for otherwise repentance would come too late.

The effect of this was not what the Nuncio expected. It roused the King's spirit, and he sent orders from his French dominions, where he then was, to England, that any persons carrying an interdict thither, should be punished as traitors, and all persons who should act in obedience to it, be banished with all their kin, and suffer confiscation of all their goods. He directed also that Peter-pence should be paid into his treasury, and no longer to the Pope; and required an oath from all his subjects to obey these orders. The laity without hesitating took this oath, which was actually an abjuration of obedience to the Primate and the Pope, and was so denominated at the time. The Clergy as generally refused, and Becket privately sent over letters to absolve the laity from observing it... But the crisis was not so near as Henry apprehended; the negotiation was again renewed, and an agreement proposed on his part, upon the general terms that each should perform what he owed to the other. Meantime, he was pursuing a business at the court of Rome, which he had greatly at heart, and which eventually brought about the shocking catastrophe of this long and perplexed drama. For many reasons, he had long wished to have his eldest son crowned,—the surest method he thought of precluding any struggle for the succession after his own death. With this intention he had obtained a bull, while the see of Canterbury was vacant, empowering him to have the ceremony performed by what Bishop he pleased; this bull had been revoked virtually though not directly: now, however, Alexander by his apostolic authority enjoined the Archbishop of York to officiate in this function, as one belonging to his see. It does not appear by what persuasions he was induced to this compliance: but there was a disgraceful duplicity in his conduct; he earnestly desired Henry to keep this permission secret from Becket, and yet shortly after, at Becket's desire, prohibited the Archbishop of York and all other English Bishops from performing the ceremony, declaring it was the privilege of the see of Canterbury. But the ports were so well watched, that Becket could find no means of introducing his inhibitory letter, and the Prince was crowned.

In giving the permission, Alexander had carefully asserted the pretensions of the Papal Court, granting by St. Peter's authority, and his own, and with the advice of his brethren, that Prince Henry should be crowned King of England. It was a severe mortification to Becket thus to be defrauded, as his friends called it, of what he had so long sighed for, and to see the Prince, who ought to have reigned by none but him, made King by another. This was their language, and it shows the entire dependence upon the Church to which they would have reduced the royal authority. He had the farther mortification of learning that the Pope had commissioned his Legates to absolve the Bishops of Salisbury and London, calling the latter, whom Becket regarded as the worst, being indeed the ablest of his enemies, a religious, learned, prudent, and discreet man. Becket's indignation at this was unbounded, and using language which he would have been the first to condemn in another, he declared that St. Peter himself, were he upon earth, could not have power to absolve such impenitent sinners; Satan, he said, was let loose to the destruction of the Church; Barabbas was freed, and Christ crucified a second time.

This temper was encouraged by some of his friends, who for the purpose of serving him more effectually, had continued about Henry's person, and communicated to him the information thus treacherously obtained. They advised him to use no farther forbearance; but to pour out his whole spirit, and unsheath his whole sword. "May the eye of God," said they, "look with favour upon you and the sheep of his pasture; and give his Church the glory of a victory over princes, rather than an insincere peace with them!" Thus excited, he wrote letters to England, peremptorily placing the kingdom under an interdict;—but here he was baffled, for the letters could not be introduced. He was in this temper, when Legates were again appointed by the Pope to effect an accommodation; and he wrote to them, warning them against the artifices of Henry, whom he called "that monster," and bidding them suspect whatever he might say, as deceitful. "If," said he, "he perceives that he cannot turn you from your purposc, he will counterfeit fury, he will swear and forswear, take as many shapes as Proteus did, and come to himself at last; and if it is not your own fault, you will be from that time a God to Pharaoh." The Legates however had received wiser instructions from Rome, and every thing was now adjusted, except that Henry still objected to give the kiss, by reason of his oath, proposing that it should be given in his stead by the young King his son; and Becket demurred at this, saying the form was essential, as one established among all nations, and in all religions, and without which peace was no where confirmed: but that if he accepted it from the young King, it might be said he was not in the father's favour. To remove this obstacle, Alexander, though unsolicited, had absolved the King from his oath. On a like occasion, Henry I. had refused to consent to such a dispensation, saying, "it was not consistent with a King's honour, for who would afterwards trust to a sworn promise, if it were shown by such an example that the obligation of an oath might so easily be cancelled?" This was too generous as well as too wise a precedent for his grandson to have overlooked, had it been in his power to pursue the same straight and dignified course; but at this time the circumstances in which he was placed were so critical that he deemed it expedient to submit in this point to his imperious subject, desiring only, that as his interview with Becket was to be in the French territories, the ceremony might be delayed till he returned to his own. To this Becket consented, and they met in a meadow near Frettevalle, in the district of Chartres, and upon the borders of Touraine, where the Kings of England and France had held conference on the two preceding days.

On Henry's part no appearance of sincerity was wanting. As soon as he saw the Primate at a distance, he galloped forward to meet him, uncovered his head, and prevented his salutation, by first greeting him. They then withdrew together, as if familiarly discoursing. But Becket's discourse, was, by his own account, (for no third person was present,) far less conciliatory than his manner. He urged the King to make public satisfaction for the great injuries which he had done the Church, and asked, whether in despoiling Canterbury of her ancient and acknowledged right, he had wished to perpetuate enmity between the Church and her children? He advised him to avert from himself and from his son, the wrath of God, and of those Saints who rested in the Church of Canterbury and were grievously injured by this proceeding; he bade him remember that, for many ages, no one had injured that Church without being corrected, or crushed, by Christ our Lord; and he also observed to him, that the consecration of a King, like other sacraments, derived its whole validity from the right of the administering person to perform that office. Becket represents the King as having replied, that Canterbury, which was the most noble of all the western Churches, should be redressed in this point, and recover its pristine dignity in all respects. But he added,..to those persons who have hitherto betrayed both you and me, I will, by the blessing of God, make such an answer as traitors deserve. It is much more likely that this should mean, those persons who, while they pretended to agree with the King, had corresponded with Becket and spurred him on to extremities, than that Henry should have alluded to the Archbishop of York, and the Bishop of London, as the Primate seems to have understood. For at these words he alighted, and threw himself at the King's feet; Henry also alighted, and ordered him to remount, and held the stirrup for him, and said, "My Lord Archbishop, what occasion is there for many words? Let us mutually restore to each other our former affection, and do one another all the good we can, forgetting the late discord." Then returning to his retinue, he said aloud, that if he did not show to the Archbishop such good will as he had now found in him, he should be the worst of men.

The business of the interview yet remained, after the first, and as it seemed the most difficult, step had been taken. Henry sent the Bishops who were with him, to desire that Becket would now, in the presence of the assembly, make his petition; these messengers advised him to throw himself and his cause upon the King's pleasure; which, as the terms had in fact already been adjusted with the Pope, would have been the wisest and most decorous course. But this he rejected, as the iniquitous counsel of Scribes and Pharisees; and determined, with the advice of his own friends, to submit nothing to the King, neither the question concerning the customs, nor of the sequestration, nor of the coronation, nor of the damages which the church had suffered in her liberties, and he in his honour. Instead of this, he petitioned by the archbishop of Sens, that the King would restore the church of Canterbury with its possessions, and his royal favour, and peace and security to him and his; and that he would graciously be pleased to amend what had presumptuously been done against him and the Church in the late coronation; promising, on his own part, love and honour, and whatever could be performed in the Lord by an Archbishop to his Sovereign. A very different form of words had been concerted with the Pope; but Henry felt that this was no place for disputing. He may have felt also, that when words were purposely made vague enough to admit of large demands, the advantage which they afforded was not to the claimant only. He agreed to all, and declared, that he received the Primate and his friends into favour. They past the evening together, and it was settled that Becket should go to take leave of the French King, and then come to Normandy, to make some abode in the court and near the King's person, that it might be publicly seen into what favour he had been received. When he was about to depart, the Bishop of Lisieux proposed to him, that on the day of indulgence he should absolve the ex-communicated servants of the King, then present, shewing thus to others such favours as he and his friends had received. But he eluded this: the persons in question, he said, were in various circumstances, and under different censures, some of which could not be removed without the Pope's authority. He must no tindiscriminately confound them; yet having sentiments of peace and charity for them all, he would, by the divine assistance, manage the matter so to the honour of the Church, the King, and himself, and also to the salvation of those for whom this was asked, that if any one of them should fail of reconciliation and peace, (which he prayed might not happen,) he must impute it to himself, not to him. A reply so evasive, and yet at the same time displaying so plainly the unallayed enmity in the speaker's heart, provoked an angry reply from one of the parties. But the King, to prevent any acrimonious contention which might otherwise have arisen, drew Becket away, and dismissed him with honour.

That the King would ever again have received Becket into favour and friendship is not to be believed, because it is scarcely possible; but there is every reason for believing that the reconciliation would have been effective to the great ends of public and private tranquillity, if there had been the same sincere intention of rendering it so on the Primate's part as on the King's. The Primate had concealed his exultation during the interview; but he had scarcely concealed his intention of renewing the contest, and making those who had offended him feel the whole weight of his authority. What his feelings were is known, not by his actions alone, but by his own letters; in these, he boasted that the King had not even presumed to mention the royal customs, that he had been conquered in every point; and that on promising to give the kiss, he had plainly shewn himself guilty of perjury: the peace, thus obtained, was such as the world could not have given or hoped for; but still the whole substance of it, as yet, consisted only in hope, and he trusted in God that something real would follow. When the Pope, at his request, again suspended those prelates who had officiated at the coronation, he said it was a measure dictated undoubtedly by the Holy Ghost, whereby his Holiness corrected the King's enormities, with an authority becoming the successor of Peter and the vicar of Christ. He was, indeed, prudent enough not to proclaim the suspension which was decreed before the form of reconciliation took place, but he requested that other letters to the same effect might be sent him, in which the injury done to the rights of Canterbury should be the sole cause assigned for the sentence; and he asked full power for himself, meaning thereby, power to excommunicate the King, and lay the kingdom under an interdict, if he should think proper; because, said he, the more powerful and the fiercer that prince is, the stronger chain and the harder staff will be necessary to bind and keep him in order.

Elated however, and bent upon extremities as he was, there was a secret feeling that his triumph was not so complete as he represented it to be, and something like an ominous apprehension that there would be danger as well as difficulty in the course which he was determined to pursue. His friends in England advised him not to return thither, until he should have well ingratiated himself with the King: his messengers to that country were generally shunned as persons with whom it was imprudent to converse; and they who had got possession of the sequestered lands, manifested a disposition to keep them as long as they could: some committed waste, in a spirit of shameless rapacity; and one powerful man, who had been enriched with the spoils of Canterbury, was said to have threatened his life if he ever set foot in England. Becket was incapable of fear. He wrote to Henry, requesting leave immediately to go over. "By your permission," said he, "I will return to my church, perhaps to perish for her; but whether I live or die, yours I am, and will be, in the Lord: and whatever befall me or mine, may God bless you and your children." And announcing his intention to the Pope, he said, that he was doubtful whether he was going to peace or punishment, and therefore he commended his soul to his Holiness, and returned thanks to him and the apostolic see for the relief administered to him and his in their distress.

The delay of which Becket complained was chiefly caused by interested and rapacious individuals. It appears, however, that Henry did not send over positive orders for enforcing the restitution which he had engaged to make; and in this he was influenced by a suspicion or knowledge of the implacable disposition which Becket still cherished against those who had offended him, and which, indeed, had been but too plainly indicated at their first interview. At their second meeting, which was not till several weeks had elapsed, during which Henry had been dangerously ill, the kiss was not given, though they were then within the King's dominions; his reception was cold and ceremonious; expostulations and recriminations past between them, not without acrimony; and Henry declared, that before the full restitution which he again engaged to make, he would have Becket return to England, that he might see how he conducted himself there. When next they met, the King was in a kinder mood, and there came from him an expression which seems to bear the stamp of sincerity..."Oh, my lord, why will you not do what I desire? I should then put every thing into your hands." The exclamation seems to imply an emotion of affectionate regret that Becket had not co-operated with him in those necessary and beneficial reforms which he had designed, and for the purpose of effecting which he had raised him to the primacy. So Becket himself appears to have understood it; but the king had touched a string to which, in his heart, there was no responsive chord; and an expression which resented of old affection, had no other effect upon him than to call up a thought not less arrogant than unprovoked: it reminded him, he says in a letter, of the devil's words to our Saviour, "All this will I give thee if thou wilt fall down and worship me."

He had now received from Rome letters, either to suspend or excommunicate at his own discretion the Bishops of London and Salisbury, for having assisted at the coronation; and for suspending the Archbishop of York on the same grounds, the power of relaxing the sentence in his case being reserved to the Pope himself, at Becket's own desire. The Pope was inexcusable in this; the act for which he thus punished these prelates was one which he had authorized them to do: and though he had revoked that authority, the revocation was not known to them when they performed the ceremony. This Becket knew, and the Pope must have known also, if Becket had lain the whole circumstances before him. The farther powers for which he had applied were not granted him. Alexander, indeed, had already granted but too much. On his way to the court Becket, took leave of the King, who still delayed giving the kiss, and is said to have visibly been careful to avoid it: an apprehension was expressed by Becket that he should see him no more; his eye implied more than the words declared, and Henry hastily answered, "Do you think me a traitor?" He promised to meet him at Rouen, provide him with money for discharging his debts, and either accompany him to England, or send the Archbishop of Rouen with him. None of these promises were fulfilled: political circumstances called the King in a different direction; the money was not forthcoming, and the person charged to attend Becket was John of Oxford, whom he regarded as one of his greatest enemies. The Archbishop lent him 300*l.* and he proceeded on his journey to the coast, believing, as he said to Louis, when he took leave of that Monarch, that he was going to England to play for his head.

He was going, in fact, not to complete the reconciliation, which had been begun, but to renew the contest, and try whether the kingly or the ecclesiastical power were strongest. It irritated him to learn, that the Prelates, who were the objects of his especial animosity, consistent as himself, and upon better grounds, were advising Henry to require, as a necessary condition of his return, that the presentations to benefices belonging to Canterbury made during his exile, should hold good; and also that the royal customs should be observed. Resolving therefore to proceed without delay against these Priests of Baal, and standard-bearers of the Baalamites, (for thus he called them,) he sent the sentence of excommunication before him into England. The law which made this a treasonable act was still in force. It was therefore a dangerous service to convey these letters, but he found a messenger well fitted for such work, who undertook to deliver that for the Archbishop. This was a nun, by name Idonea, who appears, before her conversion, to have led a dissolute life. The manner in which he wrought upon this fit instrument would be most dishonourable to him, if it did not belong less to the man, than to the age. He reminded her that God had chosen the weak things of the world to confound the strong, and bade her remember Esther, and what, when the chiefs were dismayed, and the Priests had well nigh forsaken the law, a woman's hand had done to Holofernes; and that when the Apostles had forsaken our Lord, they who followed him to his cross and sepulchre were women. The Spirit, he said, would make those things which the Church's necessity required, arduous though they might seem, not only possible, but easy to her, having faith. He commanded, therefore and enjoined her, as she desired the remission of her sins, to deliver these letters into the hands of the Archbishop, in the presence of the other Prelates, if that could be effected;

otherwise, before any persons who might happen to be with him, and to deliver them a copy of the sentence, and also tell them its purport. "A great reward," said he "my daughter, is proposed to your labour; the remission of your sins, the unfading fruit and crown of glory, which the blessed sinners, Magdalene and Mary the Egyptian, received at length from Christ our Lord, the stains of their whole former lives being wiped out. The Mistress of Mercy will assist thee, and entreat her Son, God and Man, whom she brought forth for the salvation of the world, to be the guide, companion, and protector of thy journey. And may He who, breaking the gates of Hell, crushed the power and curbed the license of the Devils, restrain the hands of the wicked, that they may not be able to hurt thee! Farewell, spouse of Christ, and think that He is always present with thee!"

The day after this fanatical messenger departed, he himself embarked from the port of Whitsand in Flanders: some persons advised him not to venture, after a measure of such direct defiance to the King; but he replied,—"I see England before me, and go thither I will, let the issue be what it may. It is enough that the pastor has been seven years absent from his flock." He landed at Sandwich, a port belonging to his see, and inhabited by his tenantry; they, he well knew, would receive him with sincere joy, the transfer of church-property to lay hands being always to the detriment of the tenants. His reception was such as he expected; but the Nun had performed her unhappy commission, and the Sheriff of Kent, with a body of knights, armed under their tunics, as expecting violence, but not intending it, hastened thither. The people fled to arms, to support their Lord. John of Oxford interposed, commanding the Sheriff, in the King's name, to do no manner of injury to the Primate or any of his followers. None was offered; but he was truly told, how by excommunicating the Bishops for having done their duty, it appeared that he was entering the land with fire and sword to uncrown the King, and that it would be safer for him to remain on board, unless he took better counsel. From one of his retinue, the Archdeacon of Sens, being a foreigner, they required an oath of allegiance, which Becket forbade him to take, because it contained no saving clause in favour of the papal and ecclesiastical authorities. The point was not pressed by the Sheriff, who feared the temper and the numbers of the people. Becket then proceeded to Canterbury. He was met by all the poor and peasantry of the country; sore experience had made them feel the difference between living under an intrusive Lord, whose tenure was uncertain, and the regular system of the Church, which was always liberal and beneficent. Hope, gratitude, and personal attachment, led them to welcome him, with every demonstration of joy; but the impious application of Scripture must have been suggested by the Priests, when these simple people spread their garments in the way before him, and sung, "Blessed is he, who cometh in the name of the Lord!" The parochial Clergy of Canterbury went out in solemn procession to meet him, and finally the Monks received him into their convent, bells ringing, the organs pealing, and the quire echoing with hymns of triumphant thanksgiving.

On the morrow, came messengers from the suspended Prelates, notifying to him that they appealed from the sentence to the Pope. There came also officers from the young King, requiring him to absolve them from their censures, the act itself being injurious to the King, and subversive of the laws. He replied, "that it was not in the power of an inferior judge to release from the sentence of the superior; though in fact he possessed that power in two of the cases, and would have possessed it in the third, if by his own especial desire it had not been withheld...

They contended warmly on both sides, the men with whom he disputed being as resolute as himself. He offered at length, for the peace of the Church, and in proof of respect for the King, to absolve them at his own peril, provided they would take an oath before him to obey the Pope's injunctions in this affair. The Bishops of Salisbury and London, when this was notified to them, were disposed to have consented; but the Archbishop of York observed to them, that it was against the laws to take such an oath without the King's permission; and he declared that, if it were necessary, he would spend eight thousand marks of silver, which he had by him, to restrain the obstinate arrogance of that man. It was their duty and their interest, he said, to be true to the King, and to him he advised that they should go. Accordingly they embarked for Normandy.

Before their departure, they despatched an account of these proceedings to the young King, representing that the end of Becket's conduct would be to tear the crown from his head. Becket also sent to justify his conduct, but his messenger was not admitted to an audience. He then set out himself to see the young King at Woodstock, and to visit his whole province, for the purpose of plucking and rooting out, what had grown up in disorder during his absence; that is, to turn out all persons who had been presented to benefices during that time. The Clergy of Rochester attended him to London, where the populace received him with acclamations. But on the following morning came an order from Woodstock, forbidding him to enter any of the King's towns or castles, and ordering him to retire with all his retinue within the verge of his Church. He answered haughtily, "that believing himself bound in duty to visit the whole of his province, he would not have obeyed the order, had not Christmas been close at hand, on which festival he meant to officiate in his cathedral." To Canterbury therefore he returned. The government had shewn more firmness than he had expected. The higher clergy and the better citizens who had gone out to meet him, were summoned to give bail upon a charge of sedition, for having thus received the King's enemy. Persons of rank kept away from him; and men, who for their own sakes desired to render any accommodation impossible, endeavoured, even at Canterbury, to provoke him and his servants, by studied indignities. Becket wrote to the Pope that the sword of death was hanging over him, and desired his prayers. He told his Clergy that the quarrel could not now end without blood, but that he was ready to die for the Church; and in his sermon on Christmas-day, said to his congregation, that his dissolution was near, and he should quickly depart from them: one of their Archbishops had been a martyr, and it was possible they might have another. And then, in a strain of bold, fierce, fiery indignation, (for so his admiring friends and biographers have described it,) he thundered out his invectives against most of the King's counsellors and friends, and excommunicated three of his enemies by name, with all the appalling forms of that execrable rite.

Meantime the Archbishop of York, and the two Bishops, had repaired to the father King in Normandy, imploring justice for themselves and the whole clergy of the kingdom. Henry was incensed at hearing what had passed, and observed with an oath, that if all who consented to his son's coronation were to be excommunicated, he himself should not escape. He asked their advice. "It was not for them," they replied, "to say what ought to be done." Indeed they knew not what to advise, and no evil meaning can be imputed to them for saying, "that there would be no peace for him or his kingdom, while Becket was alive." This was the plain truth; and Henry in his despair of ever being suffered to rest by this ungrateful and treacherous friend (for as such he regarded him), and in his indignation at this fresh instance of unprovoked hostility, called himself unfortunate in having maintained so many cowardly and thankless men, none of whom would revenge him of the injuries he had sustained from one turbulent Priest; .... words which expressed, with culpable indiscretion, a wish for Becket's death, and were too hastily understood as conveying an order for it. It is certain that no such order was intended; but it is not surprising that men who were zealous in his service, and no way scrupulous how they served him, should have imagined that what the King wished, he would gladly have them perform. Reginald Fitzurse, William de Tracy, Richard Brito, and Hugh de Moreville, who were all gentlemen of his bedchamber, knights and barons of the realm, bound themselves by an oath, that they would either compel the Primate to withdraw the censures, or carry him out of the kingdom, or put him to death, if he refused to do the one, and they found it impossible to effect the other; with this determination, they hastened to England, unknown to the King or any other person, and unsuspected.

The result of Henry's counsel was the legal and proper measure of sending over three Barons to arrest Becket. These messengers were too late. The ministers of vengeance, who were before them, landed near Dover, and past the night in Ranulf de Broc's castle,..one of the persons whom Becket had excommunicated on Christmas-day, and to whom interested motives for his marked enmity to the Primate are imputable, because he was in possession of great part of the sequestered lands. He supplied soldiers enough to overpower the knights of Becket's household, and the people of Canterbury, if resistance should be attempted. They entered the city in small parties, concealing their arms, that no alarm might be excited. The Abbot of St. Augustine's, who was of the King's party, received them into his monastery, and is said to have joined counsel with them. About ten in the morning, they proceeded with twelve knights to Becket's bedchamber; his family were still at table, but he himself had dined, and was conversing with some of his monks and clergy. Without replying to his salutation, they sat down opposite to him, on the ground, among the monks. After a pause, Fitzurse said they came with orders from the King, and asked whether he would hear them in public or in private? Becket said, as it might please him best,.. and then at his desire, bade the company withdraw; but presently apprehending some violent proceeding, from Fitzurse's manner, he called them in again from the antechamber, and told the Barons, that whatever they had to impart might be delivered in their presence. Fitzurse required him to absolve the suspended and excommunicated Prelates: He returned the old evasive answer "that it was not he who had passed the sentence, nor was it in his power to take it off." A warm altercation ensued, in which Becket insisted that the King had authorized his measures, in telling him he might, by ecclesiastical censures, compel those who had disturbed the peace of the Church to make satisfaction; this, he affirmed, had been said in Fitzurse's presence. Fitzurse denied that he had heard any thing to that purport;—and indeed Becket himself must have known that if such permission had ever been given, it certainly was not in the latitude which he now chose to represent.

The four Barons then, in the King's name, required, that he, and all who belonged to him, should depart forthwith out of the kingdom, for he had broken the peace, and should no longer enjoy it. Becket replied, "he would never again put the sea between him and his Church." Their resolute manner only roused his spirit, and he declared, that if any man whatsoever infringed the laws of the Holy Roman See, or the right of the Church, be that man who he would, he would not spare him.—"In vain," said he, "do you menace me! if all the swords in England were brandished over my head, you would find me foot to foot, fighting the battles of the Lord!" He upbraided those of them who had been in his service as Chancellor. They rose, and charged the monks to guard him, saying, they should answer for it if he escaped; the knights of his household they bade go with them, and wait the event in silence. Becket followed them to the outer door, saying, he came not there to fly, nor did he value their threats. "We will do more than threaten!" was the answer.

Becket was presently told that they were arming themselves in the palace-court. Some of his servants barred the gate, and he was with difficulty persuaded by the monks to retire through the cloisters into the cathedral, where the afternoon service had now begun. He ordered the cross to be borne before him, retired slowly, and to some who were endeavouring to secure the doors, he called out, forbidding to do it, saying, "You ought not to make a castle of the Church; it will protect us sufficiently without being shut; neither did I come hither to resist, but to suffer." By this time the assailants, after endeavouring to break open the abbey gates, had entered, under Robert de Broc's guidance, through a window, searched the palace, and were now following him to the cathedral. He might still have concealed himself, and not improbably have escaped. But Becket disdained this: with all its errors, his was an heroic mind. He was ascending the steps of the high altar, when the Barons, and their armed followers, rushed into the choir with drawn swords, exclaiming, "Where is Thomas à Becket? where is that traitor to the King and kingdom?" No answer was made; but when they called out with a louder voice, "Where is the Archbishop?" he then came down the steps, saying, "Here am I; no traitor, but a priest; ready to suffer in the name of Him who redeemed me. God forbid that I should fly for fear of your swords, or recede from justice." They required him, once more, to take off the censures from the Prelates. "No satisfaction has yet been made," was the answer, "and I will not absolve them." Then they told him he should instantly die. "Reginald," said he to Fitzurse, "I have done you many kindnesses; and do you come against me thus armed?" The Baron, resolute as himself, and in a worse purpose, told him to get out from thence, and die; at the same time laying hold of his robe. Becket withdrew the robe, and said, he would not move. "Fly, then," said Fitzurse, as if at this moment a compunctious feeling had visited him, and he would have been glad to see the intent frustrated, in which his pride more than his oath constrained him to persist. "Nor that either," was Becket's answer; "if it is my blood you want, I am ready to die, that the Church may obtain liberty and peace: only, in the name of God, I forbid you to hurt any of my people." Still it appears, that in some, at least, there was a wish to spare his life: one struck him between the shoulders with the flat part of the sword, saying, "Fly, or you are dead!" And the murderers themselves, afterwards declared, their intention was to carry him prisoner to the King; or if that was impossible, put him to death in a place less sacred than the Church; but he clung to one of the pillars, and struggled with the assailants. Tracy he had nearly thrown down, and Fitzurse he thrust from him with a strong hand, calling him pimp. Stung by the opprobrious appellation, Fitzurse no longer hesitated whether to strike. A monk, Edward Grimes, of Cambridge, was his name, interposed his arm, which was almost cut off by the blow. Becket, who had bowed in the attitude of prayer, was wounded by the same stroke in the crown of his head. His last words were, "To God, to St. Mary, and the Saints, who are patrons of this Church, and to St. Dennis,

I commend myself, and the Church's cause!" The second blow brought him to the ground, on his face, before St. Benedict's altar; he had strength and composure enough to cover himself with his robes, and then to join his hands in prayer, and in that position died under their repeated strokes, each pressing near, to bear a part in the murder. Brito cleft his skull; and an accursed man, the subdeacon, Hugh of Horsea, known by the appellation of the Ill Clerk, scattered the brains over the pavement from the point of his sword.

CHAPTER IX.

PROCEEDINGS UPON BECKET'S DEATH.—KING JOHN.—TRIUMPH OF THE PAPAL POWER.

As soon as Henry was informed that the four Barons had suddenly left the court, and taken the road to the coast, he apprehended some mischief, knowing the characters of the men, and probably, remembering also, the rash expressions which had escaped him in his anger. Immediate orders for stopping them were despatched to all the sea-ports of Normandy, but they had found a fair wind, unhappily for all parties, and had thus outstript pursuit. They looked for no reward or favour from the atrocious act which they had committed. On the contrary, they hastened to Knaresborough, a castle belonging to Moreville, believing that they had rendered the King good service, but not daring to appear before him.

When the news reached Henry, he was at once struck with remorse for the cause of the crime, and alarmed for its consequences. At first, he broke out into loud and passionate lamentations, then seemed to be overpowered and stupified by the violence of his emotions: he put on sackcloth and ashes, and for three days was incapable either of consolation or counsel. At length, by the advice of those who, meantime, had consulted what might best be done in these unexpected and most critical circumstances, an embassy was sent to the Pope, and messengers to Canterbury. The latter were instructed to inform the clergy of that Church, how deeply the King grieved for the death of Becket, and abhorred the murder: to say, that if any guilt attached to him for words rashly spoken in his anger, it might best be expiated by their prayers; and to command that the body should be honourably buried; for, though the Primate had been his enemy while living, he would not prosecute him when dead, but remitted to his soul whatever offences he had committed against him and his royal dignity. This was acting as became him, convinced as he was, that in the grounds of the dispute he stood justified to his own heart, and to his people. If he did not persevere in this dignified and becoming course, it is because a sane opinion may be subdued, though insanity is invincible when the world appears combined against it.

The King of France failed not to improve this opportunity for distressing his enemy. He called upon the Pope to unsheathe the sword of St. Peter, and therewith signally avenge the martyr of Canterbury, whose blood, not so much for itself, as for the Catholic Church, cried out for vengeance. The Archbishop of Sens, who had been commissioned, with the Archbishop of Rouen, to interdict Henry's continental dominions, if the agreement with Becket were not executed, called upon his colleague now to join with him in so doing; but he replied, that he would do nothing to aggravate his master's affliction; and he interposed an appeal to the Pope. Upon this, the former, who had been Becket's friend, and seems to have partaken no small portion of his immitigable spirit, pronounced the interdict; but no regard was paid to this unwarrantable act: the appeal was believed to suspend its force; and it is probable, that in Normandy there prevailed a fair and temperate opinion, both concerning the dispute, and the death of Becket.

The Pope, like the King of France, regarded the murder as an event which might be made subservient to his views. It was not till after long and humble entreaties, that he admitted two of Henry's embassadors to an audience; and when they saluted him in their master's name, the assembled Cardinals interrupted them by clamours, as if the very mention of that name had been an abomination. They obtained a private hearing in the evening; but though Becket was dead, his cause had not died with him, rather it had acquired tenfold strength: two of his former chaplains, sent by the Archbishop of Sens, appeared to plead against the reconciliation which Henry solicited, and all countenances looked so darkly upon his embassadors, that they almost despaired of success. Holy Thursday was at hand,..the day whereon it was customary for the Pope to excommunicate notorious offenders; and they were informed, that on that day the sentence passed by Becket against the Bishops would be confirmed, the whole of Henry's dominions placed under an interdict, and he himself excommunicated by name. In those days, when men were as licentious upon great points as they were scrupulous in indifferent ones, embassadors did not hesitate to exceed their commission where any great advantage was to be gained, and pledge their Sovereign to terms which they were far from being certain that he would perform. Thus, to prevent the impending stroke, they assured the Pope that the King would submit wholly to his mandates in this affair: this they said they were empowered to confirm by an oath in his presence, and their master would swear to the same effect.

Their object was answered by this unwarrantable expedient; and the Pope contented himself, on the dreaded day, with excommunicating the murderers of Becket in general, and all who advised, abetted, or consented to their crime, or who should, knowingly, receive and harbour them. Shortly afterwards, other members of the embassy who had been detained on the road, arrived; these, more scrupulous, refused to take the same oath; upon which the Pope confirmed the interdict which the Archbishop of Sens had imposed, and interdicted Henry himself from entering any Church. The intermediate time had not been misemployed, or these measures would not have fallen so far short of what was threatened; in fact, some of the Cardinals had been gained over, and money was said to have been largely distributed. The Pope absolved the Bishops, whose sentence he had just before ratified, and wrote himself to Henry, (a mark of special favour,) exhorting him to humility. Every thing was thus composed till Urban should send legates into Normandy; and it was plain that an accommodation would then be effected by the disposition which the Pope had thus manifested.

The terms of accommodation were such as saved appearances for both parties. They were, that Henry should give the Knights-Templars a sum sufficient to maintain 200 knights for the defence of the Holy Land, one year: that he should take the cross for three years himself, and go in person to Palestine the ensuing summer... unless it were deemed a more urgent duty to go to the assistance of the Christians in Spain: that he should not prevent appeals in ecclesiastical causes from being made freely, with good faith, and without fraud or evil intention to the Roman Pontiff; nevertheless he might require security, from any suspected appellants, that they would not attempt any thing to the prejudice of him or his kingdom: that he should absolutely give up those customs which had been introduced in his time against the English church: that any lands which had been taken from the see of Canterbury, should be fully restored, as they were held by that see a year before Becket went out of the kingdom; and that he should restore his peace and favour, with all their possessions, to all the clergy and laity of either sex, who had been deprived of their property on Becket's account. Henry also took a voluntary oath before the legates, that he had neither ordered, nor desired the murder; but was exceedingly grieved when the report thereof was brought him; yet, he said, he feared the perpetrators took occasion to commit that wicked act from the passion and perturbation which they had seen in him. Other things, the legates informed the Pope, he was to do of his own free accord, but it was not proper to set them down in writing.

Whatever these secret conditions may have been, the ostensible terms were better than Henry had reason to expect; nothing for which he had contended was, in reality, yielded by them, and the obligation of taking the cross was one from which the Pope would easily release him upon such excuses as were sure to occur. The conditions, which were concealed from public knowledge, related probably to the price which was paid for the Pope's moderation, and perhaps to certain acts of imaginary expiation which the King was willing to perform. For Becket was already regarded as a saint and martyr, and upon this point Henry's understanding was subdued by the spirit of the age. The craft in which Dunstan had excelled, and in which his successors had been no mean proficients, was still exercised at Canterbury, with equal audacity and equal success. The martyred saint, on the morning after he was killed, had lifted up his hand after the service and given the monks his blessing. His eyes which had been injured by the blows of the assassins, miraculously disappeared, and were replaced by others, smaller in size, and of two different colours. He had appeared in his pontificals at the altar on the third day, and directed that a verse from the psalms should, in future, be recited instead of sung in the mass;—and, at his requiem, angels had visibly assisted at the quire. The persons who had been his followers and counsellors asserted these things as eye-witnesses, and affirmed, that upon the spot where he was slain, and before the altar where his corpse was laid out, and at his tomb, paralytics recovered strength, the lame walked, the blind obtained sight, the deaf heard, and the dumb spake. The ministers, who were about the young king, endeavoured at first to stop these impudent and impious impostures; but they took no measures for exposing them, and the delusion spread, many being interested to support it, and the multitude, as usual, believing with eager credulity.

So effectually were these frauds practised, and so villainously encouraged by the papal court, that within two years after his death, St. Thomas of Canterbury was canonized in form, and the 29th of December, being the day of his martyrdom, dedicated to him in the kalendar. It was affirmed, that till the murderers were absolved from the excommunication which had been past against them, dogs would not take food from their hands; and that even when they had been released from these censures, upon contrition, they remained, as long as they lived, trembling as if with palsy, and disturbed in mind like men whom horror had distracted. What marvel? The martyr himself had said that his blood cried from the earth for vengeance more than that of Abel; and it was revealed that his place in Heaven was higher than that of St. Stephen, and of all other martyrs! His brains were sent to Rome; and devout persons at Canterbury were shown his skull, in one part of the church, and in a chapel behind the high altar, what was said to be his face, set in gold. The Abbey of St. Augustine's exchanged several houses and a piece of ground for a portion of his scalp. The rust of the sword that killed him was tendered to pilgrims, that they might kiss it; and a fraternity of mendicants stationed themselves by the wayside on the road to London, where they levied contributions upon pious travellers, by virtue of the upper-leather of his shoe. No arts, no falsehoods, no blasphemies were spared which might raise the reputation of the new shrine above all others in England: lost members were said to be restored there, and the dead, even birds and beasts, restored to life: parallels were drawn between this turbulent, ambitious, unforgiving churchman, and our Lord and Saviour himself; and a prayer was introduced in the service of his day, for salvation through the merits and blood of St. Thomas à Becket. These abominable artifices were successful. A jubilee was accorded every fifty years, when plenary indulgence was to be obtained by all who visited his tomb: 100,000 pilgrims are known to have been present at one of these seasons; and at this day, it may be seen where their knees have worn the marble steps. The cathedral itself was commonly called St. Thomas's; and in the account of one year it appeared, that more than 600*l.* had been offered at Becket's altar, when at the altar of Christ nothing had been presented.

If at the commencement due vigilance had been exerted, this superstition might have been crushed in the germ, and the exposure of the tricks and falsehoods which were systematically practised, might have produced a salutary effect upon public opinion. But the Prelates, who were most interested in the detection of these artifices, were with the King in Normandy; possibly, too, had they been on the spot, the fear of injuring the craft, and the knowledge that they had to make their peace with the Pope, might have withheld them. We should remember also, that those disorders, over which the imagination possessed any power, were actually healed at Becket's shrine in many cases, and in very many were suspended or relieved for a time; and they who had witnessed or experienced one such fact, were ready to believe any exaggeration or any falsehood; what they knew to have happened was to them miraculous, and therefore nothing could appear impossible. Not having opposed the delusion in time, Henry yielded to it. His sons had taken arms against him; France and Flanders were allied against his continental dominions, and the Scotch invaded England. If Henry himself did not account the death of St. Thomas of Canterbury among the evils which had brought these calamities and dangers upon him, such an opinion was encouraged by his enemies, and likely to have a disheartening influence upon his friends. And as the Pope had authorized and enjoined prayers to the new saint, that he should intercede with God for the clergy and people of England, Henry, either from prostration of mind, or in policy far less to be excused, determined to implore his intercession in the most public manner, and with the most striking circumstances. Landing at Southampton, he there left his court and the mercenaries whom he had brought over, and set off on horseback with a few attendants for Canterbury. When he came within sight of its towers he dismounted, laid aside his garments, threw a coarse cloth over his shoulders, and proceeded to the city, which was three miles distant, barefoot over the flinty road, so that in many places, his steps were traced in blood. He reached the church trembling with emotion, and was led to the martyr's shrine; there, in the crypt, he threw himself prostrate before it, with his arms extended, and remained in that posture, as if in earnest prayer, while the Bishop of London solemnly declared in his name, that he had neither commanded nor advised, nor by any artifice contrived the death of Thomas à Becket, for the truth of which he appealed to God; but because his words, too inconsiderately spoken, had given occasion for the commission of that crime, he now voluntarily submitted himself to the discipline of the Church. The monks of the convent, eighty in number, and four bishops, abbots, and other clergy who were present, were provided each with a knotted cord; he bared his shoulders, and received five stripes from the Prelates, three from every other hand. When this severe penance had been endured, he threw sackcloth over his bleeding shoulders, and resumed his prayers, kneeling on the pavement, and not allowing a carpet to be spread beneath him: thus he continued all that day, and till the midnight-bell tolled for matins. After that hour, he visited all the altars of the church, prayed before the bodies of all the saints who were there deposited, then returned to his devotions at the shrine till day-break. During this whole time he had neither ate nor drank; but now, after assisting at mass, and assigning, in addition to other gifts, forty pounds a year for tapers, to burn perpetually before the martyr's tomb, he drank some water, in which a portion of Becket's blood was mingled. He then set off for London, where he found himself in a state incapable of exertion, and it was necessary to bleed him. The believers in Becket have not failed to remark, that on the morning when Henry completed his reconciliation with the canonized martyr, the King of Scotland was defeated and taken.

There is good reason for affirming, that Henry had not changed his opinion either concerning Becket's conduct, or the original cause of their dispute, but his mind was subdued by the ingratitude of his children: some remorse he justly felt, for the expression of a wish which had led to the murder; and above all, his extreme licentiousness of life degraded him intellectually, as well as morally, and made him catch at all the substitutes for repentance which the Romish superstition has provided. Some centuries after his death, the terms upon which he had made his peace with the church were published at Rome; and an article then appeared among them, whereby he and his eldest son engaged, for themselves and their posterity, to hold the kingdom of England in fee from the Pope and his successors. There were stronger motives for forging such a condition at the time when it was brought to light, than there could have been for concealing it when it was made, and keeping it secret during the reign of his son John. Without such an act of submission, without obtaining even the direct cession of any of the points in contention between Becket and the King, the court of Rome had gained more in England by the progress of the dispute, than it had ever been able to effect against the steadier policy of the Norman Kings. For, by pursuing a just cause violently and precipitately, through right and wrong, Henry involved himself in such difficulties, that the appeal to Rome, which he would not allow in his subjects, as being derogatory to the royal dignity, was resorted to in his own case, as a resource; and the authority of the Pope to interfere and determine between Kings and their subjects, was thus acknowledged by the most powerful Prince in Europe, for such unquestionably Henry was when this dispute began. And in the case of Becket's canonization, a more important victory had been gained over the public mind: the cause for which he was worshipped as a saint and martyr, and which heaven had ratified and approved by a profusion of miracles, was not the cause of christian faith or christian practice, but of the Roman Church; its temporal power had been the sole point in dispute, and they who venerated St. Thomas of Canterbury, as they were now enjoined to do, necessarily believed that the authority of the Pope was supreme on earth.

It is not sufficiently remembered, in Protestant countries, how often that authority (though as little to be justified in itself as in the means whereby it was upheld) was exercised beneficially, and to those ends which form the only excuse for its assumption. An instance of its proper exertion occurred, when Richard Cœur-de-Lion, having been villainously seized, on his return from the Holy Land, by the Duke of Austria, was villainously purchased from him by the Emperor, and put in chains. The indignation which this excited in the other German princes, honourable as it is to them, would hardly have sufficed to obtain his release, unless the Pope had interfered and threatened the Emperor with excommunication, if he persisted in thus wrongfully and inhumanly detaining the hero of Christendom. The fear of such a measure, which might have armed all Germany against him, overcame the feelings of personal hatred, and the base intrigues of Philip Augustus of France, for perpetuating Richard's captivity; and the unworthy Emperor restored him to his subjects, upon payment of an enormous ransom.

Upon Richard's death, the clergy acted as unjust a part as they had done in raising Stephen to the throne: they assisted in electing John, to the exclusion of Arthur, his elder brother's son; Hubert the Primate, in a speech which has not unfitly been called a seed-plot of treasons, arguing that the crown was elective, and that the worthiest member of the royal family ought to be chosen. For the former part of the assertion there was some ground; the right law of succession had often been departed from, and the evil of so doing had been severely proved: the latter position would have excluded the very person in whose behalf it was advanced, for John's character was already notorious; and perhaps there is no other King recorded in history, who has rendered himself at once so despicable and so odious. The motives for this choice were, the weighty one, of obedience to King Richard's will: the specious one, that the nobles would be able to maintain their rights against a sovereign of whom they exacted a promise to respect them, and who derived his own right from their suffrages;—and the wicked one, of the Queen-mother's hatred for her daughter-in-law, the mother of Prince Arthur. The Primate did not live to witness the whole consequences of this unhappy election, but he saw enough to repent of the part which he had borne in it, as the worst action of his life.

Upon his death, a dispute arose concerning the appointment of a successor. Some of the younger monks of the cathedral assembled at night, and without the knowledge of their seniors, or the King, elected their sub-prior Reginald, a man as indiscreet as themselves, who having sworn as they required, that he would not disclose what they had done without their permission, set off immediately for Rome, to obtain from the Pope a ratification of his appointment. Too vain to keep his own secret, Reginald proclaimed himself for Primate-elect as he went: and the juniors were brought to their senses by resentment: they, therefore, joined with the superiors, and with the King's approbation, in customary form elected the Bishop of Norwich, who was accordingly invested by John. As, however, it was possible that Reginald might meet with some success at Rome, the King sent a deputation of monks with Elias de Branfield at their head, to represent the case, and obtain the Pontiff's confirmation of the King's choice. A third party also appealed; the suffragan Bishops claimed a concurrent right in the election with the monks; and despatched their agent to Rome. Their claim was decided against them, on the ground of a long established privilege enjoyed by the monks of Canterbury. When the question between the two elected candidates was examined, it was pleaded on behalf of Reginald that the second election must necessarily be null, as being made before the former had been set aside. It became now a matter of casuistry and angry contention, which Innocent determined by declaring that both claimants had been uncanonically chosen, and therefore both appointments were void. He then signified to the deputies that they might proceed forthwith to elect any qualified person, provided he were a native of England, recommending to their choice, Stephen de Langton, Cardinal of St. Chrysogonus, and formerly Chancellor of the University of Paris. John thinking it likely that a new election would be advised, had authorized the deputies to make one, but required an oath that they should re-elect the Bishop of Norwich. They represented, therefore, to Innocent, that they could not defer to his recommendation without the consent of their master; and that to act otherwise would be contrary to the laws and privileges of him and of his kingdom. Innocent replied, that the consent of a King was not thought necessary, when an election was made in the presence of the Pope; and he commanded them, on pain of excommunication, to choose Langton. Elias de Branfield, with proper spirit refused obedience; the others reluctantly obeyed, and singing Te Deum while they murmured in their hearts, led the Cardinal to the altar.

Innocent III., who thus provoked a dispute with the King of England, was a man of great ability and activity, but haughty and ambitious above all men. The appeal which had been made, recognised his right of confirming or annulling an election, not of making one. Having taken this unwarrantable step, he sent the King a present of four rings, accompanied by two letters. The first was complimentary, and explained the allegorical import of the present, entreating him rather to regard its mystery than its value; the rings in their round form, typified eternity; constancy in their square number: their stones also were significant; the emerald denoted faith, the sapphire hope, the garnet charity, and the topaz good works. One was wanting which should have read a lesson of patience; for the second letter required him to receive Langton as the elected and consecrated Primate.

The best cause may be rendered unjust and odious, if it be pursued by violent and iniquitous means. John had a valid reason for objecting to Langton's elevation, because having been bred and beneficed in France, his French connexions and attachments might prove injurious to the interest of England, and of the King's foreign dominions. The Pope's assumption of power also would have been regarded in its true light by the clergy as well as the Barons, if it had been resisted with calmness and dignity... But John was one of those men in whom base motives predominate whatever part they may take. Rapine was the first thing he thought of in his anger; an armed force was sent to expel the monks of Canterbury from the kingdom, or set fire to the convent, if they refused to leave it; and he seized the whole of their effects. Then he wrote a letter to the Pope, which, if it had not been accompanied by the news of this rapacious injustice, was such as became a King of England. It stated his determination to support the rights of his crown, and to cut off all correspondence with Rome, and all remittance of money from this kingdom thereto, if the Pope persisted in the obnoxious measure. The clergy of his own dominions he said were of sufficient learning, and he had no need to look to strangers either for advice or judgement. Innocent replied in the true papal style. The Servant of the Servants of God informed the King of England, that in what he had done there was no cause why he should tarry for the King's consent; and that as he had begun, so he would proceed, according to the canonical ordinances, neither inclining to the right hand, nor to the left ... "We will for no man's pleasure," said he, "defer the completion of this appointment; neither may we, without stain of honour and danger of conscience. Wherefore, my well-beloved son, seeing we have had respect to your honour above what our privileges and duty required, do you in return study to honour us according to your duty; that thereby, you may deserve the more favour both at God's hand, and at ours. For this know of a truth, that in the end, He must prevail unto whom every knee of heavenly, earthly, and infernal creatures doth bow, and whose place, unworthy though I be, I hold on earth. Commit yourself, therefore, to our pleasure, which will be to your praise and glory; and imagine not, that it would be for your safety to resist God and the Church, in a cause for which the glorious martyr Thomas, hath lately shed his blood."

The Bishops of London, Ely, and Worcester, were now charged to lay the kingdom under an interdict, unless the King would admit the Primate, and recall the exiled monks of Canterbury. When they waited upon him and announced the alternative, he swore by God's teeth, that if any one dared interdict his territories, he would send them and all their clergy packing to Rome, and confiscate all their property: and if he found any subjects of the Pope, he would put out their eyes, slit their noses, and in that condition despatch them to his Holiness. They retired trembling from his presence; but after waiting some weeks, in hope that some change might take place, in a mind as fickle as it was depraved, they obeyed their spiritual master, pronounced a sentence of interdict, and fled the realm; the Bishops of Bath and Hereford, acting with them. Even now, when the ceremonials of worship have been too much abridged, and the public influences of religion grievously lessened by the disuse of all its discipline, and of too many of its forms,.. even now, it may be understood what an effect must have been produced upon the feelings of the people, when all the rites of a church, whose policy it was to blend its institutions with the whole business of private life, were suddenly suspended;..no bell heard, no taper lighted, no service performed, no church open; only baptism was permitted, and confession and the sacrament for the dying. The dead were either interred in unhallowed ground, without the presence of a priest, or any religious ceremony,...or they were kept unburied, till the infliction, which affected every family in its tenderest and holiest feelings, should be removed. Some little mitigation was allowed, lest human nature should have rebelled against so intolerable a tyranny. The people, therefore, were called to prayers and sermon on the Sunday, in the church-yards, and marriages were performed at the church-door.

John, with his characteristic recklessness, cared nothing for all this. Had he proceeded temperately at first, the clergy would have stood by him, as they did by his father, and he might have made an honourable, perhaps a successful, stand against the papal usurpation. But he was incapable of generosity or justice, and the wickedness of his heart corrupted his understanding,—if indeed he were altogether free from insanity. He seized all the ecclesiastical revenues, imprisoned the relations of the obnoxious prelates, and defied the Pope. But the sentence of excommunication was hanging over him. He would have averted it by admitting Langton now, but the just condition was required that he should refund the ecclesiastical revenues which he had seized,...and this was impossible, for the whole had been expended. Prevented thus from an accommodation when he felt it necessary for his safety, by his own improvidence and injustice, he sought to guard against the dreaded effects of a sentence which was not to be averted; and for this end, he exacted hostages from the family of every baron whose fidelity he distrusted, and required his subjects, even children of twelve years old, to renew their oath of homage.

Some years had elapsed in this miserable dispute, when the sentence of excommunication was past, whereby all persons were forbidden to eat, drink, talk, converse, or counsel with King John, or to do him service at bed or board, in church, hall, or stable: he was declared to be deposed from his regal seat: his subjects were absolved from their allegiance, and the King of France, Philip Augustus, was invited to kill or expel him, and take for his reward the kingdom of England to himself, and his heirs for ever: to which, moreover, a full remission of his sins was added. To aid Philip in this holy war, all adventurers, of all countries, were called upon as to a crusade. These measures were taken at the desire of Langton, and a strong party of the Barons, who seemed to think, that as John had received the crown by election rather than descent, they had a right to depose him and choose another king in his stead. There might, perhaps, have been fair cause for setting him aside as a madman. Had it indeed been known, that the miscreant had actually sent a secret embassy to that powerful chief of the Almoravides, known in Spanish history by the title of the Miramamolin, offering to turn musselman, and pay him tribute, if the Moor would assist him against the Pope and his own rebellious subjects, it is hardly possible that he could have escaped from the general indignation which would have burst forth.

Philip, who had already dispossessed John of the greater part of his continental dominions, prepared now to take possession of England. But it was not the wish of Innocent that the acquisition which he had so liberally offered, should fall into his hands. Philip Augustus was no submissive son of the Church; and more obedience might be expected from John when he should have been thoroughly intimidated, than from a politic and powerful Prince, who was neither likely to shrink from his resolutions, nor to afford any advantages by his folly. A confidential minister, therefore, Pandulph by name, was intrusted with terms of submission, which, if John should accept, he would find the arm of

Rome as powerful to uphold, as it was to pluck down. Philip was assembling his forces at the mouth of the Seine; to oppose them, John collected a more formidable host than had ever been assembled in England,...an army of sixty thousand knights,...who here, upon their own ground, might have defied the world, if their hearts had been with the Prince who summoned them. But that unworthy sovereign knew that the bond of allegiance had been loosened, and that at any moment, in obedience to the dreadful voice of the Church, they might forsake him. This well-founded fear was increased by the bold prediction of a hermit in Yorkshire, known by the name of Peter of Pomfret, that before Ascension-day his crown should be given to another. The prophecy appeared of such possible fulfilment, that it obtained a wide belief, and John sent for the hermit, demanding of him in what manner it was to be accomplished, by his death, or his deposal? Peter was not so crazy as to imagine he could answer this question, but he persisted in affirming that when the day appointed arrived, John would no longer be king, and willingly staked his life upon the issue.

Impiety is no preservative against superstition. The day of Ascension was at hand when Pandulph landed at Dover, and tendered to John the alternative of submitting to the Pope upon all the points for which he had contended, or abiding the event of invasion. In fear and trembling he affixed his seal to the instrument which Pandulph had prepared, and swore to observe what he had thus subscribed. But such was the character of this worthless prince, that his signature and his oath were not deemed sufficient securities; and the most powerful of the nobles who were present, swore by the King's soul that as far as in them lay, they would compel him to perform what he had promised. His humiliation was not yet completed. He still dreaded the French King and his own nobles, and the hermit's prophecy terrified him. The apprehension of death produced a startling thought of eternity; and whether the prophecy pointed at his death or his deposal, if in any way it could be averted it must be, by the authority of the Vicar of God intrusted to his representative. With these feelings in the prostration of a heart as abject in adversity, as it was insolent in power, on the day before the festival of the Ascension he laid his crown at Pandulph's feet, and signed an instrument by which for the remission of his sins, and those of his family, he surrendered the kingdoms of England and Ireland to the Pope, to hold them thenceforth under him, and the Roman see ... For himself, his heirs, and successors, he swore liege homage to that see, bound his kingdom to the annual payment of a thousand marks, for ever, in token of vassalage, and renounced for himself or his successors all right to the throne, if the agreement should on their part be infringed. The money, which was delivered in earnest of this tribute, Pandulph trampled under foot, to indicate how little the Pope regarded worldly wealth, and he kept the crown five days before he restored it to John. Peter of Pomfret's prediction had now been fairly fulfilled, and there can be little doubt but that the hope of averting a worse fulfilment had been one motive which induced John to the unworthy act; nevertheless, with the malignity of a mean mind, he ordered the hermit to be hanged as a false prophet, and his son with him.

The deed of conveyance stated, that in subjecting his kingdom to the Roman see, John had acted with the general advice of his Barons; and there is reason to believe that they encouraged, if they did not urge, him to a measure by which they expected to diminish his power and to increase their own. Whatever their motives may have been, this act which now appears so revolting to the feelings of an Englishman, led, in its speedy consequences, to that event which may perhaps be regarded as the most momentous and beneficial in English history,..the acquisition of Magna Charta.

Langton, during the preceding contest, had for a time taken up his abode at Pontigny as if intimating thereby to the King of England, that he was prepared to tread in the steps of Becket. But Langton had neither Becket's singleness of purpose, nor his intemperance of mind. He had been the occasion of the struggle, not the cause; and had so little personal part in it, that he had in no degree rendered himself obnoxious to the nation. It was otherwise with regard to John, who would always regard him as the means of his humiliation, and Langton well knew there was no crime of which that miscreant was not capable. It behoved him therefore to look for protection against his perfidious resentment; and he seems to have thought that this might more certainly be found in the English Barons, and in the laws of England, than in the Pope, whose policy it would be to treat his vassal King with condescension and favour. Arriving in England with the other exiles, he proceeded to Winchester, there to absolve the King. John came out to meet them, fell at their feet, and asked their forgiveness. After the absolution had been pronounced, the Primate made him swear to defend the Church and her ministers, to renew the good laws of his predecessors, and especially of Edward the Confessor, and to annul bad ones, to administer justice according to the rightful judgement of his courts, to give every man his rights, and to make full satisfaction before the ensuing Easter, for all the damages he had caused on account of the interdict, or in default to fall again under the sentence from which he was now released. The interdict was not wholly to be removed, till these conditions had been observed. Langton exacted, likewise, a renewal of the oath of fealty to the Pope.

The business of restitution was not so easy. John ordered commissioners to inquire into the amount of the damages sustained, and report it to the Great Council which had been summoned to meet at St. Albans. He then joined his army which he had collected at Portsmouth, for the purpose of prosecuting the war in France. They had tarried for him so long that their means were spent, and they told him, therefore, that unless he supplied them with money they could not follow him. To do this was, probably, as little in his power, as in his will. He embarked with his own household, and sailed, expecting that a sense of shame, if not of allegiance, would make them put to sea after him. But in this he was deceived;...they had performed all to which the feudal system bound them; no honour was to be expected under such a leader, and as no feeling of personal attachment towards him existed, they broke up and returned home. The Great Council meantime had met. The Earl of Essex, Geoffry Fitz-Peter, to whom with the Bishop of Winchester, the government had been intrusted during the King's absence, laid before them the terms to which he had sworn; and, in pursuance of his engagement, it was ordered that all injurious ordinances should be abrogated, that no sheriff, forester, or other minister of the King should offer injury to any man, or extort fines as they had been used to do; and that the laws of Henry I. should be observed throughout the realm.

The King had sailed to Jersey; being then convinced that his Barons would not follow him, he returned to England in the bitterness of disappointment and rage, and with such forces as he could collect, marched to take vengeance upon them. The Primate met him at Northampton, and observed to him that his present conduct was a violation of the oath which he had taken. The vassels must stand to the judgement of his court, and he must not thus, in his own quarrel, pursue them with arms. Impatient of such an opposition, and, probably, astonished at it, John replied "that these matters did not belong to the

Archbishop, and should not be impeded by him; and the next morning he marched towards Nottingham. Langton followed him, and told him that unless he desisted he would excommunicate all who should bear arms, till the interdict was withdrawn, himself alone excepted. The King had felt the effect of such weapons too lately again to encounter them: he yielded to the threat, and in obedience to Langton, appointed a day on which the Barons should appear and answer to his charges.

These events past in rapid succession, and the Great Council, within three weeks after its meeting at St. Albans, assembled again at London in St. Paul's Church. The King was not present; his intention was to demand escuage from his Barons, in commutation for the personal service which they had refused to perform: their plea was, that they were not bound to pay it for any wars beyond sea; but he insisted that it had been paid in his father's time and in his brother's, and that it was his rightful due. The consideration that the money raised by the two preceding Kings was expended in upholding the honour of England, but that under him nothing but loss and ignominy could be purchased, availed nothing against the validity of his claim: the hope, therefore, of evading this payment became an additional motive for combining to limit those undefined powers which the Sovereign hitherto had exercised ; and when on this occasion Langton produced a copy of that charter which Henry the first had granted, and which, though confirmed by the two succeeding Kings, had become out of use, and almost out of mind, they bound themselves by an oath to contend for the rights which were there secured to them, and if need were to die in the cause. At this time the chief Justiciary died; he was a man whose dignity of character commanded respect even from King John; that worthless Prince rejoiced, therefore, at his death, and swore that now for the first time he was Lord of England. He lost in him the only person to whom all parties might have deferred, and who might have prevented fatal extremes on either side. But John expected that by help of the Pope he should succeed in curbing all opposition to his will. The papal court has ever been equally ready to confirm the absolute authority of devoted sovereigns, and to stir up rebellion against those who resisted its usurpations. Innocent readily espoused the King's cause, but he chose in Cardinal Nicholas, Bishop of Tarentum, a legate inferior to the service on which he was sent. When the question of damages was debated, it was perceived that he acted, not as a just arbitrator, but as one determined upon favouring the King; the act of submission was renewed in his presence, and the deed of resignation was authenticated with a seal of gold, and delivered into his hands, to be sent to Rome. His policy should now have been to conciliate the Primate and the other prelates; instead of this, he invaded their rights, and without consulting them, filled up the vacant sees and abbeys, committing also the farther imprudence of promoting persons altogether unworthy of advancement. Upon this Langton required him not to interfere with his jurisdiction, and interposed an appeal to Rome. Pandulph, who was sent to justify the new legate's proceedings, extolled John as a humble and dutiful son of the Church, charged Langton and the Bishops with demanding more in reparation than they ought to expect, and accused the Barons of seeking to oppress their sovereign, and to curtail the liberties of the realm. With the Pope the merit of obedience was every thing, and regardless of all other considerations, he supported his royal vassal, and empowered his legate to settle the damages, and withdraw the interdict.

These were minor interests; Langton had stirred a more momentous question, and the Barons for their own security, persevered resolutely in the course which they had begun. They held secret meetings at St. Edmundsbury, which they could do without exciting suspicion, because St. Edmund's shrine was frequented by pilgrims; and there, before the altar of the saint, they pledged themselves by a vow, that if the King did not confirm the laws which Langton had laid before them, and grant them the rights which they claimed ... they would make war upon him, till they should have obtained their demands in a charter under his own seal. This was about the middle of November. At Christmas, they engaged to present themselves before the King, and make their petition; meantime they were to provide force for going through with what they had begun. Had they failed in their undertaking, this would have been deemed a treasonable compact: such in reality it was; nor were the Barons justified by the plea which they appear to have taken as their popular ground of defence, that the King had virtually released them from their allegiance when he surrendered his kingdom to the Pope; for they had themselves consented to that resignation, if not urged him to it. But these things must not be tried strictly by the standard of better times. It was a struggle for power between a bad King and a turbulent nobility; the latter found it necessary to strengthen their side, by conciliating those whom they were in the habit of oppressing themselves ... and from this necessity the good which ensued arose.

If there was any man who contemplated that good, it was the Primate. He it was who had raised the storm, and he now stood aloof, the better to direct it. At Christmas, John met his Barons in London; their forces were so distributed as to secure themselves, and intimidate the King; and when they required him to confirm the charter of Henry I., and reminded him that to this he had in fact bound himself by oath, when he was absolved at Winchester, he perceived that denial would be dangerous, and, therefore, required time for deliberation, till Easter. They understood this, and consented to it only when his son-in-law the Earl of Pembroke, the Bishop of Ely, and the Primate, promised as sureties for him, that he would satisfy them at the time appointed. John had no such intention. He, who regarded no oath, employed the interval in exacting new oaths of fealty from his people, fortifying his castles, and raising forces. He also took the cross, hoping to excite the popular ardour for a crusade in opposition to the spirit which the Barons had called forth, and perhaps, by getting abroad under that pretext, to escape from a contest in which he had no chance of success.

These artifices were unavailing. In the Easter week, five and forty Barons, with two thousand Knights, and all their retainers, met in arms at Stamford; they proceeded to Brakesley, in the direction of Oxford, where the King then was; and at Brakesley, on Easter Monday, the Primate, and the Earl of Pembroke met them, and required on the King's part to know their specific demands. They delivered a roll, containing the ancient liberties, privileges, and customs of the realm; and they declared, that if the King did not at once confirm these, they would make war upon him till he did. When their demands were stated to John by Langton, he asked, why they did not demand his kingdom also, and swore that he would never grant them liberties, which should make himself a slave. Langton and Pembroke represented to him, that what was required, was in the main for the general good, and that it behoved him to yield: he was too violently incensed to be capable of reasonable counsel, and the Barons giving their force the appellation of the army of God and the holy Church, commenced war by laying siege to Northampton. Being without engines, they wasted fifteen days before the walls; then broke up, and marched against Bedford, which was delivered into their hands, for the governor was confederate with them. They now were invited to London, with assurance that the gates should be opened in the night, by some of the chief citizens. The gates accordingly were thus betrayed; and the mob, rejoicing in the temporary dissolution of all restraining power, rose against those who were believed to favour the King, and took that welcome opportunity for falling upon the Jews, and plundering them. The possession of the metropolis decided the contest; the other Barons being called upon to make their choice, and either join the confederation, or be proclaimed enemies to God, and rebels to the Church, and suffer accordingly with fire and sword, declared in favour of their peers. John then felt the necessity of submission; he met the Barons at Runnymead, and there Magna Charta was signed.

By this famous charter, the fundamental principles of free government were recognised; and wise provisions were established for the security of the subject, and the administration of justice. It is a charter for which England has just reason to be thankful; but had all its parts been carried into full effect, it would have transferred the actual sovereignty from the King to five-and-twenty

Barons, and thus have brought upon the kingdom the worst and most incurable of all governments. There is not one stipulation in favour of the servile class; and this may prove at once, that the rights of humanity in that age were not regarded; and that the condition of this class was not such as to excite compassion. The opportunity for determining the limits of the royal and ecclesiastical authorities was not taken; instead of this, the first article declared that the Church of England should be free, and enjoy its whole rights and liberties inviolable. This language, which left the pretensions of the Church unlimited, may be ascribed to Langton. Perhaps the Barons also carefully abstained from requiring any thing which might offend the Pope.

But the plain tangible benefits conferred upon the great body of the people by this charter, were such, that in their gratitude they thought God had mercifully touched the King's heart, and that they were delivered as it were out of the bondage of Egypt; for so great had been the abuses which it was now intended to correct, that they promised themselves, from these laws, a new order of things. The King's feelings were widely different; though to him, had he wisely considered it, it would have been in reality as desirable as to his subjects, except in the fatal stipulation which placed him in reality under the power as well as the inspection of his Barons. That stipulation afforded ground for imputing to the Barons motives of selfish ambition; in every other part, the charter was its own justification. Upon this, therefore, the Pope seized, when John, by his faithful agent, Pandulph, (for such the Cardinal was now become,) implored aid against his rebellious Barons, protesting, that by compulsion only had he yielded to their demands; and that holding his kingdom as a fief of the Roman Church, he had no authority to enact new statutes without the Pontiff's knowledge, nor in any thing to prejudice the rights of his Lord. Innocent looked upon the obnoxious provisions which were presented to him, and exclaimed with a frown, "Is it so? Do then these Barons go about to dethrone their King, who hath taken the cross, and is under the protection of the Apostolic See? By St. Peter, we will not suffer this outrage to go unpunished!" He then issued a Bull, declaring that though England was become a fief of the Papal see, and the Barons were not ignorant that the King had no power to give away the rights of the crown, without the consent of his feudal lord; they nevertheless, being instigated by the Devil, had rebelled against him, and extorted from him concessions to the degradation of the crown. Wherefore, as he, whom God had appointed over nations and kingdoms, to pluck up and to destroy, to build and to plant, he reprobated and condemned what had been done; forbade the King to observe the Charter, the Barons to require its execution, and pronounced it, in all its clauses, null and void.

The Bull being disregarded by the Barons, he ordered Langton to excommunicate them. The character of that Primate might have appeared doubtful, if it had not thus been put to an unerring ordeal. He had embarked, but not sailed, for Italy, to assist at the fourth Lateran Council, when Pandulph, and the persons associated in commission with him, communicated to him the Pope's orders: the Pope, he said, had been deceived by false representations, and he desired that the sentence might be suspended, till he should have seen him. But when they would admit of no delay, he refused to promulgate it; upon which he was himself suspended from his office. To this injustice he submitted as a dutiful son of the Church, and proceeded on his voyage. At the Council he appeared, not as a member, but as one accused of conspiring against the King, and of committing manifold injuries against the Roman Church. The sentence of suspension was confirmed by the Pope and Cardinals, and he was not relieved from it till after the death both of Innocent and John. In the ensuing reign, he was permitted to return and resume his functions; and then acting again in concert with the Barons, and directing their measures, he assisted them in obtaining from Henry III. a confirmation of that charter, which is to be considered as his work. When we call to mind the character of the old Barons, their propensity to abuse an undue power, and the little regard which they manifested to their country in their transactions with France, it can hardly be doubted, but that those provisions in the Great Charter which related to the general good, and had their foundation in the principles of general justice, were dictated by him. No man, therefore, is entitled to a higher place in English history, for having contributed to the liberties of England, than Stephen Langton. It is no disparagement to him, that he was devoted to the Church of Rome, more than was consistent with the interests of his country; for while, under a sense of professional and religious duty, he was ready to suffer any thing in submission to its authority, he resolutely refused to act in obedience to its orders, when he believed them to be unjust, affording thus the surest proof of integrity, and bequeathing to his successors the most beneficial of all examples.

Unhappily it was the tendency of these transactions to strengthen the papal power, which being alternately appealed to by all parties, found means to establish all its usurpations; and being withheld by no considerations of principle or prudence, abused to the utmost the victory which it had obtained.

CHAPTER X.

VIEW OF THE PAPAL SYSTEM.

The corruptions, doctrinal and practical, of the Roman Church were, in these ages, at their height. They are studiously kept out of view by the writers who still maintain the infallibility of that Church; and in truth, that a system, in all things so unlike the religion of the Gospel, and so opposite to its spirit, should have been palmed upon the world, and established as Christianity, would be incredible, if the proofs were not undeniable and abundant.

The indignation, which these corruptions ought properly to excite, should not, however, prevent us from perceiving that the Papal power, raised and supported as it was wholly by opinion, must originally have possessed, or promised, some peculiar and manifest advantages to those who acknowledged its authority. If it had not been adapted to the condition of Europe, it could not have existed. Though in itself an enormous abuse, it was the remedy for some great evils, the palliative of others. We have but to look at the Abyssinians, and the Oriental Christians, to see what Europe would have become without the Papacy. With all its errors, its corruptions, and its crimes, it was, morally and intellectually, the conservative power of Christendom. Politically, too, it was the saviour of Europe; for, in all human probability, the west, like the east, must have been overrun by Mahommedanism, and sunk in irremediable degradation, through the pernicious institutions which have everywhere accompanied it, if, in that great crisis of the world, the Roman Church had not roused the nations to an united and prodigious effort, commensurate with the danger.

In the frightful state of society which prevailed during the dark ages, the Church every where exerted a controlling and remedial influence. Every place of worship was an asylum, which was always respected by the law, and generally even by lawless violence. It is recorded, as one of the peculiar miseries of Stephen's miserable reign, that during those long troubles, the soldiers learned to disregard the right of sanctuary. Like many other parts of the Romish system, this right had prevailed in the heathen world, though it was not ascribed to every temple. It led, as it had done under the

Roman empire, to abuses which became intolerable ; but it originated in a humane and pious purpose, not only screening offenders from laws, the severity of which amounted to injustice, but, in cases of private wrong, affording time for passion to abate, and for the desire of vengeance to be appeased. The cities of refuge were not more needed, under the Mosaic dispensation, than such asylums in ages when the administration of justice was either detestably inhuman, or so lax, that it allowed free scope to individual resentment. They have therefore generally been found wherever there are the first rudiments of civil and religious order. The church-yards also were privileged places, whither the poor people conveyed their goods for security. The protection which the ecclesiastical power extended in such cases, kept up in the people, who so often stood in need of it, a feeling of reverence and attachment to the Church. They felt that religion had a power on earth, and that it was always exercised for their benefit.

The civil power was in those ages so inefficient for the preservation of public tranquillity, that when a country was at peace with all its neighbours, it was liable to be disturbed by private wars, individuals taking upon themselves the right of deciding their own quarrels, and avenging their own wrongs. Where there existed no deadly feud, pretexts were easily made by turbulent and rapacious men, for engaging in such contests, and they were not scrupulous whom they seized and imprisoned, for the purpose of extorting a ransom. No law, therefore, was ever more thankfully received, than when the Council of Clermont enacted, that, from sunset on Wednesday to sunrise on Monday, in every week, the truce of God should be observed, on pain of excommunication. Well might the inoffensive and peaceable part of the community (always the great, but in evil times the inert, and therefore the suffering part) regard, with grateful devotion, a power, under whose protection they slept four nights of the week in peace, when otherwise they would have been in peril every hour. The same power by which individuals were thus benefited, was not unfrequently exercised in great national concerns; if the monarch were endangered or oppressed either by a foreign enemy, or by a combination of his Barons, here was an authority to which he could resort for an effectual interposition in his behalf; and the same shield was extended over the vassals, when they called upon the Pope to defend them against a wrongful exertion of the sovereign power.

Wherever an hierarchal government, like that of the Lamas, or the Dairis of Japan, has existed, it would probably be found, could its history be traced, to have been thus called for by the general interest. Such a government Hildebrand would have founded. Christendom, if his plans had been accomplished, would have become a federal body, the Kings and Princes of which should have bound themselves to obey the Vicar of Christ, not only as their spiritual, but their temporal lord; and their disputes, instead of being decided by the sword, were to have been referred to a Council of Prelates annually assembled at Rome. Unhappily, the personal character of this extraordinary man counteracted the pacific part of his schemes; and he became the firebrand of Europe, instead of the peace-maker. If, indeed, the Papal chair could always have been occupied by such men as S. Carlo Borromeo, or Fenelon, and the ranks of the hierarchy throughout all Christian kingdoms always have been filled, as they ought to have been, by subjects chosen for their wisdom and piety, such a scheme would have produced as much benefit to the world as has ever been imagined in Utopian romance, and more than it has ever yet enjoyed under any of its revolutions. But to suppose this possible, is to pre-suppose the prevalence of

Christian principles to an extent which would render any such government unnecessary, . . . for the kingdom of Heaven would then be commenced on earth.

That authority, to which the Church could lay no claim for the purity of its members, it supported by its arrogant pretensions, availing itself of all notions, accidents, practices, and frauds, from which any advantage could be derived, till the whole monstrous accumulation assumed a coherent form, which well deserves to be called the mystery of iniquity. The Scriptures, even in the Latin version, had long become a sealed book to the people; and the Roman See, in proportion as it extended its supremacy, discouraged or proscribed the use of such vernacular versions as existed. This it did, not lest the ignorant and half-informed should mistake the sense of scripture, nor lest the presumptuous and the perverse should deduce new errors in doctrine, and more fatal consequences in practice, from its distorted language; but in the secret and sure consciousness, that what was now taught as Christianity was not to be found in the written word of God. In maintenance of the dominant system, Tradition, or the Unwritten Word, was set up. This had been the artifice of some of the earliest heretics, who, when they were charged with holding doctrines not according to Scripture, affirmed that some things had been revealed which were not committed to writing, but were orally transmitted down. The Pharisees, before them, pleaded the same supposititious authority for the formalities which they superadded to the Law, and by which they sometimes superseded it, " making the word of God of none effect," as our Saviour himself reproached them. And upon this ground the Romish Clergy justified all the devices of man's imagination with which they had corrupted the ritual and the faith of the Western Church.

One of the earliest corruptions grew out of the reverence which was paid to the memory of departed Saints. Hence there arose a train of error and fraud which ended in the grossest creature-worship. Yet, in its origin, this was natural and salutary. He, whose heart is not excited upon the spot which a martyr has sanctified by his sufferings, or at the grave of one who has largely benefited mankind, must be more inferior to the multitude in his moral, than he can possibly be raised above them in his intellectual, nature. In other cases, the sentiment is acknowledged, and even affected when it is not felt; wherefore, then, should we hesitate at avowing it where a religious feeling is concerned?

Could the Holy Land be swept clean of its mummeries and superstitions, the thoughts and emotions to be experienced there would be worth a pilgrimage. But it is the condition of humanity, that the best things are those which should most easily be abused. The prayer which was preferred with increased fervency at a martyr's grave, was at length addressed to the martyr himself; virtue was imputed to the remains of his body, the rags of his apparel, even to the instruments of his suffering; relics were required as an essential part of the Church furniture; it was decreed that no Church should be erected unless some treasures of this kind were deposited within the altar, and so secured there, that they could not be taken out without destroying it: it was made a part of the service to pray through the merits of the Saint whose relics were there deposited, and the Priest, when he came to this passage, was enjoined to kiss the altar.

There is, unquestionably, a natural tendency in the human mind toward this form of superstition. It prevailed among the Greeks and Romans, though in a less degree: it is found among the Eastern nations; and the Mahommedans, though they condemned and despised it at first, gradually fell into it themselves. But no where has it been carried to so great a length as in the Roman Church. The Clergy, presuming upon the boundless credulity of mankind, profited by it in those ages with the utmost hardihood of fraud, and with a success at which they themselves must sometimes have been astonished. For it is not more certain that these relics in most cases were fictitious, than that in many instances cures, which both to priest and patient must have appeared plainly miraculous, were wrought by faith in them. Sometimes, also, accident accredited this kind of superstition. If a corpse were found which, owing to the nature of the soil wherein it was laid, or to any other natural cause, had not undergone decomposition, but retained in some degree the semblance of life, this was supposed to be an indication of sanctity, confirming, by the incorruption of the saint, the important and consolatory truth of the resurrection of the body. In these cases no deceit is to be suspected. Perhaps, too, the opinion that the relics of the holy dead were distinguished by a peculiar fragrance, may have arisen from embalmed bodies: at first, it might honestly have obtained among the Clergy; but when they saw how willingly it was received by the people, whenever a new mine of relics was opened, care was taken that the odour of sanctity should not be wanting.

At one time, relics or entire bodies used to be carried about the country and exhibited to the credulous multitude; but this gainful practice gave occasion to such scandalous impostures, that it was at length suppressed. What was still encouraged is sufficiently disgraceful to the Romanists. The bodies of their Saints are even now exposed in their churches; some dried and shrivelled, others reduced to a skeleton, clothed either in religious habits, or in the most gorgeous garments, . . . a spectacle as ghastly as the superstition itself is degrading! The poor fragments of mortality, a skull, a bone, or the fragment of a bone, a tooth, or a tongue, were either mounted or set, according to the size, in gold and silver, deposited in costliest shrines of the finest workmanship, and enriched with the most precious gems. Churches soon began to vie with each other in the number and variety of these imaginary treasures, which were sources of real wealth to their possessors. The instruments of our Lord's crucifixion were shewn, (the spear and the cross having, so it was pretended, been miraculously discovered,) the clothes wherein he was wrapt in infancy, the manger in which he was laid, the vessels in which he converted water into wine at the marriage feast, the bread which he brake at the last supper, his vesture for which the soldiers cast lots. Such was the impudence of Romish fraud, that portions were produced of the burning bush, of the manna which fell in the wilderness, of Moses's rod and Samson's honeycomb, of Tobit's fish, of the blessed Virgin's milk, and of our Saviour's blood! Enormous prices were paid by sovereigns for such relics; it was deemed excusable, not to covet merely, but to steal them; and if the thieves were sometimes miraculously punished, they were quite as often enabled by miracle to effect the pious robbery, and bring the prize in triumph to the church for which it was designed. In the rivalry of deceit which the desire of gain occasioned, it often happened that the head of the same Saint was shewn in several places, each Church insisting that its own was genuine, and all appealing to miracles as the test. Sometimes the dispute was accommodated in a more satisfactory manner, by asserting a miraculous multiplication, and three whole bodies of one person have been shewn; the dead Saint having tripled himself, to terminate a dispute between three churches at his funeral! The catacombs at Rome were an inexhaustible mine of relics. But the hugest fraud of this kind that was ever practised was, when the contents of a whole cemetery were brought forth as the bones of eleven thousand British virgins, all bound from Cornwall, to be married in Armorica, carried by tempests up the Rhine to the city of Cologne, and there martyred by an army of Huns under Attila! Even this legend obtained credit; all parts of Christendom were eager to acquire a portion of the relics, and at this day a church may be seen at Cologne, literally lined with the bones!

With the reverence which was paid to relics, arising thus naturally at first, and converted by crafty priests into a source of lucre, Saint-worship grew up. If such virtue resided in their earthly and perishable remains, how great must be the power wherewith their beatified spirits were invested in Heaven! The Greeks and Romans attributed less to their demigods, than the Catholic Church has done to those of its members who have received their apotheosis. They were invoked as mediators between God and man; individuals claimed the peculiar protection of those whose names they had received in baptism, and towns and kingdoms chose each their tutelary Saint. But though every Saint was able to avert all dangers, and heal all maladies, each was supposed to exert his influence more particularly in some specific one, which was determined by the circumstances of his life or martyrdom, the accidental analogy of a name, or by chance and custom, if these shadows of a cause were wanting. The virtue which they possessed they imparted to their images, in which indeed it was affirmed that they were really and potentially present, partaking of ubiquity in their beatitude. For the Monks and Clergy promoted every fantastic theory, and every vulgar superstition, that could be made gainful to themselves; and devised arguments for them, which they maintained with all the subtleties of scholastic logic. Having thus introduced a polytheism little less gross than that of the heathens, and an actual idolatry, they hung about their altars (as had also been the custom in heathen temples) pictures recording marvellous deliverances, and waxen models of the diseased or injured parts, which had been healed by the Saint to whose honour they were there suspended. Cases enough were afforded by chance and credulity, as well as by impostors of a lower rank; and the persons by whom this practice was encouraged, were neither scrupulous on the score of * decency nor of truth. Church vied with church, and convent with convent, in the repu-

* The curious reader is referred to Sir Thomas More's *Dialoge*, for an example of the scandalous practices arising from this superstition. St. Valory's, in Picardy, was the scene: p. 76, Ed. 1530.

tation of their wonder-working images, some of which were pretended to have been made without hands, and some to have descended from Heaven! But the rivalry of the monastic orders was shewn in the fictions wherewith they filled the histories of their respective founders and worthies. No language can exaggerate the enormity of the falsehoods which were thus promulgated; nor the spirit of impious audacity in which they were conceived: yet some of the most monstrous, and most palpably false, received the full sanction of the Papal authority; the superstitions founded upon them were legitimated by Papal Bulls; and festivals in commemoration of miracles which never happened,—nay, worse than this,—of the most blasphemous and flagitious * impostures, were appointed in the Romish kalendar, where at this day they hold their place.

While the monastic orders contended with each other in exaggerating the fame of their deified patriarchs, each claimed the Virgin Mary for its especial patroness. Some peculiar favour she had bestowed upon each. She had appointed their rule of life, or devised the pattern of their habit; or enjoined them some new practice of devotion, or granted them some singular privi-

* For example, the five wounds of St. Francis.

lege. She had espoused their founder with a ring, or fed him like a babe at her breast! (it is fitting, and necessary that this abominable system of imposture should be displayed :)—and each of the popular orders had been assured by revelation, that the place in Heaven for its departed members was under her skirts. All, therefore, united in elevating her to the highest rank in the mythology of the Romish Church, for so in strict truth must this enormous system of fable be designated. They traced her in types throughout the Old Testament: she was the tree of life; the ladder which Jacob had seen leading from heaven to earth; the ever-burning bush; the ark of the covenant; the rod which brought forth buds and blossoms, and produced fruit; the fleece upon which alone the dew of Heaven descended. Before all creatures and all ages, she was conceived in the Eternal Mind; and when the time appointed for her mortal manifestation was come, she of all human kind alone was produced without the taint of human frailty. And though indeed, being subject to death, she paid the common tribute of mortality, . . . yet, having been born without sin, she expired without suffering, and her most holy body, too pure a thing to see corruption, was translated immediately to Heaven, there to be glorified. This had been presumed, because, had her remains existed upon earth, it was not to be believed but that so great a treasure would have been revealed to some or other of so many Saints, who were worthy to have been made the means of enriching mankind by the discovery; and that all doubt might be removed, the fact was stated by the Virgin herself to Saint Antonio. Her image was to be found in every church throughout Christendom; and she was worshipped under innumerable appellations,...devotees believing that the one which they particularly affected, was that to which the object of their adoration most willingly inclined her ear. As an example of the falsehoods by which this superstition was kept up, it may suffice to mention the brave legend of Loretto, where the house in which the Virgin lived at Nazareth is still shewn, as having been carried there by four Angels. The story of its arrival, and how it had been set down twice upon the way, and how it was ascertained to be the genuine house, both by miracles, and by the testimony of persons sent to examine the spot where it was originally built, and to measure the foundations,...received the sanction of successive Popes, and was printed in * all languages, for

* I have seen it in Welsh, brought from Loretto.

pilgrims of every Christian nation, who were attracted thither by the celebrity of the shrine, and by the indulgences promised to those who should visit it in devotion.

By such representations and fables, the belief of the people became so entirely corrupted, that Christ, instead of being regarded as our Mediator and Redeemer, appeared to them in the character of a jealous God, whom it behoved them to propitiate through the mediation of his Virgin Mother, for through her alone could mercy and salvation be obtained. The Pantheon, which Agrippa had dedicated to Jupiter and all the Gods, was by the Pope, who converted it into a Church, inscribed to the blessed Virgin, and all the Saints. Nor was it in idolatry, polytheism, and creature-worship alone, that the resemblance was apparent between the religion of Pagan and of Papal Rome. The Priests of the Roman Church had gradually fallen into many of the rites and ceremonies of their heathen predecessors, profiting in some cases by what was useful, in others, not improperly conforming to what was innocent, but in too many points culpably imitating pernicious and abominable usages. The incense which was employed in Christian Churches, as profusely as it had been in honour of the discarded Gods, was grateful, and perhaps, salutary; the lamps, which burnt perpetually before the altar, an allowable mark of reverence to the place; the holy water, to be censured, not as symbolical in its use of that inward purification which is required, but for the purposes of gross superstition, to which it was so easily abused. The open shrine, and the rustic chapel, give a character of humanity to the wild, of religion to the cultivated, country; they are good in their intention, and in their uses; and it is only to be desired that the Romish Saints which are there installed, as they have superseded the objects of earlier idolatry, shall themselves be removed, and the Cross alone be seen there.

Some, even of the reprehensible resemblances between Popery and Paganism, were accidental, having arisen in both from the excess and misdirection of the same natural feelings. But the greater number arose from a desire of accommodating the new profession of the converts to their old ceremonies, and of investing the Clergy with the authority and influence possessed by the Pagan priesthood. Both motives led to the toleration of customs which ought not to have been permitted, to the introduction of ceremonials more burthensome than those of the ritual law which had been abrogated, and to the adoption of so many outward and visible signs of

Paganism, that, had it not been for the Cross, the appearances of the old system would have predominated. The change meantime which took place in the spirit of the religion thus strangely corrupted, was not less remarkable than that which had been effected in its forms. To trace this worse deterioration, it will be necessary to look back upon the earlier ages of the Church.

Britain has the credit or discredit (whichever it may be deemed) of having given birth to Pelagius, the most remarkable man of whom Wales can boast, and the most reasonable of all those men whom the ancient Church has branded with the note of heresy. He erred, indeed, in denying that there is an original taint in human nature, . . a radical infirmity, . . . an innate and congenital disease, . . . to the existence whereof the heart of every one, who dares look into his own, bears unwilling but unerring testimony; a perilous error this, and the less venial, because it implies a want of that humility which is the foundation of wisdom, as well as of Christian virtue. But he vindicated the goodness of God, by asserting the free-will of man; and he judged more sanely of the Creator than his triumphant antagonist, St. Augustine*, who, retaining too much of the

* "When Pelagius had puddled the stream," says Jeremy Taylor, "St. Austin was so angry, that he stamped and dis-

philosophy which he had learnt in the Manichean school, infected with it the whole Church during many centuries, and afterwards divided both the Protestant and the Catholic world. Augustine is too eminent a man to be named without respect; but of all those ambitious spirits, who have adulterated the pure doctrines of revelation with their own opinions, he, perhaps, is the one who has produced the widest and the most injurious effects.

Augustine was victorious in the controversy: his indeed was the commanding intellect of that age . . . The opinions of Pelagius were condemned, but it was not possible to suppress them; and the errors of both soon became so curiously blended, that it would be difficult to say which predominated in the preposterous consequences to which their union led. From the African theologue, more than from any other teacher, the notion of the absolute wickedness of human nature was derived; and the tenet of two hostile principles in man, which had led to such extravagancies among the Eastern Christians, was

turbed it more." (Vol. ix. 396.) "Whoever shall think himself bound to believe all that this excellent man wrote, will not only find it impossible he should, but will have reason to say, that zeal against an error is not always the best instrument to find out truth." (Vol. ix. p. 399.)

established in the Western Church. Through the British heresiarch, the more reasonable opinion, that the actions of good men were meritorious in themselves, obtained. Cassian, whose collations were the great fount of monastic legislation in Europe, held that modified scheme, which has been called the Semi-Pelagian. But with him, and with the Monks, the opinion ceased to be reasonable: the extremes were made to meet; and the practical consequences, deduced from the Monkish doctrine of merits, coalesced perfectly with the Manichean principle, which had now taken root in the corruptions of Christianity.

The Romish Church did with the religions of the Roman world, what Rome itself had done with the kingdoms and nations over whom it extended its dominion: it subdued and assimilated them; and as the conquered people were in most parts raised in civilization by their conquerors, so of the ceremonies which the Church borrowed from Paganism, some were spiritualized, and others ennobled by the adoption. Even idolatry was, in some degree, purified; and gained in sentiment, more than it lost in the degradation of the arts.

But it was otherwise when Christianity combined with the philosophy of the Orientals.

Dualism, among the early Persians first, and afterwards by Manes (the most creative of enthusiasts or impostors), had been wrought into a wild imaginative scheme of allegorical mythology. The Christians, when it crept into their creed, were more in earnest; and they founded upon it a system as terrible in practice, as it was monstrous in theory. They believed that the war of the Two Principles existed in every individual, manifesting itself in the struggle between the flesh and the spirit. The flesh, therefore, was a mortal enemy, whom it behoved the spirit, as it valued its own salvation, to curb and subdue by unremitting severity, and to chastise as a vicious and incorrigible slave, always mutinous and ready to rebel.

The consequences of this persuasion brought into full view the weakness and the strength of human nature. In some respects, they degraded it below the beasts; in others, they elevated it almost above humanity. They produced at the same time, and in the same persons, the most intense selfishness and the most astonishing self-sacrifice, . . so strangely were the noblest feelings and the vilest superstition blended in this corrupt and marvellous mixture of revealed truth and the devices of man's insane imagination. The dearest and holiest ties of nature and society were set at nought, by those who believed that the way to secure their own salvation, was to take upon themselves the obligations of a monastic life. They regarded it as a merit to renounce all intercourse with their nearest friends and kin; and, being by profession dead to the world, rendered themselves, by a moral suicide, dead in reality to its duties and affections. For the sake of saving their own souls, or of attaining a higher seat in the kingdom of Heaven, they sacrificed, without compunction, the feelings, and, as far as depended upon them, the welfare and happiness of wife, parent, or child: yet, when the conversion of others was to be promoted, these very persons were ready to encounter any danger, and to offer up their lives with exultation as martyrs. The triumph of the will over the body was, indeed, complete; but it triumphed over the reason also; and enthusiasts, in order to obtain Heaven, spent their lives, not in doing good to others, but in inflicting the greatest possible quantity of discomfort and actual suffering upon themselves.

In pursuance of this principle, practices not less extravagant than those of the Indian Yoguees, and more loathsome, were regarded as sure indications of sanctity. It was deemed meritorious to disfigure the body by neglect and filth, to extenuate it by fasting and watchfulness, to lacerate it with stripes, and to fret the wounds with cilices of horsehair. Linen was proscribed among the monastic orders; and the use of the warm bath, which, being not less conducive to health than to cleanliness, had become general in all the Roman provinces, ceased throughout Christendom, because, according to the morality of the monastic school, cleanliness itself was a luxury, and to procure it by pleasurable means, was a positive sin. The fanatics in Europe did not, indeed, like their predecessors in Syria and Egypt, cast off all clothing, and, by going on all-fours, reduce themselves to a likeness with beasts, as far as self-degradation could effect it, in form and appearance, as well as in their manner of life; but they devised other means of debasing themselves, almost as effectual. There were some Saints, who never washed themselves, and made it a point of conscience never to disturb the vermin, who were the proper accompaniments of such sanctity; in as far as they occasioned pain while burrowing, or at pasture, they were increasing the stock of the aspirant's merits, that treasure which he was desirous of laying up in Heaven; and he thought it unjust to deprive his little progeny of their present paradise, seeing they had no other to expect! The act of eating they made an exercise of penance, by mingling whatever was most nauseous with their food; and it would literally sicken the reader, were the victories here to be related which they achieved over the reluctant stomach, and which, with other details of sanctimonious nastiness, are recorded in innumerable Roman Catholic books, for edification and example! They bound chains round the body, which eat into the flesh; or fastened graters upon the breast and back; or girded themselves with bandages of bristles intermixed with points of wire. Cases of horrid self-mutilation were sometimes discovered; and many perished by a painful and lingering suicide, believing that, in the torments which they inflicted upon themselves, they were offering an acceptable sacrifice to their Creator. Some became famous for the number of their daily genuflections; others for immersing themselves to the neck in cold water during winter, while they recited the Psalter. The English Saint, Simon Stock, obtained his name and his saintship for passing many years in a hollow tree. St. Dominic*, the Cuirassier, was

* I have given an account of this Saint in the *Quarterly Review*, vol. xxii. p. 79. And the reader who is desirous of seeing another example, not less curious, of Roman Catholic superstition in its excess, is referred to the sketch of P. Joam d'Almeida's life, in my *History of Brazil*, vol. ii. p. 684.

distinguished for his iron dress, and for flogging himself, with a scourge in each hand, day and night; and the blessed Arnulph of Villars, in Brabant, immortalized himself by inventing, for his own use, an under-waistcoat of hedgehog-skins, of which it appears five were required for the back, six for the front and sides.

The strength of the will was manifested in these aberrations of reason, as prodigiously as strength of body is sometimes displayed in madness; nor can it be doubted, that these fanatics, amid their pain, derived pleasure as well from the pride of voluntary endurance, as from the anticipation of their reward in Heaven. The extremes of humiliation and debasement produced also a pride and self-sufficiency not less extravagant in their kind. They whose austerities were the most excessive, were regarded by the people as living Saints, and exhibited as such by other members of the community, who had the same belief, but not the same fervour; or who, not having the same sincerity, considered only in what manner the madness of their fellows might be turned to advantage.

There prevailed an opinion, industriously promoted by the priesthood, which was excellently adapted to this purpose. Heroic piety, such as that of the Saints, was not indispensable for salvation; the degree of faith and good works, without which a soul could not be saved, must be at a standard which all mankind can reach. This was not to be denied. Here then was a large and accumulating fund of good works, which though supererogatory in the Saints, were nevertheless not to be lost. But indeed, if strictly considered, all human merits were in this predicament. Atonement having once been made for all, good works, in those who entitled themselves to the benefit of the covenant, were needful only as the evidence and fruits of a saving faith. There was, however, some use for them. The redemption, which had been purchased for fallen man, was from eternal punishment only; sin was not, therefore, to go unpunished, even in repentant sinners who had confessed and received absolution. The souls of baptized children, it was held, past immediately to heaven; but for all others, except the few who attained to eminent holiness in their lives, Purgatory was prepared; a place according to the popular belief, so near the region of everlasting torments, though separated from it, that the same fire pervaded both; acting indeed to a different end, and in different degrees, but even in its mildest effect, inflicting sufferings more intense than heart could think, or tongue express, and enduring for a length of time, which was left fearfully indefinite. Happily for mankind, the authority of the Pope extended over this dreadful place. The works of supererogation were at his disposal, and this treasury was inexhaustible, because it contained an immeasurable and infinite store derived from the atonement. One drop of the Redeemer's blood being sufficient to redeem the whole human race, the rest which had been shed during the passion was given as a legacy, to be applied in mitigation of Purgatory, as the Popes in their wisdom might think fit. So they in their infallibility declared, and so the people believed! The Popes were liberal of this treasure. If they wished to promote a new practice of devotion, or encourage a particular shrine, they granted to those who should perform the one, or visit the other, an indulgence, that is, a dispensation for so many years of Purgatory; sometimes for shorter terms, but often by centuries, or thousands of years, and, in many cases, the indulgence was plenary, . . . a toll-ticket entitling the soul to pass scot free.

All persons, however, could not perform pilgrimages; and even the accommodating device of the Church, which promised large indulgences for saying certain prayers before the engraved portrait of a miraculous image, was liable, in numerous instances, to be frustrated. The picture might not find its way to remote places; the opportunity of acquiring it might be neglected, or it might remain in the possession of its unthinking owner, a forgotten thing. The Romish Church, in its infinite benevolence, considered this; and therefore sold indulgences, making the act of purchasing them, and thus contributing to its wants, a merit of itself sufficient to deserve so inestimable a reward. It was taught, also, that merits were transferable by gift or purchase: under this persuasion, large endowments were bestowed upon convents, on condition that the donor should partake in the merits of the community; and few persons who had any property at their own disposal, went out of the world without bequeathing some of it to the Clergy, for saying masses, in number proportioned to the amount of the bequest, for the benefit of their souls. The wealthy founded chantries, in which service was to be performed, for ever, to this end. Thus were men taught to put their trust in riches: their wealth being thus invested, became available to them beyond the grave; and in whatever sins they indulged, provided they went through the proper forms, and obtained a discharge, they might purchase a free passage through Purgatory, or at least, an abbreviation of the term, and a mitigation of its torments while they lasted. How severe these torments were to be, might in some degree be estimated by the scale appointed for those who were willing to commute, at a certain rate, while they were alive. The set-off for a single year was fixed at the recitation of thirty psalms, with an accompaniment of one hundred stripes to each: the whole psalter, with its accompaniment of fifteen thousand, availing only to redeem five years. The chronicles of the middle ages are filled with horrible legends, invented to promote a superstition so profitable to the Priests: and that it might be the more deeply impressed upon the people, the representations of souls weltering in fire were exposed in churches, and in streets, and by the way-side; fraternities were established to beg for them; and to give money for their use is part of the penance which is usually, at this day, appointed by the Confessor.

But Purgatory was not the only invisible world over which the authority of the Church extended; for to the Pope, as to the representative of St. Peter, it was pretended that the keys of Heaven and Hell were given; a portion of this power was delegated to every Priest, and they inculcated, that the soul which departed without confession and absolution, bore with it the weight of its deadly sins to sink it to perdition. This also was a practice of priestcraft, ingrafted upon a wholesome discipline, which had grown out of a just religious feeling. The primitive Christians, when their conscience smote them for the neglect of duty, or the commission of sin, used to take shame to themselves, by acknowledging the fault before God and man, in the face of the congregation. While they were a small community, each known to the others, this was no inconvenience: but when numbers increased, and zeal abated, the confession was then made privately to the Priest alone; and the Clergy so clearly perceived the influence which they derived from this, that they soon insisted upon it as a peremptory duty, imperative upon all persons; and, according to the usual craft, they propagated a thousand tales of ghosts who had visited earth to reveal their horrible doom for having left it unperformed. Of all the practices of the Romish Church, this is the one which has proved most injurious; and if it be regarded in connexion with the celibacy of the Clergy, the cause will be apparent why the state of morals is generally so much more corrupt in Catholic than in Protestant countries. This obvious and enormous mischief is not its only evil consequence. The uses of conscience were at an end when it was delivered into the keeping of a Confessor. Actions then, instead of being tried by the eternal standard of right and wrong, on which the unsophisticated heart unerringly pronounces, were judged by the rules of a pernicious casuistry, the intent of which was to make men satisfied with themselves upon the cheapest terms. The inevitable effect was, that the fear of human laws became the only restraint upon evil propensities, when men were taught to believe that the account with Divine Justice might easily be settled. Tables were actually set forth by authority, in which the rate of absolution for any imaginable crime was fixed, and the most atrocious might be committed with spiritual impunity for a few shillings. The foulest murderer and parricide, if he escaped the hangman, might, at this price set his conscience at ease concerning all farther consequences!

If the boundless credulity of mankind be a mournful subject for consideration, as in truth it is, it is yet more mournful to observe the profligate wickedness with which that credulity has been abused. The Church of Rome appears to have delighted in insulting as well as in abusing it, and to have pleased itself with discovering how far it was possible to subdue and degrade the human intellect, as an Eastern despot measures his own greatness by the servile prostration of his subjects. If farther proof than has already appeared were needful, it would be found in the prodigious doctrine of Transubstantiation. This astonishing doctrine arose from taking figurative words in a literal sense; and the Romanists do not shrink from the direct inference, that if their interpretation be just, Christ took his own body in his own hands, and offered it to his disciples. But all minor difficulties may easily be overlooked, when the flagrant absurdity of the doctrine itself is regarded. For, according to the Church of Rome, when the words of consecration have been pronounced, the bread becomes that same actual body of flesh and blood in which our Lord and Saviour suffered upon the Cross; remaining bread to the sight, touch, and taste, yet ceasing to be so, . . . and into how many parts soever the bread may be broken, the whole entire body is contained in every part.

Of all the corruptions of Christianity, there was none which the Popes so long hesitated to sanction as this. When the question was brought before Hildebrand, he not only inclined to the opinion of Berenger, by whom it was opposed, but pretended to consult the Virgin Mary, and then declared that she had pronounced against it. Nevertheless, it prevailed, and was finally declared, by Innocent III., at the fourth Lateran Council, to be a tenet necessary to salvation. Strange as it may appear, the doctrine had become popular,...with the people, for its very extravagance,...with the Clergy, because they grounded upon it their loftiest pretensions. For if there were in the sacrament this actual and entire sole presence, which they denoted by the term of transubstantiation, it followed that divine worship was something more than a service of prayer and thanksgiving; an actual sacrifice was performed in it, wherein they affirmed the Saviour was again offered up, in the same body which had suffered on the Cross, by their hands. The Priest, when he performed this stupendous function of his ministry, had before his eyes, and held in his hands, the Maker of Heaven and Earth; and the inference which they deduced from so blasphemous an assumption was, that the Clergy were not to be subject to any secular authority, seeing that they could create God their Creator! Let it not be supposed that the statement is in the slightest part exaggerated, it is delivered faithfully in their own words.

If such then were the power of the Clergy, even of the meanest priest, what must be attributed to their earthly head, the successor of St. Peter? They claimed for him a plenitude of power; and it has been seen that he exercised it over the Princes of Christendom in its fullest meaning. According to the Canons, the Pope was as far above all Kings, as the sun is greater than the moon. He was King of Kings, and Lord of Lords, though he subscribed himself the Servant of Servants. His power it was which was intended, when it was said to the Prophet Jeremiah, "Behold, I have this day set thee over the nations and the kingdoms, to root out, and to pull down, and to destroy, and to throw down, to build, and to plant." It was an incomprehensible and infinite power, because, "great is the Lord, and great is his power, and of his greatness there is no end." The immediate and sole rule of the whole world belonged to him by natural, moral, and divine right; all authority depending upon him. As supreme King, he might impose taxes upon all Christians; and the Popes declared it was to be held as a point necessary to salvation, that every human creature is subject to the Roman Pontiff. That he might lawfully depose Kings, was averred to be so certain a doctrine, that it could only be denied by madmen, or through the instigation of the Devil; it was more pernicious and intolerable to deny it, than to err concerning the Sacraments. And, indeed, God would not have sufficiently provided for the preservation of his Church, and the safety of souls, if he had not appointed this power of depriving or restraining apostate princes. All nations and kingdoms were under the Pope's jurisdiction, for to him God had delivered over the power and dominion in Heaven and Earth. Nay, he might take away kingdoms and empires, with or without cause, and give them to whom he pleased, though the sovereign, whom he should depose, were in every respect not merely blameless, but meritorious: it was reason enough for the change that the Pope deemed it convenient. The Spouse of the Church was Vice-God: men were commanded to bow at his name, as at the name of Christ; the proudest sovereigns waited upon him like menials, led his horse by the bridle, and held his stirrup while he alighted; and there were ambassadors, who prostrated themselves before him, saying, O thou, that takest away the sins of the world, have mercy upon us!

The advocates of the Papal power proclaimed, that any secular laws which might be passed against a decree of the Roman Pontiff, were in themselves null and void; and that all pontifical decrees ought for ever to be observed by all men, like the word of God, to be received as if they came from the mouth of St. Peter himself, and held like canonical scripture. Neither the

Catholic faith, nor the four Evangelists, could avail those who rejected them, this being a sin which was never to be remitted. Christ had bestowed upon the Pope, when he spake as such, the same infallibility which resided in himself. And were he utterly to neglect his duty, and by his misconduct drag down innumerable souls to Hell with him, there to be eternally tormented, no mortal man might presume to reprove him for his faults. Even this monstrous proposition has been advanced, that although the Catholic Faith teaches all virtue to be good, and all vice evil; nevertheless, if the Pope, through error, should enjoin vices to be committed, and prohibit virtues, the Church would be bound to believe that vices were good, and virtues evil, and would sin in conscience were it to believe otherwise. He could change the nature of things, and make injustice justice. Nor was it possible that he should be amenable to any secular power, for he had been called God by Constantine, and God was not to be judged by man: under God, the salvation of all the faithful depended on him, and the commentators even gave him the blasphemous appellation of our Lord God the Pope! It was disputed in the schools, whether he could not abrogate what the Apostles had enjoined, determine an opinion contrary to theirs, and add a new article to the Creed; whether he did not, as God, participate both natures with Christ; and whether he were not more merciful than Christ, inasmuch as he delivered souls from the pains of purgatory, whereas we did not read that this had ever been done by our Saviour. Lastly, it was affirmed, that he might do things unlawful, and thus could do more than God!

All this was certain, because the Church was infallible. Where this infallibility resided, the Romanists have differed among themselves, some vesting it in the Pope, others requiring the concurrence of a General Council. Infallible, however, it was determined that the Roman Catholic Church must be, and thus the key-stone was put to this prodigious structure of imposture and wickedness.

CHAPTER XI.

RISE OF THE REFORMATION.—THE MENDICANT ORDERS.—WICLIFFE.—PERSECUTION UNDER THE HOUSE OF LANCASTER.

The corrupt lives of the Clergy provoked inquiry into their doctrines. Reformers arose, who found followers in the Alpine and Pyrenean countries, where the truth of better ages had been preserved; and the scattered but numerous relics of various heretical sects, which, though subdued, still secretly existed, fraternized with them. Agreeing in their detestation of Romish tyranny, they disregarded lesser differences; and their assimilated opinions assumed a systematic form, wherein the general principles of the Reformation are distinctly to be traced, and the germs also of those schisms, which so lamentably impeded and disgraced its progress. They taught that the Pope was the head of all errors: that the Romish Church is that woman who is described in the Apocalypse, as sitting on the beast, arrayed in purple and scarlet, decked with gold and precious stones, having the golden cup of her filthiness in her hand, and upon her forehead written, "Mystery, Babylon the Great, the Mother of harlots and abominations of the earth." The book itself explained, that the seven heads of her beast, were the seven mountains upon which her seat was placed, a designation manifestly betokening Rome. They declared against all the abuses of the Church, and condemned most of its ceremonies, comprehending what was innocent and useful, in the same proscription with what was superstitious and injurious. Because the Monks deceived the people, they proclaimed that Monkery was a stinking carrion, and monasteries an evil. Because the churches were profusely adorned, they would have stript them bare. Because the doctrine of merits was preposterous, they maintained the not less preposterous tenet, that the best works of man are sinful in themselves. And because the Clergy arrogated a monstrous power, they were for a levelling system, which, in its direct and certain consequences, extended from religious to political opinions.

Indignation against spiritual tyranny and imposture, uncompromising sincerity, and intrepid zeal, made them formidable to the hierarchy. Their numbers rapidly increased, for both the truth and the errors which they taught, rendered them popular, while they commanded respect by the purity and even austerity of their lives. The Papal Church was seriously endangered, and a religious revolution might perhaps have been effected, which would have produced more evil than good, because Europe was not ripe for it, if a counter and stronger spirit of enthusiasm had not been called forth in its defence. The person by whom this signal service was rendered to the Papacy, was the son of a rich merchant at Assissi: he was called by his acquaintance Francesco, because of his familiar knowledge of the French tongue, which was at that time a rare accomplishment for an Italian; and Hercules is not better known in classical fable, than he became in Romish mythology, by the name of St. Francis. In his youth, it is certain, that he was actuated by delirious piety; but the web of his history is interwoven with such inextricable falsehoods, that it is not possible to decide whether, in riper years, he became madman or impostor; nor whether at last he was the accomplice of his associates, or the victim. Having infected a few kindred spirits with his first enthusiasm, he obtained the Pope's consent to institute an order of Friars Minorite; so, in his humility, he called them; they are better known by the name of Franciscans, after their founder, in honour of whom they have likewise given themselves the modest appellation of the Seraphic Order,—having in their blasphemous fables installed him above the Seraphim, upon the throne from which Lucifer fell!

Previous attempts had been made to enlist, in the service of the Papal Church, some of those fervent spirits, whose united hostility all its strength would have been insufficient to withstand; but these had been attended with little effect, and projects of this kind were discouraged, as rather injurious than hopeful, till Francis presented himself. His entire devotion to the Pope,... his ardenta doration of the Virgin Mary, as the great Goddess of the Romish faith,... the strangeness, and perhaps the very extravagance, of the institute which he proposed, obtained a favourable acceptance for his proposals. Reclusion, for the purpose of religious meditation, was the object of the earlier religious orders; his followers were to go into the streets and highways to exhort the people. The Monks were justly reproached for luxury, and had become invidious for their wealth; the Friars were bound to the severest rule of life, they went barefoot, and renounced, not only for themselves individually, but collectively also, all possessions whatever, trusting to daily charity for their daily bread. It was objected to him that no community, established upon such a principle, could subsist without a miracle: he referred to the lilies in the text, for scriptural authority; to the birds, for an example; and the marvellous increase of the order was soon admitted as full proof of the inspiration of its founder. In less than ten years, the delegates alone to its General Chapter exceeded five thousand in number; and, by an enumeration, in the early part of the eighteenth century, when the Reformation must have diminished their amount at least one-third, it was found that even then there were 28,000 Franciscan nuns in 900 nunneries, and 115,000 Franciscan friars in 7000 convents; besides very many nunneries, which, being under the immediate jurisdiction of the Ordinary, and not of the order, were not included in the returns.

The rival order of St. Dominic was instituted nearly at the same time, for the same purpose, and upon the same principle. The temper of its founder engaged it in the bloody service of extirpating the Albigenses by fire and sword:... in this work both orders co-operated, and though they soon began cordially to hate each other, they were both equally zealous in serving the Papal Church, and in persecuting its enemies. The tide of popular opinion was effectually turned by their exertions; but in process of time they became the opprobrium and scandal of the church which they had preserved: the opportunities which their manner of life afforded, made their vices notorious; and the falsehoods which they fabricated in rivalry of each other, were, in a spirit of blasphemous impiety, beyond all former example, as it is almost beyond belief. The wildest romance contains nothing more extravagant than the legends of St. Dominic: and even these were outdone by the more atrocious effrontery of the Franciscans. They held up their founder, even during his life, as the perfect pattern of our Lord and Saviour; and, to authenticate the parallel, they exhibited him with a wound in his side, and four nails in his hands and feet, fixed there, they affirmed, by Christ himself, who had visibly appeared for the purpose of thus rendering the conformity between them complete! Two miserable wretches, only two years before, had attempted the same dreadful fraud in England, and having been detected in it, were punished by actual crucifixion! But in the case of St. Francis, it succeeded to the fullest extent of expectation. Whether he consented to the villainy, or was in such a state of moral and physical imbecility, as to have been the dupe or the victim of those about him; and whether it was committed with the connivance of the Papal Court, or only in certain knowledge that that

Court would sanction it when done, though it might not deem it prudent to be consenting before the fact,.. are questions which it is now impossible to resolve. Sanctioned, however, the horrible imposture was by that Church which calls itself infallible; a day for its perpetual commemoration was appointed in the Romish Kalendar; and a large volume was composed, entitled the Book of the Conformities between the lives of the blessed and seraphic Father Francis and our Lord!

Jealous of these conformities, the Dominicans followed their rivals in the path of blasphemy,..but with unequal steps. They declared that the five wounds had been impressed also upon St. Dominic; but that, in his consummate humility, he had prayed and obtained that this signal mark of Divine grace might never be made public while he lived. They affirmed that the Virgin Mary had adopted him for her son, and that his countenance perfectly resembled the authentic description and miraculous portrait of our Saviour. The envious enmity between these orders displayed itself in these competitions of falsehood, and in theological or scholastic controversy, upon those points whereon it was allowable to dispute: on all such questions the Dominicans and Franciscans were always opposed to each other; but they held a common cause against the Reformers, and against the secular clergy, whose rights and privileges they invaded in many ways, in some respects to the benefit of the Church, in others to its injury. As itinerant preachers they called forth devotional feelings, which would otherwise never have been excited, and performed some of that duty which the parochial clergy in those ages very generally neglected; as itinerant confessors, they lessened the influence of the resident priest, and the little good which may arise from the demoralizing practice of confession; and as licensed and incorporated beggars, they preyed at large upon the public. Being exempt from episcopal jurisdiction, that salutary restraint was wanting of which such preachers stood in need. But what most offended the secular clergy, because it most injured them, was that, as the earlier Regulars had done before them, the Mendicants obtained from their opulent patrons the advowsons of livings, which they served by some of their own members, or allowing a secular priest a small portion of the income, appropriated the larger part to the uses of the convent in which the patronage was vested. For it was soon found convenient to dispense with that part of their institution which forbade them to possess any thing as a community.

The influence which these orders obtained was, for a time, prodigious; it was produced partly by the pure enthusiasm of the virtuous members,... partly by the reputation of others; (for they could boast some of the subtlest and profoundest intellects that the world has ever seen;)... and partly by the implicit belief with which their enormous fables were received. Elated by success, and, as it seems, secretly conscious how little the system which they taught resembled the religion of the Apostles, they conceived a plan for superseding the Gospel; and this was so congenial to the temper of both orders, that it is doubtful whether it proceeded from a Dominican or Franciscan. The opinion which they started was, that as there were three Persons in one Godhead, the scheme of Providence was, that there should be three dispensations, one from each Person. That of the Father had terminated when the Law was abolished by the Gospel; that of the Son was now drawing, in like manner, to its close, and was to be superseded by that of the Holy Spirit. The uses of the Gospel, therefore, were obsolete; and in its place they produced a book, in the name of the Holy Ghost, under the title of the Eternal Gospel. The first dispensation had been for married persons; this had prepared the way for the Clergy in the second; the Regulars, being as much purer than the Clergy, as these were than the Jews and Patriarchs, were, under the third, to become rulers of the Church, with greater authority than had ever been granted to the Apostles. Under the first, men had lived after the flesh; under the second, in a mixed state between the flesh and the spirit; in the third, they would live wholly according to the spirit, and the scheme of Providence would be fulfilled. In this, however, they went too far: the minds of men were not yet subdued to this. The Eternal Gospel was condemned by the Church; and the Mendicants were fain to content themselves with disfiguring the religion which they were not allowed to set aside.

The Church of Rome cleared itself of this infamy; but the reproach remained of having sanctioned the impostures which emboldened the Friars to so blasphemous an attempt; and circumstances arose which converted some of these auxiliaries into dangerous enemies. When the successors of Francis relaxed the rigour of his rule, they were opposed by brethren more sincere, but less reasonable, than themselves. These pure enthusiasts maintained, that the utter renunciation of all possessions was enjoined by Christ himself, whose Gospel their Patriarch had renewed; and when the Pope condemned this opinion as an heresy, they denied his authority, and attacked him as vehemently as the Waldenses and Albigenses had done, who by their means had been crushed. Irritated at this, the Pope let loose the Dominicans against them; and that Order, for ever infamous as having founded the Inquisition, had the satisfaction of persecuting these Spiritual Franciscans, and seeing many hundreds of them expire in the flames, with constancy worthy of a better cause. A schism in the Papal Church, and a fortunate dispute between the Popes and Emperors, enabled others to find an asylum in Germany, where in safety they continued their attacks upon the Papacy; and by exposing its rapacity, its inconsistency, and its crimes, prepared the way for the great reformation which was at hand.

The first discontent in England was provoked by the manner in which the Popes abused their victory in that country. They had acted with consummate policy during the struggle; but rapacity is short-sighted, and a people who gave full credit to all their frauds, and yielded implicit obedience to their pretensions, felt and resented the merciless extortions which were practised upon them by the Pope's agents, and by the foreigners upon whom the best benefices were bestowed.

In the reign of Henry III., the Italians, who were beneficed here drew from England more than thrice the amount of the King's revenues, fleecing, by means of Priests, who were aliens also, the flock which they never fed. Repeated statutes were made against this evil. A set of Lombards, too, established themselves here, in connexion with the Legates, to advance money upon all sums due to the Pope, for which they exacted the most exorbitant usury, though all usury was prohibited as a sin by the Canon Law. The Government also began to apprehend serious injury from the multiplication of Religious Houses; apprehensions were expressed that men would be wanting for the service of husbandry and for war, if so many were collected in convents; and a real diminution in the revenue was felt in the failure of knight-service, and of the rights accruing to the Crown upon marriages, deaths, and wardships;. . . accidents to which Church lands were not liable. The statute of mortmain was passed to prevent farther foundations; and from the various devices for evading it, the greater number of our fictions in law have arisen.

This law appears to have given what had now become a more useful direction to the spirit of munificent bounty which prevailed during those ages; dark ages we call them, and dark they were . . . but in this splendid virtue they have never been surpassed, and all subsequent times are shamed by comparison with them. It was now that the Universities received their chief endowments; their utility was clearly perceived, and persons who were desirous of contributing to their improvement or advancement, easily obtained a dispensation from the statute, for so good an object. The Friars, who, by their assiduity and boldness, forced themselves every where, interfered here as much with the rights of the Universities, as they had done with those of the Secular Clergy. Their desire was, to recruit their numbers with the most hopeful subjects; and as the most promising youth were brought together to these schools of learning, there were no places where they collected so many novices. The boys whom they inveigled were taught to disregard filial duty; . . the more averse, indeed, their parents were to their taking the vows, the greater the merit was represented of the children who made the sacrifice. This was carried to such an extent, that parents became afraid to trust their sons at Oxford; and the number of students is said to have been diminished, in consequence, from thirty thousand, to six. The Friars, therefore, were regarded with an evil eye by the members of that University, from the duties of which they endeavoured to exempt themselves, as they had obtained an exemption from its jurisdiction. And when there appeared a man bold enough to attack them upon the principle of their institution, and the errors which they taught, and skilful enough in disputation to baffle them at their own weapons, he was encouraged by the persons in authority there.

This man was John Wicliffe, whom the Roman Church has stigmatized as a heretic of the first class, but whom England and the Protestant world, while there is any virtue and while there is any praise, will regard with veneration and gratitude. He is supposed to have been born at a village of the same name, in the North Riding, upon the Tees, (near the place where that river, in the most beautiful part of its course, receives the Yorkshire Greta): and having been a Commoner at Queen's College, at that time newly founded, and then a Probationer at Merton, was appointed Master of Balliol. At first he exercised himself in disputing against the Friars upon scholastic subtleties and questions which, ending in nothing, as they begin, exercise the intellect without enriching it. But such being the manner of controversy then in use, this was a necessary preparation for him; and the reputation, which thus only could be obtained, was available to a better purpose, when feeling his own strength, and that the opinion of the place was with him, he charged them with maintaining false doctrine. For they taught, that the religion which they inculcated was more perfect than that of the Gospels; that Christ had not only enjoined a life of mendicity, but set the example of it, by begging for his own livelihood; and that the members of their Order were sure of obtaining salvation, and would sit in judgement with our Lord upon all other men at the last day.

While he confined himself to such questions, success was certain, and he stood upon safe ground. But even then, his opponents saw good reason for suspecting his opinions upon points which he had not yet ventured to attack; and the Monks, hostile as their feelings were toward the Friars, made common cause with them against Wicliffe. Canterbury Hall had been founded by the Primate Simon de Islip, who appointed a Monk of his own church Warden; but, finding him an unfit person, on account of his hasty temper, ejected him, and placed Wicliffe in his stead. Upon Islip's death, his successor, Simon Langham, took part with the Monks, and ejected Wicliffe. Wicliffe appealed to Rome. That Court was prepossessed against him, and yet might perhaps have pursued the policy of winning him by favourable treatment, if a circumstance had not occurred while the cause was pending, which led him to take a decided part. Edward III. had refused that homage to which King John had subjected his successors, and Urban V. threatened, that, if it were not performed, he would cite him to Rome, there to answer for the default. A sovereign of Edward's ability and renown was not thus to be intimidated; the feeling of the country was with him, and the Parliament affirming that what John had done in this matter was a violation of his coronation oath, declared that if the Pope proceeded in any way against the King, he and all his subjects should with all their power resist him. The Papal claims were defended by a Monk, in a treatise, published as books were before the discovery of printing, by the dispersion of numerous transcripts, and written with such ability that it produced considerable impression upon those into whose hands it came. But he ventured to challenge Wicliffe upon the question, who, coming forward with superior ability in a better cause, produced a conclusive reply; in reward for which, when the appeal concerning the Wardenship was decided against him, he was appointed Professor of Divinity. And as a farther mark of favour, the living of Lutterworth in Leicestershire was given him.

Hitherto his opposition to the Papal authority had been purely constitutional, and if he had yet satisfied himself concerning the corruption of the Romish doctrines, that judgement was rather implied than expressed in his discourses from the pulpit and his exercises in the schools. Implied it was by his silence upon some of those doctrines, and his constant reference to Scripture, in which he was so well versed, that when contemporary teachers were designated each by some epithet characteristic of their scholastic talents, the Gospel Doctor was the appellation by which he was known. But certainly it could not have been avowed when, two years after his appointment to the Divinity chair, he was named, with other embassadors, to meet the Pope's representatives at Bruges, and resist his pretensions to the presentation of benefices in England, an injurious practice, against which several statutes had been past. The negotiation lasted nearly two years; and it is probable that what he then had opportunities of discovering, convinced him that the system of the Papal Court and its doctrines were equally corrupt. For, on his return, he attacked it in the boldest manner, maintained that the Scriptures contained all truths necessary to salvation, and that the perfect rule of Christian practice was to be found in them only; denied the authority of the Pope in temporal matters; proclaimed that he was that Man of Sin, the Son of Perdition, whom St. Paul prophetically describes, "sitting as God in the temple of God, shewing himself that he is God," and denounced him as Antichrist. These opinions he openly preached and published, appealing to the Scriptures for their proof; and they were propagated by his disciples, who attacked the Friars in their own manner, preaching to the people, and going about, as he himself did, barefoot, and in plain frieze gowns. It was not long before he was accused of heresy, and orders came to Sudbury the Primate, and Courtney the Bishop of London, to have him arrested, and kept in close custody till they should receive further instructions. But the Duke of Lancaster, John of Gaunt, who was then governing the kingdom during the latter days of his father, protected him with a high hand; and he was still so popular in Oxford, that when a Nuncio was sent thither, requiring the University, under pain of the severest penalties, to deliver him up for justice, the threats were disregarded. The Archbishop, finding it impossible to proceed in the summary manner which the Pope ordered, summoned him to appear within thirty days before him and the Bishop of London, at a Synod held in St. Paul's; and Wicliffe, confident in his cause and in his protectors, hesitated not to obey. During the interval between the citation and appearance, a circumstance occurred which contributed alike to incense the Prelates against him, and to strengthen his interest with the Government. Richard II. had just succeeded to his grandfather's throne, and in his first Parliament the question was debated, whether, the kingdom being then threatened with an invasion from France, they might not for their own defence detain the treasure due to the Pope, although he required it on pain of ecclesiastical censures. Opinions differing upon this question, it was referred to Wicliffe for decision; . . . less, it may be presumed, for his celebrity as a casuist, than because the ruling party knew in what manner he would decide. His answer was, that, both by the law of the nation and of the Gospel, it might be withheld when self-preservation required it. The Pope could only claim it as alms; but charity begins at home, and it would be madness, not charity, to send that money out of the realm, which was wanted for its defence.

On the day appointed, Wicliffe appeared before the Synod, with four Bachelors of Divinity, one from each of the Mendicant Orders, to assist him,...thus shewing, that even among the Friars themselves, he had found disciples and coadjutors; and with John of Gaunt, and Lord Percy the Earl Marshal, as his friends and protectors. With whatever intent these powerful Barons accompanied him, their conduct was such as discredited the cause. Before the proceedings could begin, they engaged in an angry altercation with Bishop Courtney, who appears to have preserved both his temper and his dignity, when Lancaster had lost all sense of both. Here, however, the feeling of the people was against Wicliffe, probably because he was supported by an unpopular Government; and when the citizens who were present heard Lancaster mutter a threat of dragging their Bishop out of the Church by the hair of his head, they took fire; a tumult ensued; the Synod was broken up, and the Barons were glad to effect their escape as they could. In consequence of this disturbance, an imprudent bill was brought forward the same day in Parliament, by Lord Percy, that London should be governed by a Captain, as in former times, instead of a Mayor, and that the sole power of making arrests within the city should be vested in the Earl Marshal. The member for the city, John Philpot, manfully opposed this attempt upon the liberties of London: a riot ensued the next day;

Lancaster and the Earl Marshal escaped up the river to Kingston; and the mob, to shew their detestation of the Duke, hung his escutcheon upon gibbets in the open places of the city, as if he had been a convicted traitor. By the interference of the Court, and of the Bishops, who, notwithstanding the occasion of these troubles, supported the cause of Government as that of order, with the whole strength of their authority, the Duke and the City were reconciled; one of the conditions being that, in atonement, probably, for the death of a Priest in his service, whom they had murdered in their fury, the citizens should maintain a great wax taper marked with the Duke's arms, to burn continually before the image of our Lady in St. Paul's.

These tumults having been appeased, Wicliffe was cited to appear before the same Prelates, at Lambeth. He obeyed; and delivered in a written explanation of the points upon which the charges of heresy against him were founded. The strength of his defence would have availed him little, if Sir Lewis Clifford had not suddenly entered with authoritative orders, forbidding them to proceed to sentence. It is not, however, likely that any protection could long have upheld him against the ecclesiastical authority, if a schism had not at this juncture occurred to weaken the

Papal power, and shake its very foundations. Wicliffe seized the advantage which was thus offered him, and set forth a tract upon the schism, exposing the absurdity of ascribing Infallibility to a divided Church. He published, also, a treatise upon the Truth of Scripture; and that his countrymen might be enabled to try his doctrines by that test, he translated both the Old and New Testament into the English tongue. There were several partial versions in the Anglo-Saxon language, but these had long become obsolete; and the portions of Scripture*, which had previously been rendered into English, were in few hands.

It is related of him, that before he had completed this most important undertaking, he fell dangerously ill at Oxford, and some of the Friars,

* I cannot but consider Sir Thomas More's authority as decisive upon this subject: his words are,—"Myself have sene and can shew you Bybles fayre and old, wryten in Englyshe, whych have ben knowen and sene by the Byshop of the dyocyse, and left in ley mennys handys and womens, to suche as he knew for good and catholyke folke, that used it with devocyon and sobernesse." (*Dialoge*, book iii. ch. 15.) He had previously said, that these translations "were allredy well done of olde, before Wyclyffys days." Lewis has endeavoured to disprove this;—but I do not think any reasoning can possibly outweigh the positive affirmation of such a man as Sir Thomas More, upon a matter of fact, on which he could not be mistaken. His words may imply that there existed a complete translation; but are not necessarily to be taken in that extent.

hoping that the prospect of death might bring with it fear of ecclesiastical censures, waited upon him to require that he would revoke what he had taught against the Mendicant Orders. Having listened to them patiently, he desired his attendant to raise him on his pillow, and then looking at them sternly, replied, "I shall not die, but live still further to declare the evil deeds of the Friars!" When he attacked them, he had the Secular Clergy and the better class of the Regulars in his favour: and when he opposed the Papal authority, he acted in unison with the wishes of the Government and the spirit of the country. But he now proceeded to impugn the doctrine of Transubstantiation, shewing what absurdities and contradictions it involved, . . . and then all favour failed him: for the people implicitly believed this doctrine, the Clergy rested their loftiest pretensions upon it, and the Government had no inclination to interfere in points of pure theology. When Wicliffe published his "Conclusions" upon this subject, and offered to defend them in the schools, the University forbade any of its members to hold or defend such doctrines, on pain of imprisonment. He appealed, consistently with his principles, to the King in Parliament; but his appeal was rejected. His patron, Lancaster, admonished him to submit, in these matters, to his ecclesiastical superiors: and he was summoned before an ecclesiastical court at Oxford, to explain his doctrine. A retractation was expected. On this occasion his consummate skill in the language of the schools, appears to have saved him both from the consequences of avowing his opinions, and the dishonour of denying them. The doctrine which he held, is that which the Church of England afterwards adopted; and by declaring his full belief of the real presence in the Sacrament, while he kept clear of all attempt at explaining the inscrutable manner of that presence, he so far satisfied the court, that he was dismissed without censure; and yet so fairly preserved his consistency, that his confession was declared by his enemies to be, not a recantation of his heresy, but a vindication of it.

But even upon the point of transubstantiation his opinions gained ground; for his translation of the Bible was now eagerly read by all who could obtain it, and it was perceived that his doctrine bore the test. His proselytes became very numerous; and obtained the name of Lollards, which had been given, in the Low Countries, to the persecuted Franciscans and other enthusiasts, from their practice of singing hymns, . . . *lollen* or *lullen*, in one of the old German dialects, signifying to sing, as a mother when she lulls her babe. Upon the death of Sudbury, who was murdered by the rabble in Wat Tyler's insurrection, Courtney succeeded to the primacy; he was a man of ability and decision, and lost no time in citing Wicliffe before him. Wicliffe refused to appear, pleading that, by his office in the university, he was exempted from episcopal jurisdiction. Articles, however, were preferred against him, as drawn from his writings, some being fair statements of the opinions which he taught, and others gross and malicious distortions of his meaning. Just as the assembly began their deliberations, the monastery in which they met was shaken by an earthquake; they interpreted it as a mark of divine displeasure, probably because many, who were there to sit in judgement upon Wicliffe, were secretly conscious that his cause was good,... and in that fear they would have fain broken up the meeting, if Courtney had not, with great presence of mind, given the earthquake a different interpretation;... if it portended any thing, he said, it was the purging of the kingdom from heresies; for as the air and noxious spirits in the bowels of the earth were expelled by this convulsion, so was the kingdom, not without commotion, to be cleared of noxious opinions, which were in the hearts of reprobate men. The Synod, therefore, proceeded with their business; and the propositions, such as they appeared by the accuser's statement, when there was no one to explain or defend them, were censured, some as erroneous, and others condemned as heretical.

The sentence was published at Oxford; but its effect there was invalidated, by the spirit with which Wicliffe vindicated himself, and exposed the malice or the ignorance with which his opinions had been misrepresented. Courtney then brought a Bill into Parliament, for imprisoning all persons who should preach heresies and notorious errors; and, as soon as the Bill had passed the Lords, he acted upon it; upon which the House of Commons, which had now become an efficient part of the Constitution, petitioned that it should be annulled, as not having had their consent. Baffled by his own precipitance in this measure, Courtney obtained letters from the King to the Chancellor of Oxford, requiring him to banish Wicliffe from the university, and seize all writings in which his doctrines were maintained. The Chancellor represented that the peace of the university and his own life would be in danger were he to obey;...in fact, the partisans of the new doctrines were bold as well as numerous, and carried arms under their gowns, to make their cause good if they were offended. This temper, which fatally accompanied the Reformation, Wicliffe discouraged; and when Courtney insisted with the Chancellor upon obedience, he withdrew to his living of Lutterworth, where the Primate left him unmolested, for the fiery days of persecution had not yet commenced in England. Our great reformer, undaunted in his retirement, and faithful to the last, still wielded the pen; and when Urban VI. endeavoured to raise men and money here for a crusade against the rival Pope, he wrote against the wickedness of exciting war in Christendom, upon a dispute between two false priests, insisting that the Pope was plainly Antichrist. Urban summoned him for this to Rome; he replied, that an attack of palsy rendered him incapable of performing the journey. A second attack, which seized him in his church, proved fatal, when he was about sixty years of age. It is a reproach to this country that no statue has been erected in his honour, . . . and that his translation of the Old Testament should never have been printed.

Wicliffe held some erroneous opinions, some fantastic ones, and some which, in their moral and political consequences, are most dangerous. Considering the intrepidity and ardour of his mind, it is surprising that his errors were not more and greater. A great and admirable man he was; his fame, high as it is, is not above his deserts; and it suffers no abatement upon comparison with the most illustrious of those who have followed in the path which he opened. His writings were carried into Bohemia by one of the natives of that country, whom the marriage of their Princess with Richard II. brought into England. From the perusal of them, John Huss imbibed those opinions concerning the Papal Church, for which he suffered heroically at the stake, to his own eternal honour, and to the perpetual infamy of the Council which condemned him, and of the Emperor, who suffered the safe conduct which he had given him to be broken: and Huss prepared the way for Luther.

This wife of Richard's, whose memory was so dear to the people, that, long after her death, she was called the good Queen Anne, protected the followers of Wicliffe while she lived, and was herself a diligent reader of the Scriptures in the English tongue; there can be little doubt, therefore, that it was in Wicliffe's translation. She was particularly commended for this by Archbishop Arundel, the successor of Courtney in the primacy, when he preached her funeral sermon. But the prelate, who thus commended her, is branded in history as a persecutor and a traitor; becoming a traitor, and taking an active part in deposing Richard, that he might no longer be withheld from persecuting a sect, whose numbers were now formidable. It was by the aid of the Clergy that Henry IV. succeeded in usurping the throne, this being the only instance in English history, wherein their conduct as a body was disloyal. To prove himself as sincere in their cause, as they had been in his, and as little restrained by humanity or justice in supporting it, he passed a statute whereby all persons, who propagated the new doctrine by preaching, writing, teaching, or discourse, were required to renounce their heresies, and deliver in all their heretical books, and submit themselves to the Church, on pain of being delivered over to the secular arm, and burnt alive.

Undoubtedly the Lollards were highly dangerous at this time ; if there were some among them whose views and wishes did not go beyond a just and salutary reformation, the greater number were eager for havoc, and held opinions which are incompatible with the peace of society. They would have stript the churches, destroyed the monasteries, confiscated the church lands, and proclaimed the principle that the Saints should possess the earth. The public safety required that such opinions should be repressed ; and, founded as they were in gross error, and leading to direct and enormous evil, the Church would have deserved the approbation of impartial posterity, if it had proceeded temperately and justly in repressing them. But the course which the Clergy pursued was equally impolitic and iniquitous; by making transubstantiation the test of heresy, and insisting, on pain of the stake, upon the belief of a proposition which no man could believe, unless he disregarded the evidence of his senses, they gave the Lollards all the advantage which men derive from the reputation and the merit of suffering in defence of the truth.

William Sautre, the parish priest of St. Osithes, in London, and formerly of St. Margaret's, at Lynn in Norfolk, was the first victim under the new statute, and the first martyr for the Reformation in England. He had been questioned for his opinions by the Bishop of Norwich, and, under the fear of death, had formally abjured them. "Let those," says the excellent Fuller, "who severely censure him for *once* denying the truth, and do know who it was that denied his Master *thrice*, take heed they do not as bad a deed more than four times themselves. May Sautre's final constancy be as surely practised by men, as his former cowardliness, no doubt, is pardoned by God." On his removal to London, he petitioned Parliament that he might be heard before them for the commodity of the whole realm; . . . an act to which he must have been induced less by the hope of effecting any public good, than by the desire of recovering his own peace of mind. In consequence of this, he was convented before Archbishop Arundel, in the convocation, and charged with affirming that he would not worship the Cross on which Christ suffered, but only Christ who suffered on the Cross; . . . that if any man had vowed to make a distant pilgrimage, he would do better to disburse the expense of such a journey in alms, than to perform it; that it was more the duty of the Clergy to preach the word of God, than to say the canonical hours; and, finally, that the sacramental bread continued to be bread after it was consecrated. He desired time to answer the charges, and on the sixth day delivered in a scroll, explicitly declaring that these were the opinions which he held. Being then asked, if he had not formally abjured such opinions the preceding year? he is said to have denied it. The imperfect record of these proceedings has left this denial unexplained; it may have been that sort of denial, which a court of justice requires as preliminary to a trial; this, however, is certain, that it would not be less preposterous than unjust, did we impute falsehood to one who was about to give the last extreme proof of sincerity, and was actually at that time presenting himself for martyrdom. The single question with which he was prest was, whether the Sacrament of the altar, after the pronouncing of the sacramental words, remained material bread or not? It was not sufficient for him to declare a firm belief that it was the bread of life which came down from Heaven; he was required to acknowledge, that it ceased to be bread. "Thus," in the words of Fuller, "their cruelty made God's table a snare to his servants; when their other nets broke, this held; what they pretended a sacrifice for the living and the dead, proved indeed the cause of the sacrificing of many innocents; and cavils about the corporal presence, was the most compendious way to despatch them." Finding it vain to protest that he attempted not to explain what is inexplicable, his final answer was, that the bread, after consecration, remained very bread as it was before. He was then pronounced to be judicially and lawfully convicted as an heretic, and as an heretic to be punished; and being moreover a relapsed heretic, to be degraded, deposed, and delivered over to the secular arm.

This being the first condemnation of the kind in England, Arundel was punctual in all its forms, that they might serve for an exact precedent in future. They were probably derived from the practice of the accursed Inquisitors in Languedoc; and they were well devised for prolonging an impression of horror upon the expectant and awed spectators. Sautre was brought before the Primate and six other Bishops in the cathedral of St. Paul's; they were in their pontifical attire, and he appeared in priestly vestments, with the paten and chalice in his hands. Arundel stood up, and, in the name of the Father, and of the Son, and of the Holy Spirit, (thus profaned in this inhuman process,) degraded him, first from his priestly order, and, in sign of that degradation, took from him the paten and chalice, and plucked the priestly casule from his back. The New Testament was then put into his hands, and taken from him; the stole being at the same time pulled off, to degrade him from the office of deacon. By depriving him of the alb and maniple, his deprivation from the order of sub-deacon was effected. The candlestick, taper, and urceole were taken from him as acolyte; the book of exorcisms as exorcist; the lectionary as reader: he then remained in a surplice as sexton, and with the key of the church-door; these also were taken from him: the priest's cap was then to be laid aside, the tonsure rased away, so that no outward mark whatever of his orders might remain; the cap of a layman was placed upon his head, and Arundel then delivered him, as a secular person, to the secular court of the High-Constable and Marshal of England there present, beseeching the court to receive favourably the said William Sautre, unto them thus recommitted! For with this hypocritical recommendation to mercy the Romish Church always delivered over its victims to be burnt alive! Sautre accordingly suffered martyrdom at the stake; leaving a name which is still slandered by the Romanists, but which the Church of England will ever hold in deserved respect.

The second victim upon whom Arundel laid his hands, was a priest of great ability and firmness, William Thorpe by name. The same searching question was put to him, concerning the material bread in the Sacrament. "Sir," he replied, "I know no place in Holy Scripture where this term, material bread, is written, and therefore, when I speak of this matter, I use not to speak of material bread." How then did he teach men to believe in this Sacrament? "Sir," he replied, "as I believe myself, so I teach other men." And being required to tell out plainly his belief, he answered in these impressive words:—"Sir, I believe that the night before that Christ Jesu would suffer for mankind, he took bread in his holy and most worshipful hands, and, lifting up his eyes, and giving thanks to God his Father, blessed the bread, and brake it, and gave it to his disciples, saying to them, Take and eat of this, all you, this is my body. And that this is and ought to be all men's belief, Matthew, Mark, Luke, and Paul witnesseth. Other belief, Sir, I have none, nor will have, nor teach; for I believe that this sufficeth in this matter. For in this belief, with God's grace, I purpose to live and die, knowledging, as I believe and teach other men, that the worshipful Sacrament of the altar, is the Sacrament of Christ's flesh and his blood, in form of bread and wine." This, he said, had been accepted by the Church for a thousand years, as sufficient for salvation, till the Friar Thomas Aquinas introduced the term of an accident without subject,—"which term," said he, "since I know not that God's law approveth it in this matter, I dare not grant: but utterly I deny to make this Friar's sentence, or any such other, my belief. Do with me, God, what thou wilt!"

It is not related that Thorpe suffered; had he saved his life by recantation, it would not have been concealed; and, unless he had recanted, it is certain that no mercy would have been shown; probably, therefore, he died in prison. The second victim who was brought to the stake, was a tailor, from the diocese of Gloucester, by name John Badby. Prince Henry (afterwards Henry V.) was present at his execution, and urged him to save his life by submitting to the opinion of the Church. The pix was then brought forth by the Prior of St. Bartholomew's, twelve tapers being carried before it: it was presented to Badby as he stood in an empty tub, chained to the stake, with faggots piled around him,. . .and he was asked how he believed in it? He answered, that it was hallowed bread, and not God's body; and upon that the pile was set on fire. His cry for mercy, whether it were addressed to God or man, touched the Prince with such compassion, that he ordered the fire to be quenched, and the sufferer to be taken down; and in that condition he offered him his life, if he would renounce his opinions, and a daily allowance from the treasury for his support. This poor man might well have gone through the world without troubling his conscience upon such subjects: but he had come to a point at which he rightly felt that insincerity was too dear a price to pay for life . . . and maintaining constantly his rejection of a tenet, which was now become as hateful as it was preposterous, he was replaced in the tub, and there, calling upon Christ to receive his soul, expired a martyr.

The statute upon which these inhuman executions were made, required that the heretics should be burnt "in an high place before the people, to the end that such punishment might strike-in fear to the minds of others." To give farther efficacy to this bloody statute, Arundel set forth several provincial constitutions, whereby any persons preaching doctrines contrary to the determination of the Church, or calling in question what the Church had determined, were to be excommunicated *ipso facto* on the first offence, and declared heretics for the second. Whoever read the books of Wicliffe or his disciples, without a license from one of the universities, was to suffer as a promoter of heresy. The greater excommunication was to be incurred by advancing propositions, even in the schools, which tended to subvert the Catholic faith. It was declared heresy to dispute the utility of pilgrimages, or the adoration of images and of the Cross. Because Oxford was greatly infected with Lollardy, the heads of every college were enjoined, on pain of excommunication and deprivation themselves, to inquire every month whether any scholars maintained doctrines against the determination of the Church; and if any such were found who remained obstinate, forthwith to expel them. The proceedings against offenders in this case, were to be as summary as in cases of treason. And because it was difficult to retain the true sense of Scripture in translations, whoever should translate it, or read such translations, particularly Wicliffes, without the approbation of his ordinary, or of a provincial council, was to be punished as a promoter of heresy.

Twelve inquisitors of heresy,. . .for this dreadful name had been introduced among us ! were appointed at Oxford, to search out heretics and heretical books. They presented, as heresies, two hundred and forty-six conclusions, deduced, some truly and some falsely, from the writings of Wicliffe's followers and of the Lollards ; and they represented that Christ's vesture without seam could not be made whole again, unless certain great men, who supported the disciples of Wicliffe, were removed; particularizing Sir John Oldcastle, who, in right of his wife, was Lord Cobham, a man of high birth, and at that time in favour with Henry V. Him they accused to the King of holding heretical opinions concerning the Sacrament, penance, pilgrimages, the adoration of images, and the authority of the Romish Church, declaring their intention of proceeding against him as a most pernicious heretic. Henry V. was of a noble, but immitigable nature. He knew and admired the noble qualities of Lord Cobham, and requested the prelates that, if it were possible, they would reduce him to obey the Church, without rigour or extreme handling, saying, that if they would defer their proceedings, he would commune the matter with him seriously.

It happened, on that very day, that a pile of heretical books was burnt at St. Paul's Cross,... Arundel preaching to the people, and stating why they were thus destroyed. Among these was a volume belonging to Lord Cobham, which had been seized at a limner's in Paternoster-row, whither it had been sent to be illuminated. Certain extracts from this volume were laid before the King; he declared that they were the most perilous and pestilent that he had ever heard; and demanded of Lord Cobham, whether the volume had not justly been condemned? Cobham owned that it had; and being asked why then he had kept and perused such a book? replied, that he had never read in it more than two or three leaves. That the book might have contained propositions which he condemned, though he approved of its general tendency, is a probability which every man may understand; and that Lord Cobham was not one who would seek to shelter himself by a paltry subterfuge, is proved, not only by his final but by his immediate conduct. For when Henry admonished him, that as an obedient child he should acknowledge himself culpable, and submit to his mother, the Holy Church; the Christian knight made this magnanimous answer: "You, most worthy Prince, I am always prompt and willing to obey; unto you (next my eternal God) owe I my whole obedience; and submit thereunto (as I have ever done) all that I have either of fortune or nature, ready at all times to fulfil whatsoever ye shall in the Lord command me. But as touching the Pope and his spiritualty, I owe them neither suit nor service; for so much as I know him by the Scriptures to be the great Antichrist, the son of perdition, the open adversary of God, and the abomination standing in the holy place." Upon this the King turned angrily away, and authorized Arundel to proceed against him to the uttermost.

Lord Cobham, perhaps, relied at this time upon his popularity and his strength. He retired to Cowling Castle in Kent, which was his favourite place of residence; and though the age was past in which a Baron could, from his strong hold, defy with impunity the royal power, the sumner, who was sent to cite him before the ecclesiastical authorities, was afraid to perform his errand. Upon this the Archbishop introduced his sumner under the protection of a person in the King's service, who informed Cobham it was the King's pleasure that he should obey the citation. But he, who knew his life was aimed at, and for no offence, except that of disbelieving a gross and palpable superstition, replied that he would not consent to these devilish practices of the priests. His feelings were those of a powerful Baron in turbulent times; he thought himself strong in the attachment of his vassals and of the surrounding country; and the system of persecution which had been introduced with the Lancasterian dynasty, he regarded as a new and intolerable tyranny, which it behoved him to resist. It was soon represented, and probably understood, that any person who should attempt to cite him personally, would be in danger of death. Letters citatory were therefore twice affixed upon the great gates of Rochester Cathedral, and they were twice taken down and destroyed. But the ecclesiastical power was too strong to be thus baffled. Arundel excommunicated him, cited him afresh, with a threat, that if the summons were not obeyed, he would proceed to extremities,. . .and called upon the secular power, on pain of the Church's censures, to assist him against this seditious apostate, schismatic, and heretic, the troubler of the public peace, enemy of the realm, and great adversary of all holy Church.

These measures, if he had persisted in his

course, must soon have involved him in a hopeless struggle with the King's power. In better reliance, therefore, upon a good cause, than upon popular favour and his own means of resistance, he wrote a paper, which he entitled, "The Christian Belief of the Lord Cobham;" and with this he went to the King, trusting, it is said, to find mercy and favour at his hand. The writing began with the Apostles' Creed, to which a larger declaration of his faith was added. Like Wicliffe, he expressed an opinion that the Church was divided into three parts, the Saints in Heaven, the Souls in Purgatory, and the Faithful on Earth: but he qualified this admission of a Purgatory, by saying, if any such place be in the Scriptures. The latter, or Church Militant, he said, was divided, by the just ordinance of God, into the three estates, of Priesthood, Knighthood, and the Commons, who, by the will of God, ought to aid, and not to destroy, each other. The duty of the Priests was that, secluded from all worldliness, they should conform their lives to the examples of Christ and his Apostles, evermore occupied in preaching and teaching the Scriptures purely, and in giving wholesome examples of good living to the other two degrees; more modest also, more loving, gentle and lowly in spirit should they be, than any other people. The Knighthood, under which term he comprised all who bear sword by law of office, ought to defend God's laws, and see that the Gospel were purely taught; yea, rather to hazard their lives, than suffer such wicked decrees, as either blemish the eternal Testament of God, or impede its free passage, and thus give rise to heresies and schisms; for from no other source did they, in his judgment, arise, than from "erroneous constitutions, craftily first creeping in under hypocritical lies, for advantage. They ought also to preserve God's people from oppressors, tyrants, and thieves; and to see the Clergy supported, so long as they teach purely, pray rightly, and minister the sacraments freely. And if they see them do otherwise, they are bound by the law of office to compel them to change their doings." The duty of the common people was, "to bear their good minds and true obedience to the foresaid ministers of God, their Kings, civil governors, and priests;"... justly to occupy every man his faculty, be it merchandise, handicraft, or the tilth of the ground, and so one to be helper to another. He then professed his full belief that the body and blood of Christ were verily and indeed contained in the Sacrament of the altar, under the similitudes of bread and wine; that the law of God was most true and perfect; and that they which did not so follow it in their faith and works (at one time or another) could not be saved: "whereas he that seeketh it in faith, accepteth it, learneth it, delighteth therein, and performeth it in love, shall taste for it the felicity of everlasting innocency. Finally, that God will ask no more of a Christian believer, in this life, than to obey the precepts of this most blessed law. If any prelate require more, or any other kind of obedience than this, he contemneth Christ, exalting himself above God, and so becometh an open Antichrist." He required that the King would cause this his confession of faith to be justly examined by the wisest and most learned men of the realm; that if it were found in all points agreeing to the truth, it might be so allowed, and he himself thereupon holden for none other than a true Christian; or that it might be utterly condemned, if it were found otherwise, provided always that he were taught a better belief by the word of God, which word he would at all times most reverently obey.

The Edwards would have rejoiced in so high-minded and honourable a subject as Lord Cobham was proved to be by this manly declaration of his views and sentiments. But Henry V. had delivered his heart and understanding into the keeping of the Prelates, and he refused to receive the paper, ordering it to be delivered to those who were to be his judges. Cobham then desired that he might acquit himself, according to the old principle of law, from all heresies, by the oath of an hundred knights and squires, who would appear in his behalf. But the new ecclesiastical law superseded all feudal forms, as it violated all principles of justice. This, therefore, was disregarded, as was his appeal to the laws, when, in perfect accordance with the feelings of his rank and the spirit of the times, he offered to fight for life or death, with any man living, Christian or Heathen, in this quarrel of his faith, the King and the Lords of his Council alone excepted. Finally, he declared, that he would refuse no correction which should be ministered to him after the laws of God, but alway with all meekness obey it. But when the King allowed him there in his presence to be personally cited, Lord Cobham perceived that his destruction was determined on, and rejecting the Archbishop as his judge, appealed from him to the Pope. It has been seen in what light he regarded the Pope; and this appeal must have been made for the purpose of gaining time. It was disallowed, and he was immediately committed to the Tower, till the day appointed for his examination.

All hope having thus failed him, it remained only to assert the truth, like one who was about to bear witness to it in the flames. He passed the interval of his confinement in preparing accordingly. When he was brought before the Consistory, in the Chapter-House of St. Paul's, Arundel addressed him, saying, that in the last general Convocation he had, by sufficient proof, been found culpable of certain heresies, and being cited, had, for his rebellious contumacy in not appearing, been both privately and openly excommunicated. Nevertheless, he might then have obtained absolution, and even now it would not be refused, if he would meekly ask it. Without replying to this, Lord Cobham drew a writing from his bosom, and saying, that he would gladly before that assembly make rehearsal of the faith which he held, and intended always to stand to, desired leave to read it. It contained his profession upon the four points which were chiefly objected to him. As to the Sacrament, he declared his belief in a real presence in the form of bread. Concerning penance, that it was needful for every man who would be saved, to forsake sin, and do due penance for sins which he had committed, with true confession, very contrition, and due satisfaction, as God's law teacheth. Touching images, he held, that they were allowed by the Church, as kalendars for unlearned men, who might thus be reminded of the passion of our Lord, and the martyrdom and holy lives of the Saints; but whosoever did to them that worship which is due to God, or put such trust in their help, as he should do in God, or had affection in one more than in another, he committed the sin of idolatry. And for pilgrimages, it was his belief, that they who did not keep the commandments in their lives, would not be saved by pilgrimages; and they who did, would be saved without them. He then delivered in the writing.

They bade him stand aside while they consulted together. Presently, Arundel called to him, "Come hither, Sir John. In this your writing are many good things contained, and right catholic also; we deny it not. But there are other points concerning those articles, whereof no mention is made in this your bill; and therefore ye must declare your mind yet more plainly." He pressed him then with the question, whether material bread remained after consecration; and whether every Christian was not bound to make confession to a Priest. Cobham answered, that he would declare his mind no otherwise than was already expressed in that writing. "Sir John," said Arundel, "beware what you do! For if you answer not clearly to these things, (especially at the time appointed you only for that purpose,) the law of holy Church is, that compelled once by a judge, we may openly proclaim you a heretic." He answered, "Do as ye think best, for I am at a point!" And to all further question, he only replied by bidding them resort to his bill, for thereby he would stand to the very death. The business of this wicked day ended in remanding him to the Tower till the ensuing Monday, (this being Saturday,) and promising to send him these matters in writing clearly determined, that he might be prepared to answer upon them.

The writing which they sent him, declared it to be the faith and determination of the Church, that neither material bread, nor material wine, remained after the sacramental words were spoken; that every Christian man ought to be shriven to a priest; that Christ ordained St. Peter to be his vicar on earth, and granted the same power, which he had given him, to the Popes of Rome as his successors, wherefore all Christians ought to obey their laws; and that it was meritorious to go on pilgrimage to holy places, and more especially to worship holy relics and images of saints approved by the Church of Rome: and to each of these points the question was added, How feel ye this article?—On the Monday, he was again brought up, but to a different place, and before a larger assembly. At the former examination, the Bishops of London and Winchester, and the Lieutenant of the Tower, were the only persons present. Here, at the Dominican Convent, within Ludgate, many Canonists and Friars, the heads and leading persons of their respective orders, were convened to sit in judgement on him; while a number of Priests, Monks, Canons, and Friars, with a rabble of underlings, who were collected as spectators, insulted him as he came, for a horrible heretic, and a man accursed before God. Two Notaries were there to record the proceedings, and the Archbishop caused them, and all the Prelates and Doctors present, to be sworn, that they would do their duty faithfully that day; and, neither for favour or fear, love or hate, register any thing which should that day be spoken or done, but according to the truth, as they would answer before God and all the world at the day of doom.

These preparations, and the certainty of what was to ensue, could not shake the constancy of his resolved mind. But the taunts and mockery of the brutal audience, who came there as to a spectacle, and anticipated with exultation the inhuman catastrophe, disturbed that equanimity which he had hitherto preserved; and moved him, ... not to an unseemly anger, nor to aught unworthy of himself, ... but to an emotion, than which nothing nobler in its kind hath been imagined in fiction, or recorded in history. For when Arundel began the tragedy, by offering him absolution and mercy, if he would humbly desire it, in due form and manner, as the Church ordained—“ Nay, forsooth, will I not,” he replied, “ for I never yet trespassed against you, and therefore I will not do it!” Then, kneeling on the pavement, and holding up his hands toward Heaven, he exclaimed, “ I shrive me here unto Thee, my eternal, living God, that in my youth I offended thee, O Lord, most grievously in pride, wrath, and gluttony; in covetousness and in lechery! Many men have I hurt in mine anger, and done many other horrible sins! Good Lord, I ask Thee mercy!” He wept while he uttered this passionate prayer: then, standing up, said, with a mighty voice, “ Lo, good people, lo! for the breaking of God's law and his commandments they never yet cursed me! But for their own laws and traditions, most cruelly do they handle both me and other men. And, therefore, both they and their laws, by the promise of God, shall utterly be destroyed!”

When they had recovered from the surprise

which this awful appeal produced, they began to examine him concerning his belief. He replied, with the same intrepid spirit, "I believe fully and faithfully in the universal laws of God. I believe that all is true which is contained in the holy sacred Scriptures of the Bible. Finally, I believe all that my Lord God would I should believe." Such faith was not sufficient, under the Papal tyranny, to save him who professed it from the flames. They pressed him with the murderous question concerning material bread. He made answer, "The Scriptures make no mention of this word material, and therefore my faith hath nothing to do therewith. But this I say and believe, that it is Christ's body, and bread." They exclaimed against this with one voice; and one of the Bishops stood up and said, "it was a heresy manifest, to say that it is bread after the Sacramental words were spoken." The noble martyr replied, "St. Paul was (I am sure) as wise as you, and more godly learned, and he called it bread: 'the bread that we break,' saith he, 'is it not the partaking of the body of Christ?'" The Archbishop then spake of the writing which had been sent him, containing what upon that point had been clearly determined by the Church of Rome and the holy Doctors. Lord Cobham replied, "I know none holier than Christ and his Apostles; and as for that determination, it is none of theirs; for it standeth not with the Scriptures, but manifestly against them. If it be the Church's, it hath been her's only since she received the great poison of worldly possessions." He had now become the assailant, and the proceedings resembled a dispute in the schools, rather than the forms of judicial inquiry. "In your lordly laws and idle determinations," said he, "have I no belief! For ye be no part of Christ's holy Church, as your open deeds do shew: but ye are very Antichrists, openly set against his holy law and will. The laws that ye have made are nothing to his glory, but only for your vain-glory and abominable covetousness."

Upon this, the Prior of the Carmelites reproved him for judging his superiors. "Rash judgement," said he, "and right judgement all is one with you. So swift judges always are the learned scholars of Wicliffe!" Lord Cobham replied, "It is well sophistered of you, forsooth! Preposterous are your judgements evermore. For, as the prophet Esay saith, ye judge evil good, and good evil; and therefore the same prophet concludeth that, 'your ways are not God's ways, nor God's ways your ways.' And as for that virtuous man, Wicliffe, I shall say here, both before

God and man, that before I knew that despised doctrine of his, I never abstained from sin. But since I learned therein to fear my Lord God, it hath otherwise, I trust, been with me. So much grace could I never find in all your glorious instructions!" To this the Carmelite answered, "It were not well with me if I had no grace to amend my life, till I heard the Devil preach. St. Hierome saith, 'That he which seeketh such suspected masters, shall not find the mid-day light, but the mid-day Devil!'" "Your fathers, the old Pharisees," returned Lord Cobham, "ascribed Christ's miracles to Beelzebub, and his doctrines to the Devil; and you, as their natural children, have still the self-same judgement concerning his faithful followers. To judge you as you be, we need no farther go than to your own proper acts. Where do ye find in all God's law, that ye should thus sit in judgement of any Christian man, or yet give sentence upon any other man to death, as ye do here daily? No ground have ye in all the Scriptures, so lordly to take it upon you, but in Annas and Caiaphas, which sate thus upon Christ, and upon his Apostles, after his ascension!"

A lawyer upon this observed to him, that Christ judged Judas. But Cobham, who was better versed in Scripture, replied, "That Judas judged himself. Indeed," he pursued, "Christ said, 'woe unto him for that covetous act of his,' as he doth yet unto many of you; for since his venom was shed into the Church, ye never followed Christ." Arundel demanded what he meant by that venom? "Your possessions and lordship," replied Lord Cobham; "for then cried an angel in the air, as your own chronicles mention, 'Woe, woe, woe! this day is venom shed into the Church of God!' Since that time, one Pope hath put down another, one hath poisoned another, one hath cursed another, and one hath slain another, and done much more mischief, as all the chronicles tell. Let all men consider well this, that Christ was meek and merciful; the Pope is proud, and a tyrant: Christ was poor, and forgave; the Pope is rich, and a malicious manslayer, as his daily acts do prove him. Rome is the very nest of Antichrist, and out of that nest cometh all the disciples of him, of whom Prelates, Priests, and Monks are the body, and these piled Friars are the tail!" "Alas, Sir," said the Prior of the Augustines, "why do you say so? that is uncharitably spoken!" These are the only words of this Prior which are reported in the proceedings, and they imply no uncharitable temper in the speaker; one, perhaps, who would gladly have washed his hands of the innocent blood. But the martyr, who saw him only as he was, prepared to go through with the murderous business in which he was engaged, replied, "Not only is it my saying, but also the prophet Esay's, long before my time; 'the prophet,' saith he, 'which preacheth lies, is the tail behind.'"

Master as he was of the subject, strong in his cause, sure of the issue, and therefore fearless of it, and armed with Scripture, the Court felt his superiority; and one of the Canonists, that they might come without further delay to the condemnation, took from his bosom a copy of the writing which had been sent him, and interrogated him upon the four points; to all of which he replied openly and resolutely. When he denied that worship was due to images, a Friar asked him, if he would worship the Cross upon which Christ died? "Where is it?" said Lord Cobham. The Friar replied, "I put the case that it were here even now before you?" "This is a great wise man," said Lord Cobham, "to put me an earnest question of a thing, yet he himself knoweth not where the thing is. I ask you, what worship I should do unto it?" An ignorant clerk answered, "Such worship as Paul speaketh of, and that is this; 'God forbid that I should joy, but only in the Cross of Christ Jesus.'" Lord Cobham spread forth his arms, and said, "This is a very cross;

yea, and so much better than your cross of wood, in that it was created of God; yet will I not seek to have it worshipped!" (It was a favourite remark with the Reformers, when they argued against the Crucifix, that there was no other true image of God, but man, who in that image had been created.) The Bishop of London upon this observed, "Sir, ye wote well that he died on a material cross!" "Yea," answered Lord Cobham, "and I wote also, that our salvation came not in by that material cross, but by him which died thereupon!"

The Archbishop now thought proper to close an argument, in which the accused person had so palpably the advantage of his judges and accusers. "Sir John," said he, "ye have spoken here many wonderful words to the slanderous rebuke of the whole spiritualty, giving a great evil example unto the common sort. We must now be at this short point with you. Ye must submit yourself, and have none other opinion in these matters, than the universal faith and belief of the Holy Church of Rome, or else throw yourself (no remedy) into most deep danger. See to it in time, for anon it will be too late!" "I will none otherwise believe in these points," was the resolute reply, "than that I have told you hereafore; do with me what ye will!" "Well, then," said Arundel, "I see none other, but we must needs do the law!"

He stood up, all the assembly vailing their bonnets, and began, "In the name of God!" "Lord Cobham," he said, "having been detected and presented at the lawful denouncement and request of our universal Clergy, we proceeded against him according to the law, (God to witness!) with all the favour possible. And following Christ's example in all we might, which willeth not the death of a sinner, but rather that he be converted and live, we sought all ways to bring him to the Church's unity. And though we found him in the Catholic faith far wide, and so stiff-necked that he would not confess his error, nor purge himself, nor yet repent him thereof, we yet pitying him of fatherly compassion, appointed him a competent time of deliberation, to see if he would seek to be reformed; but seeing that he is not corrigible, we are driven to the very extremity of the law, and with great heaviness of heart we now proceed to the publication of the sentence definitive against him."

This issue had been so clearly foreseen, that the Archbishop came with the sentence written. It began by taking Christ to witness, that His glory was the only thing sought in these whole proceedings; and saying, that the worthiness of the cause weighed first on one side, and the unworthiness of this child of iniquity and darkness on the other, his fault also being aggravated through his damnable obstinacy, it condemned Lord Cobham for a most pernicious and detestable heretic, and committed him as such to the secular power, to do him thereupon to death. Furthermore, the sentence excommunicated and denounced him accursed; and not him alone, but all who should in any way receive, defend, counsel, help, or maintain him: and this sentence was to be published and explained from the pulpit, throughout all dioceses, in cities, towns, and villages, at such times as they should have most concourse of people; to the end that, upon the fear thereof, the people might fall from their evil opinions, conceived of late by seditious preaching.

When Arundel had finished this wicked and inhuman sentence, Lord Cobham said to him, with a firm voice and courageous countenance, "Though ye judge my body, which is but a wretched thing, yet am I certain and sure that ye can do no harm to my soul, no more than could Satan upon the soul of Job. He who created that, will of his infinite mercy and promise save it; I have therein no manner of doubt. And as concerning these articles before-rehearsed,

I will stand to them even to the very death, by the grace of my eternal God!" Turning to the spectators then, he spread his hands, and spake, with a louder voice, "Good Christian people, for God's love be well ware of these men! for they will else beguile you, and lead you blindling into hell with themselves. For Christ saith plainly unto you, 'If one blind man leadeth another, they are like both to fall into the ditch!'" Then kneeling down before them, he prayed for his enemies, "Lord God Eternal! I beseech thee, of thy great mercy's sake, to forgive my pursuers, if it be thy blessed * will!"

Their victim was now remanded to the Tower, and the remainder of his history is perplexed by contradictory statements, from which nothing certain can be collected, except the results. It is

* From the account here faithfully given of this most interesting trial, it will appear evident, as Mr. Turner has well stated in his valuable History of England, (Vol. ii. 307.) that Lord Cobham's guarded confession might have satisfied his persecutors, if conciliation had been their object; but that they pursued him with questions, which left no choice between falsehood and condemnation. It is fit, however, that the reader should know in what manner the recent Catholic historian, Dr. Lingard, speaks of this trial: he says that Lord Cobham's conduct was "*as arrogant and insulting, as that of his judge was* MILD *and dignified.*" (Hist. of England, Vol. iii. .335) It is fitting, indeed, that we should know in what manner an English Catholic historian speaks of such transactions, *at this time.*

said that a respite of fifty days was obtained for him, at Arundel's desire. An abjuration was put forth in his name, which he, by aid of his friends, contradicted; setting up bills in various parts of London, wherein he declared, that he never varied, in any point, from that confession which he had made before the Clergy, and which he had taken care to have published at the time. The Lollards were certainly numerous, and he had, as his character and talents deserved, many devoted friends, by whose help he escaped from the Tower. The ensuing transactions are inexplicably mysterious. The King was informed that the Lollards had formed a plot for murdering him and his brothers at Eltham. He removed immediately to Westminster, and was then told, that they were assembling from all quarters in the Ficket Field behind St. Giles's, to act at a certain hour under Lord Cobham, and burn the Abbey, St. Paul's, St. Alban's, and all the friaries in London. In the middle of the night, the King ordered his friends to arm, that he might anticipate these enemies. He was urged to wait till daylight, that he might see who were with him and who against him, and he was advised also to collect an army, if there was a formidable body to be opposed; but with such men as at this immediate and unseasonable summons could be got together, he went out, during a Christmas night, to the place stated by his informer, and found only a few persons there, who being asked what they wanted there, said, . . . the Lord Cobham. It is said, that unless the precaution had been taken of guarding the city gates, these people were to have been joined by fifty thousand servants and apprentices. In opposition to this most improbable story, it is asserted, that the persons whom the King found in the fields were collected there to hear a midnight preaching, because they could not assemble without danger by day; . . and this tale, considering the season of the year, is as little credible as the former. It is not unlikely that a conspiracy may have been formed for raising the rightful family to the throne, and that the Lollards had embarked in it as a party, in the expectation of obtaining toleration at least, if not the triumph of their doctrines. What secret information there may have been of this does not appear; open evidence there is none. The prisons in and about London were filled; and nine and thirty persons, the chief of whom was Sir Roger Acton, who is described as a man of great ability and possessions, were suspended by chains from a gallows in Ficket Field, and in that manner burnt alive, for heresy and treason. A large reward was offered for taking Lord Cobham alive or dead; so faithfully, however, was he sheltered, notwithstanding all who harboured him incurred the same danger as himself, that he eluded his persecutors for four years, till he was discovered, by means of the Lord Powis, in Wales. He stood resolutely upon his defence, and would probably not have been taken alive, if a woman had not broken his legs with a stool. In this condition he was carried to London in a horse-litter; and there being hung by the middle in chains, was consumed in the flames *, praising God with his latest breath.

A new statute was enacted upon the pretext of these "great rumours, congregations, and insurrections," which, it was said, were designed to destroy the Christian faith, the King, and all other estates, spiritual and temporal, all manner of policy, and, finally, the laws of the land. That the words may not imply more falsehood than was intended, it should be remarked, that by Christian faith, faith in Transubstantiation is meant. That there were, among the Lollards, some fanatics who held levelling opinions in their utmost extent, may be well believed: .. it is the extreme stage of enthusiasm, and that extremity

* He suffered as a heretic, not as a traitor. His indictment for high treason is a forgery. See HOWELL's *State Trials*, Vol. I., 254, 265.

the circumstances of the times were likely to produce. But it is worthy of notice, that in all the records which remain of this persecution, in no one instance has the victim been charged with such principles. In every case, they were questioned upon those points which make the difference between the reformed and the Romish religion; in every case they were sacrificed as burnt-offerings to the Mass. For the more effectual punishment and suppression of their opinions, the statute enjoined, that all persons employed in civil offices, from the Chancellor downwards, should swear, upon their admission to office, that they would put forth their whole power and diligence to destroy Lollardry.

The cruelties in England must not be ascribed to the personal character of Arundel and the other persons who instigated them; though, beyond all doubt, these men, had they been of a more Christian temper, might have prevented them: they proceeded from the system which the Papal Church had adopted, of supporting its authority and its abuses by fire and sword. The Council of Constance, by whose execrable sentence Huss and Jerome of Prague were burnt alive, condemned Wicliffe also as an obstinate heretic, and ordered that his remains, if they could be discerned from the bodies of other faithful people, should be dug up and consumed by fire. Accordingly, by order of the Bishop of Lincoln, as Diocesan of Lutterworth, his grave, which was in the chancel of the church, was opened, forty years after his death; the bones were taken out and burnt to ashes, and the ashes thrown into a neighbouring brook, called the Swift. "This brook," says Fuller, "conveyed his ashes into Avon, Avon into Severn, Severn into the narrow seas, they into the main ocean: and thus the ashes of Wicliffe are the emblem of his doctrine, which now is dispersed all the world over." "So," says Fox, "was he resolved into three elements, earth, fire, and water, thinking thereby utterly to extinguish and abolish both the name and doctrine of Wicliffe for ever. But as there is no counsel against the Lord, so there is no keeping down of verity; it will spring and come out of dust and ashes, ... as appeared right well in this man. For though they digged up his body, burnt his bones, and drowned his ashes, yet the word of God and truth of his doctrines, with the fruit and success thereof, they could not burn. These, to this day, remain."

The Papal Church, by its pretensions to infallibility, had precluded itself from retrieving any error into which it had fallen, or reforming any abuses and corruptions which it had sanctioned: and therefore, even those persons who conscientiously maintained its doctrines upon all other points, and even zealously defended them, if they ventured to express the slightest hesitation upon this main article, were regarded and treated as heretics. Proof of this was given in the treatment of Reynold Pecock, Bishop of Chichester, a man of great ability and rare moderation, who, perceiving errors and evils on both sides, would fain have held an even course between the extremes, and have conciliated the Lollards, by conceding to them what was untenable, while he argued against them convincingly upon some of their most popular, but least reasonable, tenets. He reasoned against a preposterous tenet which the Bible-men, as he called them, advanced, that nothing was lawful unless it were appointed in the Scriptures, by which we were to be absolutely guided, as a rule of life, even in things indifferent. The error was not derived from Wicliffe, for he expressly affirmed that human ordinances might be accepted, when they were grounded in good reason, and were for the common profit of Christian people; and Pecock justly maintained, that it was not the purport of revelation to teach any thing which might be discovered without it. That there were abuses in the adoration of images among the simple and ignorant, he admitted, but insisted that they were remediable harms;...differing in this from Wicliffe, who thought that, though not unlawful in themselves, they gave such occasion of idolatry, that they ought to be destroyed. With regard to pilgrimages, he affirmed it was not true that all places are alike in God's sight, since God chooses to dispense his favours in one place rather than in another, and in the manner of his own approving, rather than of man's advising; but he recommended those who sought for spiritual improvement, rather to seek it in reading and hearing the word of God, than by "haunting, as it were, alway the exercise in such visible signs." He agreed with the Lollards, in reprehending such preaching as that of the ignorant and superstitious Friars, whose sermons were filled with absurd legends, and who inculcated nothing so zealously as the duty of employing their order to say masses for the deliverance of souls from Purgatory. But though he censured these pulpit-bawlers, as he called them, he nevertheless maintained, that by means of such itinerants as the Friars, the people were made better than they would have been without them; and he shewed the utility of monasteries, were it only for the effect they produced, as places whither the great sometimes withdrew for the purpose of religious retirement. The charges which were brought against the Bishops for not preaching, he answered openly and fairly, by maintaining that they were not bound by their office to preach to the common people, but rather were free from that burthen; their business was to have knowledge of those matters which the inferior clergy should preach: for themselves, they had higher duties, and more useful work. He insisted also, that they were not bound to residence, when they might be better employed elsewhere.

Bishop Pecock did not, like Arundel and too many other prelates, hunt out the Lollards, for the purpose of bringing them to the stake. Many of the chief persons among them conversed familiarly with him upon subjects which it had been death to touch upon before a persecutor; he deserved their confidence, and even won their affection, by the patience with which he listened to them; . . . he could always, he says, have made their case stronger than they did themselves. But while he was thus serving his own Church effectually, by unexceptionable means, he fell under its censure himself, for declaring that the pretension of infallibility could not be maintained, and that Holy Writ was the only standard of revealed truth. The implicit faith which the Church upon this ground required in all its institutions, as he saw that it shocked the understanding of reasonable and conscientious men, so he perceived that it was deeply prejudicial to religion, and expressed his strong feeling concerning it in this prayer: "O thou Lord Jesus, God and Man, head of thy Christian Church, and teacher of Christian belief, I beseech thy mercy, thy pity, and thy charity; far be this said peril from the Christian Church, and from each person therein contained; and shield thou that this venom be never brought into thy Church: and if thou suffer it to be any while brought in, I beseech thee that it be soon again outspit. But suffer thou, ordain, and do, that the law and the faith which thy Church at any time keepeth, be received, and admitted to fall under this examination, whether it be the same very faith which thou and thine Apostles taught or no, and whether it hath sufficient evidences for it to be very faith or no."

A charge of heresy was therefore brought against him, for teaching that the Church was fallible: other accusations were added, some of which seem intended to excite a popular cry against him, and also to bring him into disgrace with the Government. Duke Humphrey had been his patron, and they who had brought about the murder of the Duke, extended their hatred to him. That which should have been a merit in the eyes of the Papal Court, was imputed to him as a crime,... his assertion, that the Pope, having a right to all benefices, might, in the disposal of them, reserve to himself what part of the revenues he thought fit, without being guilty of simony; since, as rightful lord, he sold only what was his own. Another imputed crime was, his opinion that the goods of Churchmen are not the goods of the poor, but are as much their own property, as are the temporal estates of those who have them by inheritance. Another, that it was not necessary to salvation to believe that our Saviour descended into Hell. There were other charges, which were merely frivolous, turning wholly upon verbal subtleties. He was condemned, however, upon all, and had then to choose between abjuration and martyrdom.

Let no one reproach the memory of Bishop Pecock, because martyrdom was not his choice! It was well said by the worthy Fuller, "Oh, there is more required to make a man valiant, than only to call another coward." His principles were not those which demanded that he should bear witness against the Roman Church in their behalf. He was the able and dutiful defender of that Church, not its enemy; his life had been spent in supporting it, and in endeavouring to refute or conciliate its opponents: consistently, therefore, with the tenour of that life, he chose rather to sacrifice his judgement, and perhaps truth also, in submitting, than to suffer death for opposing it, and thus strengthen, as undoubtedly such an execution would have strengthened, the cause of the Lollards. And considering the extreme humiliation to which he submitted, it can hardly be doubted but that death would have been the preferable alternative, had he not acted under a sense of duty. He was brought in his episcopal habit to St. Paul's Cross, in the presence of twenty thousand people, and placed at the Archbishop's feet, while fourteen of his books were presented to the Bishops of London, Rochester, and Dunholm, as judges. These books he was ordered to deliver with his own hands to the person by whom they were to be thrown into the fire, there ready for that purpose. Then standing up at the Cross, he read his abjuration in English, confessing that, presuming upon his own natural wit, and preferring the natural judgement of reason before the Scriptures and the determination of the Church, he had published many perilous and pernicious books, containing heresies and errors, which he then specified as they had been charged against him. "Wherefore, regarding himself as a miserable sinner, who theretofore had walked in darkness, but now by the mercy of God was reduced into the right way, and that he had wickedly infected the people, he openly revoked and renounced these heresies, committed himself as a penitent sinner to the correction of the Church and his Lord of Canterbury; and required all persons, as they tendered their souls and his, to deliver in all writings of his which they might have in their keeping; that the same might be openly burnt as an example and terror to others." As many copies as could be collected were then brought forward, and consumed in the fire.

It remains now to state, what were the tender mercies of the Romish Church to this eminent man, (the most learned of his age and country,) who had thus humbly and thoroughly submitted to its authority. That his enemies in that Church insulted him with a malice which was at once venomous and grovelling, is only what may always be expected from mean and malignant minds; but the treatment which he received can only be imputed to the immitigable spirit of the papal tyranny and its agents. He was sent to Thorney Abbey, there to be confined in a secret closed chamber, out of which he was not to be allowed to go. The person, who made his bed and his fire, was the only one who might enter and speak to him, without the Abbot's leave, and in his presence. He was to have neither pen, ink, nor paper, and to be allowed no books, except a mass-book, a psalter, a legendary, and a bible. For the first quarter, he was to have no better fare than the common rations of the convent; afterwards, the pittance of a sick or aged brother, with such further indulgence as his health might require, for which, and for fitting up his close apartment, the Prior was allowed eleven pounds. In this dismal imprisonment, Pecock died. But carefully as his writings were sought for, and destroyed, some of them remained to preserve his memory, and bear witness to his learning, his moderation, and his worth.

If such was the severity which the Romish Church exercised toward the ablest of its defenders, what were those persons to expect who detested its doctrines, when they fell into the hands of its inhuman ministers? The civil wars, which in all other respects were so frightful to humanity, had the good effect of affording them a respite. In Fuller's beautiful words, "the very storm was their shelter." But when the struggle ceased, the business of persecution was resumed, and Henry VII., while he asserted his authority over the Clergy, found it consistent with his policy, to employ them, rather than his nobles, in state affairs, and suffered them to proceed against the Lollards with the utmost rigour. Among the victims whom they brought to the stake, was a woman of some quality, Joan Boughton by name, the first female martyr in England: she was more than eighty years of age, and was held in such reverence for her virtue, that, during the night after her martyrdom, her ashes were collected, to be preserved as relics for pious and affectionate remembrance. Her daughter, the Lady Young, suffered afterwards the same cruel death, with equal constancy. At Amersworth, when William Tylsworth was burnt, his only daughter, as being suspected of heresy, was compelled not only to witness his death, but with her own hands to set fire to him! By such barbarities did the Romish Church provoke the indignation of God and man. That it should have made one real convert, by such means, is impossible; though it compelled many to abjuration. In that case, the miserable wretches whom it admitted to its mercy, were made to bear a faggot in public, while they witnessed the martyrdom of those who had more constancy than themselves. They were fastened to a stake by the neck with towels, and their hands held fast, while they were marked on the cheek with a hot iron; after which, they were for life to wear a faggot, worked or painted on the left sleeve; and if they ventured to lay aside this badge, which, if they were in humble life, consigned them to want as well as infamy, they were sent to the flames without remission:...so that it became a saying, Put it off and be burnt; keep it on and be starved. Bishop Nix, of Norwich, one of the most infamous for his activity in this persecution, used to call the persons whom he suspected of heretical opinions, men savouring of the frying-pan;...with such levity did these monsters regard the sufferings which they inflicted! A correspondent of Erasmus wrote to him, that the price of wood was considerably advanced about London, in consequence of the quantity required for the frequent executions in Smithfield. The statement is one of those hyperboles, which, in the familiarity of letter-writing, are understood as they are meant, and convey no more than the truth.

END OF THE FIRST VOLUME.

LONDON:
Printed by WILLIAM CLOWES,
Northumberland-court.